THE LIVING
& THE DEAD

The public mourning of a private tragedy. The sculptor Lev Kerbel's 1972 monument to wartime medics rendered the faces of his son and wife, both of whom had committed suicide.

THE LIVING
& THE DEAD

THE RISE AND FALL
OF THE CULT
OF WORLD WAR II
IN RUSSIA

NINA TUMARKIN

BasicBooks
A Division of HarperCollins*Publishers*

"1941" by Julia Neiman appearing on page 66 from *Dissonant Voices in Soviet Literature,* edited by Patricia Blake and Max Hayward (poem translated by Walter N. Vickery), Random House, 1965. Copyright © 1965 by Random House. Used by permission.
Material from "Babi Yar" appearing on pages 119 and 120 from *Selected Poems* by Yevgenii Yevtushenko, translated by Robin Milner-Gulland and Peter Levi, Penguin Books, 1962. Copyright © 1962 by Robin Milner-Gulland and Peter Levi. Used by permission.
Photos by Mikhail Trakhman, Georgii Zelma, and Yevgenii Khaldei from *The Russian War: 1941–1945* by Daniel Mrazkova and Vladimir Remes. Copyright © 1975 by Daniel Mrazkova and Vladimir Remes. Used by permission of Dutton Signet, a division of Penguin Books USA Inc.

Designed by Jessica Shatan

Library of Congress Cataloging-in-Publication Data
Tumarkin, Nina.
    The living and the dead: the rise and fall of the cult of World War II in Russia / Nina Tumarkin.
        p. cm.
    Includes bibliographical references and index.
    ISBN 0–465–07159–7 (cloth)
    ISBN 0–465–04144–2 (paper)
    1. World War, 1939–1945—Soviet Union—Public opinion. 2. World War, 1939–1945—Influence. 3. Public opinion—Soviet Union. 4. Cults—Soviet Union. 5. Soviet Union—History—Errors, inventions, etc. I. Title
D764.T855 1994
947.084—dc20   94–2964
                                                                                 CIP

95 96 97 98 ❖/HC 9 8 7 6 5 4 3 2 1

For my mother,

Suzanne Tumarkin

CONTENTS

Acknowledgments   ix

1 Introductory Thoughts   1
2 Valley of Death   11
3 The Last Hurrah   28
4 "No Sea Without Water, No War Without Blood"   52
5 After the War Was Over   95
6 "No One Is Forgotten, Nothing Is Forgotten"   125
7 *Glasnost* and the Great Patriotic War   158
8 Russia Remembers the War   202
9 Parting Thoughts   222

Notes   229
Index   237

ACKNOWLEDGMENTS

"When you pick up a book, be sure always to read the acknowledgments first. That's the only way to find out from what world the book has evolved," a seasoned senior colleague once told me when I had just begun graduate school in history. She passed on this sage advice more than a quarter-century ago, when history book acknowledgments made up the last part of the preface and invariably ended with profuse thanks and post hoc apologies to the author's children, who had suffered through years without their father's attention, and to his wife, who had critiqued, edited, and finally typed draft after draft of the manuscript.

I do not believe I need to apologize to anyone for this book—happily, the computer saved my spouse from having to do my typing—but there are many people and institutions I wish to thank for their support and help in every aspect of the book's preparation. I first thank the National Council of Soviet and East European Research, which—while not responsible for the contents of this book— supported my research and writing with two most generous grants and (only slightly less important) much verbal reinforcement. The National Council, the International Research and Exchanges Board, and Wellesley College funded more than a half-dozen research trips to the (then) Soviet Union. My warm thanks to all of them and to the Harvard University Russian Research Center, which has given me a scholarly home for more than half my life. In addition, Wellesley College has been generous with sabbatical leave and other support, for which I am most appreciative.

I am deeply grateful to the many individuals in this country who gave up precious time to consult with me about my book-in-progress, to provide comradely support of all kinds, and to read portions of the manuscript in draft: Jack Beatty, John Bennet, Jeffrey Brooks, Alexander Dallin, Daniel Field, Abbott Gleason, Rhea and Murray Josephson, Mark Kramer, Jack F. Matlock, Jr., Norman Naimark, the late Aleksandr Nekrich, John Pearce, S. Frederick Starr, Richard Stites, Adam Ulam, and Dan Wakefield. I would also like to mention the late Michael Cherniavsky, who was, together with Sidney Monas, my undergraduate mentor, and whose brilliant work and bizarre attitude toward life served as powerful forces in my intellectual upbringing.

"Over there" so many wonderful people contributed so much to this book that I can mention only a few of them by name: the late Ales Adamovich, Viktor Agashkov, Margarita Astafieva-Dlugach, Iulii Ikonnikov, Georgii Kumanev, Viacheslav Klykov, Viacheslav Kondratiev, V. M. Kulish, Oleg and Ada Lishin, Roy Medvedev, Daniil Mitlianskii, Anatolii Naiman, and Elena Rzhevskaia. In addition my most profound gratitude goes to Lazar Lazarev, the late Mikhail Gefter, and Valentin Gefter, who over the years have proven to be infinite providers of support, wisdom, and caring.

My able research assistants—Allison Katsev, David Woodruff, Dmitry Radyshevsky, Denis Fedosov, Sergei Reshetnikov, and Ania Narinskaia—did fine work, and I am grateful to all of them, and to Steve Fraser, my patient editor at Basic Books.

I also owe a special word of thanks to the late Konstantin Simonov, whose fine trilogy provided me with the inspiration for the title of this book.

With much love I thank my husband, Harvey Gallagher Cox, Jr., and my son, Nicholas Tumarkin Cox, both pacifists, for allowing World War II to dominate our lives for so many years. We can put away those records of Russian war songs now!

NINA TUMARKIN
Cambridge, Massachusetts

There was no one now between the squadron and the enemy except a few scattered skirmishers. An empty space of some seven hundred yards was all that separated them. The enemy ceased firing, and that stern, threatening, inaccessible and intangible line which separates two hostile armies was all the more clearly felt.

"One step beyond that boundary line which resembles the line dividing the living from the dead, lies uncertainty, suffering, and death. And what is there? Who is there?—there beyond that field, that tree, that roof lit up by the sun? No one knows, but one wants to know. You fear and yet long to cross that line, and know that sooner or later it must be crossed and you will have found out what is there, just as you will inevitably have to learn what lies the other side of death."

—LEO TOLSTOY, *War and Peace*

Note: In transliterating Russian words and proper names I have used the Library of Congress system in the notes, and a slightly modified form of that system in the text. Translations are my own unless otherwise indicated.

1

INTRODUCTORY THOUGHTS

The past isn't dead; it's not even past.

—William Faulkner

I met the sculptor Lev Kerbel, a big, beefy man with large, freckled features and curly, sandy hair, in Moscow in the summer of 1987. Kerbel had designed a dreadful statue of Lenin near what was then called October Square, and so when he invited me into his studio I expected the worst. Instead I was pleasantly surprised.

It was midafternoon, and like so many American exchange scholars loath to waste the long time necessary for a restaurant lunch, I was famished. "First you eat, then we work," he ordered sternly, as he sat me down to a table laden with plates of salami, bread, sliced cucumbers and tomatoes, cheese, and a bowl of sour cream.

After lunch we walked slowly through the enormous studio. The dissonance of dimensions produced by monumental artworks scaled down and crowded into rooms whose floors were strewn with plaster heads, legs, and other by-products of the trade made the atmosphere surreal. In those days when Moscow was still the capital of a country called the Soviet Union, Kerbel, who claimed that his name came from the French *coeur belle* (beautiful heart), had long since established himself as a successful sculptor. His studio consisted of several large rooms in a fashionable part of Moscow. He had a chauffeur-driven car and the authoritative, self-satisfied manner of a high-level bureaucrat. But his lined face bore the traces of a difficult life.

He showed me photographs of some of his works devoted to the war theme. One of them—a monument to wartime medics of the First Moscow Medical Institute—doubtless explained the deeply furrowed forehead and cheeks. Two faces and one hand had been sculpted into a large granite rectangle. One face was of a woman; stern, beautiful, with a hood covering her hair, she resembled the mother of God as depicted in Russian icons. Her hand cradled the forehead of a dead or dying young man; his eyes were shut, and his features closely resembled Kerbel's own.

"Those are my son and my wife," he said in a quiet voice. "They died one after another." When his grown son committed suicide, Kerbel's grief-stricken wife had taken her own life as well. The sculpture, erected in 1972, had been commissioned as a war memorial, but for the artist it was an expression of his anguish over a massive personal tragedy.

A double—or even more thickly layered—agenda often informs the creative process. When we paint or write or compose, some of us are impelled to recreate our personal histories, either implicitly or explicitly, in an attempt to placate or (if we are lucky) to exorcise the demons whose long reach keeps us mired in the pain of past losses. This dynamic was glaringly evident in the memorialization of World War II in the Soviet Union. As I interviewed sculptors, painters, novelists, literary critics, poets, filmmakers, and historians who had chosen the war as the creative theme of their work, I learned that many of their artistic or scholarly endeavors had been inspired by painful memories of the wartime deaths of loved ones or by other equally sorrowful events.

The Living and the Dead: The Rise and Fall of the Cult of World War II in Russia has just such a double agenda. For me this book represents both an exploration of the Soviet and post-Soviet Russian memorialization of an excruciating national ordeal and an attempt to confront and push beyond the great pain of my own life: the untimely deaths of my father, brother, and sister, all of whom died before the age of fifty.

When I was ten and my father was dying of kidney failure at age forty-seven, my Aunt Lucy, a pediatrician, explained to my sister, brother, and me that his kidneys had been irreparably damaged by a childhood bout of scarlet fever, and that the family had known all along that it was only a matter of time before they would give out. Only a matter of time. The relentless crush of time informed my earliest understanding of God—at times reassuringly predictable, at others, remote and unyielding.

I loved my father desperately and sometimes thought of myself, the youngest, as his favorite, although he was so skilled at communicating love that my sister thought *she* was his preferred child. It was unfair that Masha, twenty-two months my senior, had inherited his round face, refined features, blue eyes, and dark hair, while I was stuck with a big mouth and long blond braids.

He died on a balmy Indian summer day in October 1955. I had skipped home to West End Avenue after playing punchball in Riverside Park with my sixth-grade friends. At ten, I was small and skinny, weighing in at sixty-eight pounds. Clad in a checked shirt, navy shorts, and red Keds, I was still bouncing my little pink Spalding ball when I pressed the doorbell twice in staccato fashion, the family signal. Someone opened the door, I do not remember who, but she was big and wore a black dress. From the doorway it looked as if a flock of fat crows had alighted in our living room, together with a rabbi. In an instant I knew what had happened. Quickly I shut the door and ran to push the elevator button. But my mother ushered me back into the apartment.

The grown-ups decided that Masha and I were too young to attend Daddy's funeral, although our seventeen-year-old brother, Georgie, was allowed to go. When they returned from the cemetery, my sister and I were playing jacks on our bedroom floor and giggling about something. "How can you enjoy yourselves when your father has just been buried?" chided my distraught mother. If I close my eyes, I can still recall my feelings of shame and horror.

For years afterward I cultivated a secret fantasy: Daddy had not really died but had crawled out of his coffin and made his way back home to me. Then I grew up and wrote my first book, *Lenin Lives! The Cult of Lenin in Soviet Russia,* about the organized veneration of a man who had died but was declared to be immortal, a man who had not been buried and was "always with us." The real subject of that book was my father. To make up for the funeral I had missed decades

earlier, I obsessively charted every moment of the elaborate rites that
followed Lenin's death and then focused on the cult of his embalmed
body. For decades beyond his death, posters declared that "Lenin is
more alive than all the living."

In 1978, as I was preparing to spend six months in the Soviet
Union to gather materials for *Lenin Lives!,* Georgie drowned in the
Central Park lake at age thirty-nine. This time I had a real funeral to
manage, but even that ritual could not prevent me from falling into a
depression when I got to Moscow. For months, I found myself going
to cemeteries to look for my dead brother and father and the ghosts
of my ancestors, who had all lived and died in Russia.

Publishing books is supposed to bestow a kind of immortality, but
I had just the opposite sensation when, some months after my first
book came out, I looked it up in a library card catalog. The card
read: "Tumarkin, Nina 1945–." The other side of the dash was left
blank. All the librarians in the world, I thought, are waiting to fill in
the other date.

Long, fulfilling lives devoted to self-actualization, the kind
described in the self-help books that dominate paperback best-seller
lists, have never played a role in Russian wishful thinking. My sib-
lings and I acquired our expectations of the future, at least in part,
from our teachers and schoolbooks and 1950s television shows like
"Father Knows Best" and "Ozzie and Harriet," in which happy families with strong and healthy fathers resolved meaningless conflicts in
the living rooms of their perfect suburban homes. Our own parents,
wholly secularized Russian Jews, had spent their childhoods in prerevolutionary St. Petersburg, reared on Pushkin's otherworldly fairy
tales and the mysterious icon corners that glowed red in the beckon-
ing bedrooms of their Russian peasant nannies. "See that *bozhenka,*
that little god?" my mother's *niania* used to say to her, signaling my
mother to gaze up at a painted image of St. Sergius or St. Nicholas
the Wonderworker. "If you are a bad little girl, he will throw pebbles
at you."

Niania Polia. As a small child I was terrified of *Niania* and drawn
to her at the same time. Her long earlobes were as lined as her
cheeks, and each lobe had an elongated hole, a legacy from decades
of bearing pendulous earrings. Her long, thinning gray hair was
twisted back into a knot, which she secured with memorable metal

hairpins. "*Pik, pik, pik,*" she would say if I did not do as I was told, leaning on her wooden cane with one hand and with the other, holding out a hairpin menacingly. She invariably sent us children home with foods that looked like treats but always had a downside, like cooked grapefruit peels encrusted with crystallized sugar, and dry, biscotti-like cookies that seemed pretty pathetic compared with our beloved Mallomars and Oreos.

Niania's real first name was Pelagea. Her parents had been born into serfdom. When my grandparents hired her at the turn of the century, she was a young widow who had borne several children, only two of whom had survived. She lived with members of my family in Russia, Finland, Paris, and Manhattan until the last few years of her life, which she spent in a Russian Orthodox monastery in upstate New York. By that time it was the sixties and I was in my teens. Once a month I would ride up to see her with my uncle and his children. The monastery was a magical place, especially in winter, when the afternoon light rendered the snow-covered ground as mellow blue as the peal of the chapel bells, which called the black-robed monks, who wore their hair just as *Niania* did, to begin their noiseless glide along its snow-covered paths.

Whatever *Niania*'s real feelings about living at the monastery, I thought of the place as a kind of mezzanine between this world and the next, an intermediate step between life and death. *Niania* was old and infirm and appeared to me ready to face the end, if not with equanimity, then at least with a sober acceptance.

Almost forty years after my father's death my beloved sister, Masha, lay dying of leukemia a few months short of her fiftieth birthday. Her neck was grossly distended by painfully swollen lymph nodes, dwarfing her head, which was covered with a thin white fluff that had sprouted after chemotherapy had caused her hair to fall out. Twice a week a needle inserted into her pleural cavity drained out almost two liters—the size of one of those big soda bottles—of a milky substance that had accumulated there because enlarged thoracic nodes blocking normal passageways in the lymphatic system made her short of breath. No therapies seemed able to stop the inexorable progress of the dread disease. Her teeth grew long, her lips thinned out, and her skin took on a yellowish cast.

I wrote much of *The Living and the Dead* during Masha's illness as I watched her approach that boundary between life and death. What had her evident impending death to do with the remembrance of war in the Soviet Union and Russia? What was the link between my personal loss of a father, a brother, and now a sister and a war that took the lives of some thirty million Soviet citizens?

The link was my own search for wisdom about how to live with death. When I was a child, the loss of my father was a blow from which my family never quite recovered its sense of equilibrium, of wholeness. That wound had occurred so early in my life that I had turned it into a self-defining badge. Death, trauma, loss had made me special, different, vulnerable. When I was around twelve, someone once offered to read my palm. "You have a broken lifeline!" she cried out with a giggle. And so I did; that inner curved crease in my left palm veered off to the right about one-third of the way into its arc. I took to wearing black.

By the time Masha had become leukemic I was middle-aged and had long since abandoned a self-image based in loss. I had a husband, a child, stepchildren, challenging work, and strong ties to family and friends. It was possible to lovingly accompany Masha on her journey and nonetheless stay whole. But I am sure I could not have made that painful trip without keeping Russia in my head the whole time.

Russia is the counterworld against which I measure my own experience. When I am numbed with grief by the loss of my darling sister as I watch her two young sons make their way through life without a mother, I sometimes summon up images of Russia at war. During the Second World War, everyone's vulnerability to fate, to cruel luck, was exposed, with the stakes unutterably high. Some mothers sent eight sons to fight and lost them all. Other families remained intact. Who could predict which Russian children would live through the war in the safety of Alma-Ata or some other eastern evacuation site, and which would starve to death in Leningrad and be eaten by their crazed parents?

Our American pursuit of happiness, the promise of life and liberty as God-given rights, can arouse a bewildered rage when reality ends up differing so wildly from our cherished expectations. In the Soviet Union, communist ideology too made all sorts of extravagant promises, but the beneficiaries of those promises were purportedly large groups of people living in the future, rather than individuals in the here and now. Besides, the Russians I knew during the Soviet period ignored that ideology entirely and lived by their own homely philosophies based on a relaxed fatalism that can sometimes seem more mature than our own determination to pursue lives that are fat-free, salt-free, stress-free, and aerobic.

"Do you really love your life so much that you need to sustain it forever?" teased a Russian friend once when, after an evening in which I had, *seriatim,* refused his proffered vodka, cognac, coffee, and cigarettes, I also declined an offer of ice cream, which he knew I loved. From a superficial American perspective, the Russian attitudes toward life and death look unfashionably self-destructive. Russians—including the most progressive members of the intelligentsia—eat foods rich in animal fat (when they can get them), think sugar is healthy, smoke too much, and drink much too much. It is considered perfectly acceptable to telephone people at home until midnight or even later, because Russia is a country of owls. Those owls usually have to get up early to go to work, and an afternoon siesta is not part of the culture. So chronic fatigue is the norm. You get into the passenger seat of a car and reach for the seat belt. *"Ne nado, ne nado"* ("don't bother, don't bother"), says the driver almost invariably. During the Soviet period when police still had authority, he would point to his own belt, slung over his shoulder but not buckled in. "I just throw it over like this so it looks like I'm obeying the law." Seat belts in Russia have to do with laws and not with safety, and putting one over on the police has always taken precedence over preventing serious injury.

I think that what might appear in Russians to be a kind of negligence is in reality an acceptance of the inevitability of death. Russians do not seek death or embrace it, nor do they contend, as did some ancient Greeks, that "those whom the gods love, die young." Russian proverbs, which provide a rich repository of popular attitudes, stress the need to be aware of one's eventual death and the wisdom of being prepared for it at any time. "Death will find a reason"; "Only God can bring life into being, but any cur can take it away"; "Everyone will die when his day comes."[1]

"Of course we Russians cherish the blessing of life," opined the poet Anatolii Naiman as we chatted one summer in the Russian like setting of rural Vermont, "but we are also prepared to die and to allow others to die. The American obsession with the significance of each individual life has been played out with every hostage crisis. It is unimaginable that any Russian government could make such a fuss over the lives of some fifty or five hundred or even five thousand of its citizens. We are surely too callous, but might you in turn be expecting too much of this world?"

The great mystery about Russia, the pull that keeps me going back there year after year—despite so many inconveniences and frustrations in both work and day-to-day living, no matter who sits on the Kremlin throne—is the Russian people's capacity to assimilate a painful, indeed brutal, history and come out the other side so astonishingly authentic, courageous, and wry.

I suppose people need to value what they have, and what Russians have always had is loss. But Soviet political culture placed one kind of value on its bitter history, while traditional Russian culture generated a different kind of wisdom. Desperate to produce both an explanation for a pitifully low standard of living and a sustaining myth to maintain popular support for a failing political system, the regimes of Stalin's successors continued both to mourn the millions of war dead and to celebrate the triumph of victory, just as Lenin's successors had kept his authority going in all sorts of incarnations. As do individuals, nations feed on myths, and political systems that came into being through revolution—as happened in America, in France, in Russia— are especially dependent on the creation and maintenance of myths to bolster their legitimacy. Why did some regimes enshrine liberty or fraternity, and others the martyred millions from the Great Patriotic War? For the answer to that question we need to study their particular histories. *The Living and the Dead: The Rise and Fall of the Cult of World War II in Russia* tells the story of the development, career, and eventual demise of the organized public veneration of a legendary wartime experience. And it details the emergence of passion as a searing social force that empowered Russians to confront the pain produced by raw human memory.

On the other end of the philosophical spectrum from the cult of the Great Patriotic War is the Russian proverb "when you live near the graveyard, you can't weep for everyone." I suppose it means that people surrounded by death become somewhat inured to it. Or that you should not be expected to devote more than a limited amount of energy to mourning those who have died because the lives that continue demand your attention.

Perhaps living near the graveyard does, in fact, encourage you to weep for everyone, even if you have to get drunk first, which is fine, as long as mourning the dead is not considered to be some kind of deviant behavior. In American culture some kinds of persistent devotion to certain dead people are acceptable. When I was young I remember hearing that Joe DiMaggio sent a dozen red roses to Marilyn Monroe's grave every day. Now *that* was romantic. But it was anomalous. Although my family used to visit my father's grave twice a year, on the anniversaries of his birth and death, I was ashamed to talk about those visits because I had never heard of any of my friends going to cemeteries for any reason. Decades later, I still never hear American acquaintances talk about visiting the graves of their loved ones. Is a grave site not a fit topic for conversation? Do most people really never go, but just have, say, fifty dollars deducted yearly from their credit cards for flowers laid down by cemetery staff? Maybe cremation is the name of the game, and the dead end up in more or less tasteful urns on suburban mantles or bookcases. A rare exception to the American norm is the magnificently landscaped Mt. Auburn Cemetery in my current hometown of Cambridge, Massachusetts, a haven for bird-watchers and observers of New England's famed fall foliage.

In Soviet Russia, cemeteries were places for hanging out, for relaxed picnics with family and friends. On a spring or summer day it was customary for couples to amble arm in arm through the cemeteries of Russia's big cities and contemplate the gravestones of famed compatriots. Caring friends have taken me to see the graves of Gogol, Chekhov, Tchaikovsky, Rimsky-Korsakov, Mussorgsky, Prokofiev, Khrushchev, and Nadezhda Allilueva, Stalin's young wife, who took her own life in 1932. Together we have enjoyed the trees, patches of grass, some bread, pickles and vodka, the sense of physical and psychic remove from the tensions of daily life, and a kind of communion with friendly and accomplished ghosts from the past. In the bad old days of the Brezhnev era, those dead celebrities were a refreshingly benign contrast to the malignant authorities in the Politburo. In post-Soviet Russia, people are busier trying to make a living and seem to have less time for the dead.

In a description of the graves in her native Antigua, Jamaica

Kincaid evoked the staying power of the dead in a way that reminded me of Russia: "death is just another way of being, and the dead will not stay put, and sometimes the actions of the dead are more significant, more profound, than their actions in life, and no structure of concrete or stone can contain them."[2] Maybe *that* is what we learn when we live near the graveyard, that death is just another way of being. And if we have the wisdom to remember and respect those who have gone before us in whatever ways we can, we may thereby gain the courage—when the time comes—to face the inevitable loss of our loved ones and to stay with them as they approach the line that divides the living from the dead.

2

VALLEY OF DEATH

The Lord's hand was upon me, and he carried me out by his spirit and set me down in a plain that was full of bones. He made me pass among them in every direction. Countless in number and very dry, they covered the plain. He said to me, "O man, can these bones live?" I answered, "only you, Lord God, know that." He said, "Prophesy over these bones; say: Dry bones, hear the word of the Lord. The Lord God says to these bones: I am going to put breath into you, and you will live."

I prophesied as I had been told; breath entered them, and they came to life and rose to their feet, a mighty company.

He said to me, "O man, these bones are the whole people of Israel."

—Ezekiel 37:1–5,10,11

"Poor Yorick," murmured Sergei (Serega) Shpilianskii with a gentle smile as I carefully lifted the human skull out of the sandy soil. Twenty-one years old, tall and slender, Serega had a sunburned face brimming with health, and a thick shock of bristly black hair.

"At least Hamlet knew Yorick's identity," I responded, pushing some coagulated earth out of the right eye socket with my thumb, "but no one will ever know this poor fellow's name."

Serega and I were crouched in a trench only a few hundred meters

away from the upper reaches of the Volga River on the outskirts of
Rzhev, an ancient city to the northwest of Moscow that had been
destroyed during the Second World War. Armed with a three-foot
metal probe and hefty shovel, Serega Shpilianskii was the *komissar* of
my *brigada,* which was charged with the task of locating and
unearthing the remains of soldiers whose wounded or dead bodies
had been hastily flung into the trenches around Rzhev in the thick of
fighting. Our brigade had been sent out that morning by Oleg
Lishin, the founder and commander of *Dozor* (Patrol), one of many
hundreds of organizations dedicated to finding and burying the estimated two to three million unburied soldiers who lost their lives in
the Great Patriotic War.

I had first heard about those unburied dead in 1987 from Avgust
Mishin, a hulking, bespectacled professor of law with large, craggy
features and a frizzy beard of a greenish yellow color I had never
before seen outside of a Crayola box. He was missing an arm. "Shot
right off by German bullets in the battle of Moscow," he said. At the
end of a long evening of war talk, he was already dressed to leave, his
empty coat sleeve dangling conspicuously from his shoulder, when
he remarked, "In the woods outside of Smolensk you can see skeletons of soldiers. They had died and just stayed there. At first it was
too dangerous to retrieve them, because the area was mined, and
finally they were just forgotten. You can go and see for yourself."
Once started on the subject, Mishin did not want to let it go. "I
remember when the fighting was so thick that corpses just fell everywhere and we pushed them into pits, Germans, Russians together.
No one took the time to sort them out; they became just one great
stinking mass."

ANTIGONE'S CHILDREN

After her father's tragic death, Antigone, daughter of Oedipus, King
of Thebes, sacrificed her own life in an attempt to bury the body of
her brother, Polynices, who had been slain by his brother in a struggle over the rule of Thebes and left on the battlefield to rot. Some
of the young people of *Dozor,* and similar groups devoted to burying
their comrades-in-spirit slain a half-century earlier, displayed Antigone's
resolute sense of mission toward the dead.

"[The eighteenth-century general A. V.] Suvorov used to say that a war is not over until the last slain soldier is buried," Ada Lishin replied when I asked her how she had come to make *Dozor* her life. Avid campers and hikers, had she and her husband, Oleg, been born and raised in the United States, they might have gravitated toward Boulder or Seattle or some other such mecca for people who love the outdoors.

But Moscow was their home and just as naturally Oleg Lishin took a job as military director of a school, which placed him in charge of war games, nighttime hikes, and a cache of twenty target rifles. He even formed a "spy club," in which the teenagers went out at night on skis with their rifles, shooting at a moonlit phantom enemy. As opposed to most instructors of "military-patriotic upbringing" who emphasized the competitive aspect of battle, Lishin saw as his main goal "to bring the children together, to teach them how to organize themselves, how to persevere in achieving a common goal." In the 1960s Oleg and Ada Lishin began organizing expeditions to search for the war dead, and by the late 1980s, their grown children and oldest grandson—who had joined the company at age eight—were accompanying them on the regular expeditions of *Dozor*.[1]

Hundreds of search groups made up the MIA search movement, and they varied tremendously in size, composition, operating principles, and motivating forces. Some had mostly or only adult members; others, like *Dozor*, were primarily geared toward teenagers. The main attraction of the work varied as well, along a spectrum ranging from the simple love of weapons and excitement, all the way to a palpably spiritual commitment to a sacred mission.

The Lishins described themselves as pedagogues and their work as a kind of enlightenment for young people. "The most important thing for the young people to understand is that those bones were people, real people with hopes, desires, loves and lives," explained Oleg. "Only when we fully respect the dead can we truly respect the living."

For many years after the war, the Soviet Army was loath to address the challenge of burying its war dead. Often the work was perilous, since the battle areas were mined. Besides, if they buried the dead in military cemeteries, the upkeep of those graves would be the army's responsibility. In 1946 a directive had come down from on high that all territories that had seen battle were to be brought "into order." But the impoverished local organs of administration were supposed to pay for the work. The regime of Stalin and his successors had turned its back on its last—and most primal—duty to its fallen soldiers.

In the 1960s the Komsomol (Communist Youth Organization) involved itself in the work of "Red Pathfinders" who led schoolchildren on trips to search for human remains and wartime relics as part of their military-patriotic upbringing. But the authorities were eager to minimize the publicly acknowledged number of MIAs; to admit to a huge number of unburied war dead would clash too shockingly with the central claim of the cult of the Great Patriotic War: "no one is forgotten, nothing is forgotten." Moreover, families of those who were classified as having "disappeared without a trace" were not entitled to receive compensatory financial benefits. Indeed, those families were often ostracized since—who knows?—perhaps their loved ones had allowed themselves to be taken prisoner, which in Stalin's time was tantamount to treason. It was easier and cheaper to leave forests, hills, rocky ledges, and cliffs in northern and western Russia, Karelia, Smolensk, Crimea, and other regions littered with the detritus of human life, and death.

Like so many other unaddressed problems, that of the unburied dead came to public notice in the Gorbachev period. An article in the popular illustrated journal, *Ogonek,* "Is No One Forgotten?" suggested that the number of abandoned war dead was at least two million, almost all of whom were still listed as "missing in action." Television documentaries deplored the ugly fate of the war's neglected victims, and in 1988–89, in the throes of *perestroika,* a restructured Komsomol helped found the Association of United Search Organizations. The association supervised the activities of between ten thousand and twenty thousand members (the number of participants more than doubles in the summer months) who belonged to several hundred groups with names like *Poisk* (Search), *Iskateli* (Seekers), *Dolina* (Valley)—and *Dozor.*[2]

In the same year, the Soviet Army began to help occasionally in transporting volunteers to old battle sites and providing coffins for burial, gasoline, which it either gave away or sold at low prices, and, most important, experienced sappers to defuse mines—but no money.

The army had good reason to be wary of volunteer search organizations. Sometimes their expeditions yielded more truth than the authorities were ready to make public. In 1989, for example, when a *Dozor* detachment excavated the grounds of a military hospital not far from Novgorod and found the remains of the many sick and wounded patients together with fragments of hospital gowns, its members noted that every skull had been pierced with a bullet hole. The bullets that had been found were Soviet, and besides there was plenty of other evidence that the patients had been shot *before* the Germans had reached the site. This is what Stalin's scorched earth policy had meant: kill our own people before the enemy can make use of them.

In 1991 the Association of United Search Organizations unearthed and buried the remains of 18,349 soldiers. Most of them could not be identified. No one will ever know how many of them were German. In 1992 Iulii Ikonnikov, the head of the association's Coordinating Council, estimated that one million German soldiers still lay unidentified on the territory of the former Soviet Union, but others thought that figure inflated, citing the German Army's propensity to bury its dead and its more efficient body identification system. Ikonnikov had met with German veterans' organizations, hoping for help in finding their MIAs, but was told that while Germany would pay for the upkeep of German graves in the former Soviet Union, finding MIAs there was too risky and too expensive.

In fact, as the fiftieth anniversary of the Stalingrad battle approached in February 1993, both the German and Austrian governments had been struggling with the question of what to do about their dead soldiers whose remains were still scattered under the thinnest cover of earth in the fields and forests around that devastated city that in 1956 had been renamed Volgograd. Come and take them away? Bury them? Build memorials to them? Forget them?[3]

CAN THESE BONES LIVE?

On a terribly hot August night in 1992, eight of us boarded the train in Moscow bound for Rzhev, scene of prolonged brutal fighting during the war. Oppressed by the stifling heat and excited about the journey ahead, I got no sleep at all during the five-hour train ride. "I have, first of all, personal goals," I had written in my journal on the airplane to Moscow a few days before. "Masha is very, very sick. Her doctor has told me that 'we could lose her at any time.' My poor, dear, sweet sister. I first came to Russia in 1978 just a month after Georgie's funeral. I kept going to cemeteries and crying. Now Masha seems as close to death as she's been all year. And I'm going to see bones.

"I am eager to confront death and face it down. To put my own vanity and greed into perspective—to see how we all end up. I hope for the beauty of the woods, for adventure and camaraderie. I hope this will be the closest I ever come to really being in a war."

The party of young people traveling with me included Oleg Lishin's daughter, Tania, who was slim, indeed almost frail-looking, but with a smart-alecky tough manner, and her two children, a wiry ten-year-old boy and a six-year-old girl with strawberry blond hair who kept blowing up a blue balloon and then letting it whiz around the train compartment. We arrived in Rzhev at about 3:00 in the morning and, after some milling around, piled onto a bus, rode for half an hour, then filed out. The bus drove away, leaving us at the edge of a dirt path in total darkness. Blackened trees rustled mysteriously as we entered the woods.

We got to the campsite shortly after dawn. Most everyone was still asleep, but Oleg and Ada Lishin greeted us with hot tea, which we gratefully downed with brown bread. Some fifteen tents had been set up in a forest of tall pines adjacent to a defunct Pioneer camp that was by then used mostly as a very rustic lodge for hikers.

First I wanted to see the soldiers I had been reading about for so many years. Two dozen *Dozor* members had already spent ten days at the site and in nine of them had found the remains of fifty-three people. Just the day before we arrived they had dug up an additional twenty-six.

Soldiers from the Great Patriotic War were waiting for me in a clearing at the edge of the camp. Some crowded together in big, semitransparent plastic bags, waiting to be cleaned and sorted. Others, washed but not yet sorted, rested in piles on a large sheet. Another sheet displayed a neat arrangement of human bones spread out according to type. Leaf-filtered sunlight threw speckled shadows on the skulls aligned in neat rows at the edge of the sheet. Strange, even though no brains or eyes or mouths remained to give them pride of place, the skulls nonetheless took precedence over all the other bones—the thigh bones, pelvises, jumbled ribs, and the rest— reposing in the early morning sun. I glanced at a pile of coccyx bones. What difference did it now make that while alive they had been vestigial?

Oleg scooped up a skull. "You can tell he was very young," he said. "Look at those even white teeth. Whatever gaps you see here are from teeth that fell out after he died."

My camp mates had pitched a tent for me, a tiny, one-person construction of old-fashioned canvas. "It's called a *robinson*," they said, accenting the last syllable, "after Crusoe." I pulled on the rubber barn boots I had purchased in a Vermont country store and some rain pants over which I strapped on a leather belt with the equipment I had been issued: a large knife and a sapper's spade. A handful of us marched into the woods behind Serega Shpilianskii. His *shchup* (probe) was for experienced hands only; it gave a characteristic sound when it touched bone.

With us was Volodia Demidov, a handsome giant of a man about thirty years old. He worked as an administrator with the Association of United Search Organizations, and bore an uncanny resemblance to the "Soldier-Liberator," a 1949 monument to the Soviet troops killed in the storm of Berlin that for decades had served as a prime symbol of the cult of the Great Patriotic War. Demidov had come into the movement through the Komsomol, which had sent him to keep an eye on search activities; in time he had defected from the Komsomol.

We strode through the woods into an open meadow along whose edges grew large, rectangular masses of a beautiful plant called *ivan-chai* (willow herb), tall, graceful stalks adorned with pink flowers. "Before the war there used to be a village here called Noshkino," explained one of my companions. "And now *ivan-chai* has filled in the places where the houses stood." Houses, soldiers vanish suddenly or gradually and plants grow up where they once luxuriated.

We headed back through the woods and came out at the banks of the Volga gliding majestically in the sun. We turned right and fol-

lowed Shpilianskii as he bounded along holding his probe and shovel
on his shoulder, with the river to our left, and to the right, the most
magnificent birch forest I had ever seen.

Fifty years before, the site of that splendid forest had been a battlefield strewn with corpses. Situated northwest of Moscow, Rzhev was
the locus of some of the most horrendous fighting of the war. The
battles there raged almost without respite for the better part of two
years, beginning in 1941, continuing with the Moscow counteroffensive of early 1942 and on past the time of the Stalingrad battle,
when Stalin launched offensives in the Rzhev region—among others—to divert German forces from more strategic places. Particular
plots of land changed hands many times. Easily one million people
died there, with few prisoners taken. By the spring of 1943, according to an official Soviet report, of Rzhev's 5,443 houses only 495
remained standing.[4]

Serega Shpilianskii led us into the woods to a wartime trench that
had been partly dug out. The warm sweet air vibrated with the hum
of insects. The serene beauty clashed with the brutal history of the
site. I quickly learned that the knife I had been issued together with
my sapper's shovel was for cleaning everything we would unearth.
Our goal was to find the remains and effects of soldiers and to study
them carefully with the aim of determining, if possible, just how
each individual had died. A hole through the skull or chestbone was
self-explanatory. Ideally we aimed to identify the soldiers by name
but knew that the likelihood of such identification was slim.

During the war every Soviet soldier had been issued a *smertnyi
medalion* (death medallion), a faceted wooden capsule with a twist-off
top that contained a tightly rolled paper scroll on which their partic-
ulars had been written. Perhaps the army ought to have given those
capsules some other, more innocuous name like "dog tags," because
Soviet soldiers, believing they brought bad luck, would often throw
them away before going into battle.

That first morning I sat on the edge of the trench and, together
with a twelve-year-old boy whose conflicted feelings about the work
had earned him the epithet "hobbit," used my knife to scrape the
earth from each bone before carefully placing it in a tan jute bag.
After fifty years in the soil, the bones had turned as brown as wood. I
wondered if my father's bones were brown too after almost forty

years, or my brother's after fifteen years. I wished I could see them, touch them, talk to them.

As I cut off pieces of earth clinging to the bones, I was filled with the satisfaction of doing something for the dead at a stage when one would have thought it was no longer possible. "I'd like to gently stroke each one by the head," Serega mumbled shyly, coloring slightly as I worked on a skull. What had been that soldier's last thoughts, I wondered? It felt like traveling backward and forward in time simultaneously—backward to the war, and forward beyond death or at any rate beyond death's initial stages, so to speak. Cleaning those bones was an act of both caring and respect, like Jesus Christ washing the feet of the disciples.

Was I crouching on what Tolstoy called "the other side of death?" I felt protected and safe; it was easy to pay homage to someone who could do me no harm. Caressing those bones and skulls was an unusual, unique way of being intimate with strangers. It would give me comfort to know that fifty years after my death, loving, respectful hands would dig up my remains, carefully wash them, and rebury them, preferably with a prayer.

We returned to camp in time for a late breakfast of burnt oatmeal cooked in a big iron pot suspended over an open fire. The beverage was *chaga,* a steamy, bitter brew made from a spongy-looking brown fungus that grew on the birches in those parts. Everyone was also entitled to two slices of bread and two cubes of margarine that young Shurka Rochlin, a gawky, red-headed boy of fifteen, had carefully laid out with his filthy hands into a neat, symmetrical arrangement that brought to mind the skulls and bones lying in order on the other side of the camp.

On day two, my brigade returned to the same clearing in the woods and I felt ready to begin to dig on my own. I jumped into the trench and got to work. My hands were sheathed in those yellow rubber gloves that generations of American women have used to protect their hands from dishpan dryness. Serega had begun to dig out the skull and I finished the job, ever so carefully and gently; the once-vigorous soldier had become so fragile. We unearthed arms, ribs, cartridge cases, bullet shells, splinter fragments. I recalled words from my school days: tibia, fibula, radius, ulna; they sounded like the names of Roman children. The work was hard, messy, hot. My back hurt. I was always hungry. At night I slept so soundly that I had to be shaken awake in the mornings at 6:45, when it was time to have tea and some kind of porridge and get to work.

DOZOR

"After they bring the bags of bones back to camp," Ada Lishin had told me, "the kids make a point of washing every one as a gesture of respect. Then they sort the bones and artifacts, immediately separating out anything that might explode. They examine everything carefully to see if they can identify the individual. Then, at the end of the expedition, if we can get coffins, we put the remains of nine people into each one and hold a burial service to which we invite local inhabitants. We read poems, sing songs, and in the past few years we have usually found a priest to participate in the service. If we have no coffins, we dig a big grave and strew pine branches on the bottom; then we place the bodies on the branches, cover them up, and hold our service." According to Russian custom, evergreen branches symbolize eternal life.

The digs, which usually went on from May to October, were just part of *Dozor's* work. During the rest of the year its members researched the war in libraries and archives in an effort to piece together the military activity in the areas they were planning to excavate. They also traveled to the prospective sites and interviewed local residents who might have spent the war there as children and could share memories that would help pinpoint where fallen bodies might be lying.

On a Sunday afternoon during our dig Lena Petrova, a twenty-year-old university student of history who had spent several months researching the Rzhev battles, presented a lecture to a plenary session of the group. We all sat on logs while Lena, equipped with a map and pointer, described the results of her work in the archives of the Twenty-ninth and Thirtieth Armies.

The Germans first entered Rzhev in October 1941, envisoning it as a springboard for the attack on Moscow. In January 1942, after the battle of Moscow, Soviet forces knocked them back to Rzhev, but before the end of the month the Germans once again controlled the villages around Rzhev as well, and more than a year of fighting would ensue before the Soviets there broke out of the "bag," or encirclement. In the course of Lena's talk, again and again it became apparent just how little thought the high command of the Soviet armed forces had given to the lives of its soldiers—or civilians, for that matter. Unrealistic orders to attack were issued one after another at a time when troops were hardly capable of retreating in an orderly fashion, and besides, they had nowhere to go but down, which was where we found them fifty years later.

Mikhail Gefter, a small, wizened, elderly historian-turned-dissident who was for more than a dozen years my informal academic mentor, had fought and been severely wounded in these lands in the first half of the war. When I later told him about the work of *Dozor* in the Rzhev area, he said, "Without exaggeration, there must be a million corpses in those woods." I asked him why so many of them had been left unburied. "How could we have had time to bury our dead," he replied with a resentful chuckle, "when every moment that we weren't directly under fire we ourselves had orders to attack, attack, attack!"

After Lena's lecture, Volodia Demidov, who had come along to represent the search organizations' association, reported on events that had occurred earlier in 1992. "This has been a tragic year for our movement," he began, his round face with its high Slavic cheekbones looking tired and drawn. In April an eighteen-year-old boy was killed and several others wounded when a group of boys on an expedition in Viazma (not far from Rzhev) piled up a bunch of grenades they had found and set fire to them. Another boy died in June and several others were heavily wounded under similar circumstances in July. In addition, two teenagers had been wounded by mines. Demidov's message was meant to inform, but also to instruct, and he used the opportunity to remind the group about personal safety. In *Dozor* no one was allowed to keep any artifacts he or she had unearthed. Everything—and ammunition in particular—was handed over to one of the group's four commissars, who were at least twenty years old, and usually a good deal older.

Late evenings at camp were given over to music and sitting around on those big logs near the campfire. There was always at least one guitar and many voices. The group sang war songs, songs about the movement, and other favorite melodies. *Dozor*'s theme song, which was belted out at least once a night, had been composed by one of its members, Vladimir Yerkhov, a young composer and filmmaker from Kazan. It was called "Valley of Death."

The trench is full up to the breastwork,
With blackened water from the ground.
It's here the youth lay down forever
In the embrace of his misfortune.
Old cartridge cases near the helmet,
Burst in two places by big splinters,
Serve for us to tell the story
Of war that roamed within our country.
Valley of death, valley of pain,
Valley of mourning, valley of grief
Valley of those missing in action,
Valley of the fallen, valley of the fallen.
The campfire burns on field of battle
Lit by the soldiers' grandchildren,
But its own bright and living heat
Will give cold comfort to those youngsters,
Who perished here and disappeared,
Let their lives fall like packs off shoulders,
Oh true remembrance, true remembrance,
How hard it is to keep you safe.

At one point I picked up the guitar. Although I love to sing Russian songs, something American was called for, I thought, and found myself gravitating towards blues:

Black girl, black girl,
Don't you lie to me,
Tell me where did you sleep last night?
In the pines, in the pines
Where the sun never shines,
And I shivered the whole night through.

For several days I had worked with *Dozor* members, both at the dig and in camp; we had walked, talked, and sung together. I was enormously impressed by their capacity for work, their overall respect for one another (with some exceptions, of course), and above all their commitment to the enterprise of finding and decently burying their World War II compatriots. I believe that the shared perception of the nobility of their cause served as the prime source for the *Dozor*'s success on both common and individual levels.

"And what if these are German bones?" I asked Serega Shpilianskii one day.

"They're probably ours," he said, "since the enemy usually took their men out of the trenches and buried them. But that's really not the point. German soldiers shouldn't lie around like this either. Every civilized human being deserves a decent burial."

"And the fact that we have left our men here for so long," added Demidov, putting down his shovel and wiping the sweat off his forehead, on which his tousled blond hair was plastered, "shows that ours has been an uncivilized country." The lament that Russia was not civilized, or not normal, was common in those post-*perestroika* days. For most everyone, a civilized life meant a modest apartment with indoor plumbing, the availability of basic consumer goods, and, perhaps most important, an administrative system that treated people with respect.

When I would ask the *Dozor* youngsters of fifteen, sixteen, eighteen *why* they had committed their time (and often their own money) to finding MIAs, their answers were never particularly eloquent, and indeed sometimes verged on the monosyllabic. "The job needs to be done." "Because it's necessary, that's all."

The power of the enterprise, I believe, came from its primal, unmediated quality. In contradistinction to paying homage to war monuments, not to speak of engaging in contrived "patriotic" activities, digging for bones is elemental, direct. Indeed, I suspect that in some nearly vestigial recesses of our brains we are all wired to dig around in the earth looking for the bones of our ancestors. And we all could probably benefit from taking direct physical actions that might be initially fearsome but would enable us to pacify the restless ghosts from the past that torment us if we allow ourselves to hear their tread.

Youthful Iconoclasts

One Saturday night in the summer of 1986, in the polar region of Soviet Russia, six young men on motorcycles who were going fishing happened to pass by the "Valley of Glory," where repose the remains of thousands of Soviet fighters who died in the three-year effort to prevent the Germans from taking Murmansk. During the war it was called "Valley of Death," but some four decades later flowers surrounded the pedestal of an obelisk in what had been turned into a modest war memorial. The youths downed a case of beer, then one of them produced a rifle, and, for sport, they began to take turns shooting at empty beer bottles that they ranged along the pedestal. Then, evidently bored with those pedestrian targets, they opened fire on the monument itself. They set their sights on the date, 1941, and on the words THE MOTHERLAND REMEMBERS HER SONS. The shooting spree lasted almost three hours.

Iunost (Youth), a periodical for young people, carried an article about the incident containing a brief interview with Andrei Kulikov, the first of the youths to open fire:

> "Andrei, is it difficult to kill a person?"
> "Of course it is difficult."
> "And is it possible to kill memory?"
> "What memory?"
> "Human memory."
> Kulikov remained silent.[5]

When Andrei Kulikov and his Siberian pals went on their tipsy, gun-toting fling at the Valley of Glory, they were surely not out to kill memory. At best, their choice of location for target practice was entirely random; at worst, theirs was an act of iconoclasm, of sacrilege—the desecration of a sacred object in a civil religion. Indeed if anyone had sought to kill the real human memory of World War II in the Soviet Union, it was not the vandals but rather those who had labored to concoct out of the Valley of Death a contrived "Valley of Glory," with its predictable obelisks and ritual slogans. Perhaps those boys had taken potshots at the Murmansk war memorial precisely as a form of rebellion against years of having to perform unwanted rites, standing honor guard, congratulating veterans, laying wreaths, all by fiat.

Something similar to the Murmansk affair took place in Pavlovsk, outside Leningrad, in 1985. A Leningrad teacher had taken some of her best pupils to Pavlovsk, which is dominated by a magnificent and beautifully restored late–eighteenth-century palace. On the tour they unexpectedly came upon a "fraternal grave" of World War II dead. The teacher was shocked to see the children spontaneously act out a *parody* of wreath laying. "They were running around and laughing, someone threw an armful of dirty leaves on the grave while the others, doubling over with laughter, divided up into those who made believe they were weeping, and those who sang out funereal melodies. 'Boys! Take your caps off!' shouted a star pupil with bows in her hair . . . "

When the teacher started to explain to the children "about those who had died, about duty, about memory—about everything appropriate," she saw that they had understood only one thing: that they could not act out this way in her presence.

The next day the teacher told those children's instructor from the previous year what had happened. "She took it as a reproach to her patriotic work with them and heatedly began to list everything she had done." She had taken them to the Piskarevskoe Cemetery, the Field of Mars, had gone to lay wreaths, to play war games, to meet veterans.

"Now I understood," continued the author, "why the children had committed that sacrilege. Theirs was an unconscious reaction to having been forced to participate in incomprehensible rituals. What on earth do you think was going on in their souls during those times? Those endless, monofaceted 'patriotic' games for show, the contests for the composition of patriotic songs, poems, posters . . . ?" Children, she explained, "need real life—with real dangers and difficulties." This Leningrad teacher repeated her story in a devastating 1987 film, *This is How We Live,* about the alienation and moral depravity of Soviet youth. She shook her head and smiled sadly as she recalled a student who had submitted an essay and had later inquired whether it was satisfactory, or did she "need to add more patriotism?"[6]

LINKAGES

Once in the early 1980s I witnessed the last part of a firewalking workshop. A hundred people had each spent two hundred dollars to learn to imagine and articulate their fears of walking on hot coals, to gain the courage (and a technique, including a shouted mantra) to do that which they feared, and finally to walk across a bed of hot coals yelling "Cool moss! Cool moss!"

The goal of the investment, apparently, was to gain the confidence to do what seemed scary and difficult by doing something very scary and very difficult. As it turned out, people walked quickly, the coals did not have to be that hot to look menacingly orange, and the whole enterprise, run in a conference room and then the parking lot of a Sheraton hotel in suburban Boston, was something of a scam. At the end of the experience, people bought FIREWALKER T-shirts in order to inspire themselves and advertise their proven fearlessness.

Like firewalkers, every *Dozor* member had to confront and overcome his or her initial fear, in this case of exhuming and handling human remains, and each one was thereby strengthened, as, I believe, was I. But the cause far transcended the mere desire to do something frightening for its own sake. A sense of duty and connection to truth, to history, to the dignity of every human individual—these have inspired the years of work put in by volunteers who were and are trying to take direct action to right the wrongs of the past.

The youngsters in *Dozor* attempted in every way to identify themselves with the boys and men whose bodies they had been hacking out of the thick soil. On my last evening with them it was cool and rainy. Sitting by the campfire in our sweaters and jackets, we watched and participated in a stunning theatrical performance. The event was introduced by Oleg Lishin, who told us to imagine ourselves back exactly fifty years, to August 1942. A young soldier from that time, he said, would come to see us and tell us of his fate and aspirations. All we needed to do was listen to him and ask him questions. Then Oleg withdrew and we were left with a light rain and the fire flickering in the darkness.

Sasha Aleshin, a handsome, clean-cut seventeen-year-old group member who had spent weeks preparing, stumbled into view dressed in the full uniform of a wartime Red Army soldier. For a while a field nurse played by the Lishins' daughter, Tania, chatted with him, but then she disappeared and Sasha the wartime soldier was left to expound upon the details of the fighting he had seen and participated in, and on his hopes, his politics, his fears, his beliefs. At an age when young people tend to be hopelessly narcissistic by hormonal fiat, Sasha had made a spiritual leap into another era, into another soul.

The last thing I did before leaving camp was to say good-bye to the pile of bones and skulls I had greeted on my first morning—except that now others had been added to the neat collection. This time we did not have to repeat our long march along what would now be muddy country roads, because an army medical rescue vehicle transported us to the Rzhev railroad station. We arrived in Moscow at 5:30 in the morning.

After a wash and some breakfast I walked over to the local church, an eighteenth-century gem. It was both *Preobrazhenie* (Day of the Transfiguration) and *Iablochnyi Spas*, a Russian church holiday dedicated to the first apple harvest. I bought two of those beautiful mustard-colored candles they sell in every Russian church and, overwhelmed by the smell of incense and apples and by the glorious choral chants, I made my way over to a *Bogomater* (an icon of the Mother of God with child), and lit both candles. Then I said two prayers: one for my dying sister, the other for the boys, the hundreds of thousands of boys, men, women, and girls, who had died in the battlefields around Rzhev.

Antigone of Thebes had to sacrifice her life so that her brother's soul could go to its eternal home. But Antigone's children, the thousands of volunteers who slogged through forests and swamps to rescue their dead brothers, had received the gift of a life fraught with meaning, dignity, and that sense of connectedness with the past and future that can eventually lead to wisdom.

3

THE LAST HURRAH

In May 1985, the Soviet Union commemorated the fortieth anniversary of the Victory of the Soviet People in the Great Patriotic War with a propaganda extravaganza of monumental proportions. The event was the last flamboyant, orchestrated tribute to the old guard before the political system they were celebrating was blown apart by the winds of *glasnost, perestroika,* and *demokratizatsiia.*

During Leonid Brezhnev's eighteen-year tenure as general secretary of the Party—now known as the period of *zastoi* (stagnation)—his administration had specialized in blockbuster jubilees: in 1967, the fiftieth anniversary of the revolution; in 1970, the centennial of Lenin's birth; in 1975, the thirtieth anniversary of the Soviet victory in the Great Patriotic War. These elaborately orchestrated galas were meant to infuse the body politic with national pride and a spirit of allegiance toward the Party that in all three events congratulated itself in an outpouring of slogans, speeches, media hype, posters, and commemorative objects ranging from topical bric-a-brac for sale in kiosks to gargantuan examples of monumental art. Whether the nation was convulsed in a paroxysm of propaganda glorifying Lenin one year or extolling grieving mothers and triumphant soldiers in another, the message was pretty much the same: socialism had triumphed. The reality contrapuntal to the workers' paradise feted in the flamboyant jubilees was an inefficient economy, ailing political leadership, and a demoralized populace, all of them rife with corruption.

In 1985 the media were saturated with the war theme for the first four months, but the focus of public ritual was Victory Day, May 9. By that time, the new general secretary of the Party, Mikhail Gorbachev, had been in office for only two months; the jubilee had been planned during the tenure of his immediate predecessor, Konstantin Chernenko, and may well have been conceived before Brezhnev's death in the fall of 1982.

I visited Leningrad, Moscow, and Volgograd to witness the jubilee and returned home with a suitcase full of newspapers, magazines, commemorative books, cards, posters, and a stack of records of wartime songs that I had purchased in the Volgograd department store in whose basement Field Marshal Paulus had surrendered to Soviet forces on February 2, 1943.

The fortieth anniversary celebration turned out to be the last full-scale, overblown Soviet megaholiday. The Soviet Union is gone, and besides, how many veterans are going to be around to enjoy their fiftieth in 1995? For most, 1985 was their last hurrah.

LENINGRAD

Arriving in Leningrad felt like coming home to mourn. My parents were both born in St. Petersburg in the early part of this century. Together with my grandparents and all of my aunts and uncles, they left their stately Petersburg homes in the maelstrom of the 1917 revolution and its aftermath. But many relatives stayed behind. One, the foreman in my maternal grandfather's enormous macaroni factory, had married his employer's sister. When, by 1918, the confiscation of the factory was imminent, my grandfather, Nikolai Goldberg-Rudkovskii, expressed the desire to retain ownership, protesting to his foreman that he had always been a fair and generous employer. "Indeed you have," replied his brother-in-law, "but now our paths must diverge; yours leads to the right, and ours to the left."

Grandfather moved to Finland, the foreman retained his job, and Ivanov and Goldberg Macaroni Factory (Ivanov was a fiction, meant to legitimate the factory in those times of official anti-Semitism), purveyor of pasta to the Imperial Army, became the Leningrad State Macaroni Factory. Grandfather Goldberg died of cancer in New York City shortly after the outbreak of World War

II. Many members of his family who had stayed in what became
the Soviet Union perished of hunger, cold, and disease in the great
siege of Leningrad.

During my first visit to Leningrad, a month-long sojourn seven
years before, I had fallen in love with that beautiful city of canals and
shabby, nineteenth-century houses hiding intricate systems of smelly
courtyards. The city is known for its Dostoevskian mists and fog, but
during that entire month of May 1978, it was bathed in sunlight that
threw sharp shadows on the wide streets. In mid-May a cold sun
slowly broke up the ice on the river Neva, and two weeks later a
warm and fragrant balm forced the birches into a glorious and dramatic birth of spring. It seemed to me a poor city but one that was
blessed with extraordinary elegance, the home of the most beautifully
spoken Russian in the world, the imperial capital of all the Romanov
emperors, the city that would likely now be my home had it not
been for the world-shaking events of 1917.

I returned to Leningrad on May 5, 1985 (the very afternoon that
President Ronald Reagan was in Bitburg, Germany, paying his
respects at the graves of the German enemy, including the graves of
members of the SS). On my way into the city from the airport I
stopped at the major memorial to the blockade, completed in 1975.
Mournful music from a loudspeaker alternated with the ticking of a
metronome, a heartlike sound carried on the airwaves during every
minute of the siege. Embedded, cavelike, in the memorial was a
spooky museum featuring tacky mosaics of wartime scenes on its
windowless walls. One of them depicted Dmitrii Shostakovich composing the Leningrad Symphony. The funereal music and metronome provided a dramatic background to my lone heels as they
clicked along the polished floor. Although Leningrad was already
filled with bemedaled veterans, I was alone in the museum with the
museum guard, an animated elderly woman who was glad to show
me the exhibit. She proudly showed off part of the original score of
the Leningrad Symphony, but I kept coming back to a glass-covered
case devoted to hunger: it contained a worn ration card and a 125-
gram daily ration piece of black bread, a pathetically diminutive
dark-brown rectangle on a tiny bread board.

Outside, ranged on a high wall, were silhouetted statues in stylized
poses. Sailors and soldiers brandished bayoneted rifles; a helmeted

soldier embraced a clinging child with his enormous hands; a grieving mother gazed up at her tall son in a piteous farewell. On the
monument's lower level, I photographed the jagged ends of a black
granite semicircle engraved with gold letters: 900 DAYS 900
NIGHTS. Suddenly a pimply faced young policeman grabbed my
arm, and claiming that I had broken the law by photographing him,
marched me over to his superior. "What the hell are you bothering
me for? Get her out of here!" snapped the captain, a surly giant,
without even looking up from his cramped desk. "With the f-film?"
stammered the policeman. His angry boss lifted his head and glared
at me. "Of course, with the film! Now get out!" And he waved us
both away. That was that. Nothing had occurred except the mindless
harassment of a foreigner, so characteristic of the bad old days under
Brezhnev. Why, I wondered, was there a police station in a war
memorial? To prevent vandalism? To demonstrate that this was the
state's and not the people's place?

Like every other city in the Soviet Union, Leningrad was in the
grip of the agitation and propaganda campaign commemorating the
fortieth anniversary. Red banners emblazoned with self-congratulatory slogans fluttered incongruously from resplendent buildings
erected in the era of Catherine the Great. But the city's mood was as
somber and cold as the gray skies and swaying bare trees still
untouched by the promise of spring.

The primary site of both official and informal mourning ceremonies, that year as every year for more than a quarter-century, was
the Piskarevskoe cemetery, where more than a half-million victims of
the siege are buried. It is the largest of the city's repositories of its
war dead. Intending to spend Victory Day itself in Moscow, I visited
the Piskarevskoe cemetery three days before that event.

Like most visitors to the cemetery, I first stopped for a minute of
silence at the eternal flame that burns in a massive square of gray
granite. To the sound of Chopin's Funeral March lugubriously
resounding throughout the cemetery over loudspeakers, I slowly
made my way to the mass graves, enormous plots covered with grass
and each marked with a stone slab engraved with a leaf, a hammer
and sickle or a star, and the year in which the Leningraders buried
there died 1941, 1942, 1943, 1944. A simple bunch of flowers,
mostly tulips, casually draped the top of each slab. As I walked I

thought about my own relatives and family friends lying nameless and silent somewhere under those large expanses of grass. These musings intensified a bit later when I came upon a section of named graves, mostly of military officers, and saw one bearing my paternal grandmother's last name, Gurevich.

My funereal mood was repeatedly interrupted by the grating and hissing noises made by giant cleaning and hosing machines, out in full force to prepare the cemetery for the holiday. Packs of school-children trotted past in pairs, the girls walking arm in arm, as was their charming habit. Many carried flowers. They paused at the eternal flame and then moved on to the nearby pool where their teacher showed them the mosaic of a flame glistening at the bottom. Soon the children were replaced by a solemn group of military offi-cers and then by a jolly handful of American veterans who, forty years earlier, had met their Soviet counterparts at Torgau, on the Elbe. Eventually everyone ended up at the far end of the cemetery to lay flowers at the foot of the statue called "Motherland," erected in the late 1950s.

The statue shows a fulsome young woman balancing a garland of leaves on open hands that look at once welcoming and powerful. Behind her stretches a mushroom-colored wall on which are engraved the words of a poem by Leningrad poet Olga Berggolts, a poem whose last line had become the watchword of the war cult:

Here lie the people of Leningrad.
Here lie its citizens, men, women, children.
Near them are Red Army soldiers.
They defended you, Leningrad,
Cradle of the revolution.
We cannot here enumerate their noble names,
So many are there under the eternal protection of granite.
But know as you look upon this stone
No one is forgotten, nothing is forgotten.

Leningrad did not need monuments, museums, slogans, posters, or exhibits of commemorative art. Its cemeteries eloquently told the whole story.

Moscow

On May 7, 1985, I wandered into the restaurant of Moscow's National Hotel in search of lunch, and was seated at a table with a couple in their thirties. Zhemel, hirsute and swarthy, was consuming an appetizer—ovals of white bread topped with butter and smoked fish. Ira, an overly made-up woman in a turquoise dress and dangling earrings, with a small garnet cross at her neck and a mop of curly blond hair, was trying to talk without too much obvious slurring. Next to her plate was a two-thirds-empty bottle of vodka. Responding to their questions, I explained that I was an historian who had come to Moscow for *Den Pobedy* (Victory Day). At this, Ira, who had been laughing quite a bit, grew serious, even maudlin.

"*Den Pobedy* is the only *real* holiday, the only one that means anything," she said thickly, fumbling clumsily in her purse for a cloth handkerchief. "As for *their* holidays—*their* May Day, *their* anniversary of the revolution—you can send them all to hell! But *Den Pobedy* . . . can you imagine, twenty million dead? Twenty million! So much suffering." She dabbed at her eyes, heavily laced with smeared mascara. "I always cry on *Den Pobedy*." Considering myself lucky to get away with joining them for only two rounds of vodka, I escaped into downtown Moscow, which was even more flamboyantly decked out in red than Leningrad. Shop windows, especially in bookstores, were given over to Victory Day in much the same way as American stores blare out Christmas in the late fall. Most notable were the many veterans strolling, mainly in twos and threes, along the streets. They were largely civilians, though some wore current military uniforms. All proudly sported their medals on the right side of their jackets and, on the left side, collections of *znachki*, the formerly ubiquitous little metal pins indicating membership in or support for an organization, cause, or place.

The weather was gray and cold, although the graceful birch trees I had seen on my way into Moscow from Vnukovo airport were already resplendent in delicate leaves of the lightest green. On May 8, virtually all radio and television programs were devoted to the holiday. They ranged from groups of children singing lilting, lyrical ditties about the happy holiday to poetic declamations about the dead, ponderously contrived to sadden the heart.

Like Jewish holidays, important Soviet celebrations often began the evening before the actual targeted day. The May 9 rituals began on May 8, at 3:00 in the afternoon, with the big ceremonial meeting of the Party and government held in the Kremlin's Palace of Congresses. It was a televised, carefully orchestrated quasi-religious service. After the playing of the national anthem, everyone rose as the Victory Banner was carried into the hall by a naval honor guard to the rousing march, *Den Pobedy,* the holiday's inappropriately bouncy theme song. Sometimes called the "holy of holies" (the epithet also given to the innermost sanctuary of the Jewish Temple in Jerusalem), this flag is the one that Soviet forces hoisted onto the Berlin Reichstag building on April 30, 1945.

I watched the television coverage of the meeting in the apartment of the historian Mikhail Gefter. His face pale and wrinkled behind large spectacles, Gefter had on his at-home uniform—blue sweatpants, a plaid flannel shirt, and those floppy felt slippers that everyone wears in Russian apartments. Gorbachev was still an unknown, having become Party chairman only two months earlier, but one of the many rumors afloat in Moscow was that to honor the fortieth anniversary of victory, the bad old guard in the Party leadership had wanted to change Volgograd's name back to Stalingrad, and that Mikhail Gorbachev had personally vetoed the move. Gefter believed the rumor and was eager to listen for the general secretary's allusions to Stalin in his formal address; the savvy historian rightly considered Stalin the great barometer of political continuity and change.

Gorbachev's speech was called "The Soviet People's Immortal Valiant Deed." His style of delivery was refreshingly crisp and unpretentious, but the speech was a string of clichés: the heroic Soviet people saved Europe from fascist enslavement; the victory has not receded into the past but is embodied in our present and future; congratulations to our front-line soldiers, partisans, and resistance fighters. "Glory to your great deed, in the name of the motherland, in the name of life on earth!" The audience was filled with some women and many men—veterans of front and labor—their jackets encrusted with medals.

> The mortal danger hanging over the homeland and the tremendous force of patriotism elevated the entire country to fight a people's war, a holy war. Soviet people drew strength from the great Leninist ideas.

They rose to the defense of their motherland. . . . The roots of the victory are in the nature of socialism, in the Soviet way of life. . . . It was a victory of our ideology and morality.

Gefter and I kept waiting for some mention of Stalin. Would Gorbachev possibly leave him out altogether? No, he uttered the name once: "The gigantic work at the front and in the rear was guided by the Party, its Central Committee, the State Defense Committee headed by the General Secretary of the CPSU Central Committee Joseph Vissarionovich Stalin." Only one mention, that was good. But, to my shock, when Gorbachev uttered the name Stalin, the audience exploded in applause so loud and so pro- longed—lasting seventeen seconds—that Gorbachev had to stop his speech and ask for quiet.[1]

What did this applause mean? I glanced at Gefter's wife, Lela, a retired librarian whose grown children had long teased her about her loyalty to the regime. She tearfully shook her head and said that the audience—representing her own generation—was expressing its longing for a revival of the strong Party to which the official saga attributed the great victory. Gefter soberly added that it was impossi- ble to disassociate Stalin from the victory, because May 9 had been, in fact, a victory for the dictator himself.

During this fortieth anniversary year, Mikhail Gefter was brim- ming with sadness and love for his Moscow University history faculty classmates who had perished in the war. He had spent months visit- ing their widows, relatives, and friends and collecting their letters from the front. "To remember is to resurrect and also to understand (anew and for the first time) those whom memory has brought back to life," Gefter wrote in his introduction to these letters, which he hoped to publish as a book. With the pompous, self-congratulatory ceremonial meeting soundlessly blinking on the television screen, he spread out onto a brown-and-white checked oilcloth a fistful of let- ters and photographs of their authors. I swallowed hard as I gazed on the intelligent, hopeful, painfully young faces.

All frontline letters were triangular for instant recognition. My colleague's arthritic hands lovingly unfolded the yellowed triangles. "Friendship was the religion that sustained these boys and girls," he murmured. "Nothing was more important. Listen to the end of the poem young Musia Ginzburg wrote to his sister in 1940: 'Honestly now, what is happiness?/A friend's smile, and nothing else.'"

I asked Gefter whether he thought the letters would see print.

"Not likely," he responded. "First of all, too many of the boys who wrote them have Jewish names. Besides, the letters are too personal, too lyrical. Our readers are supposed to learn that our young men fought 'for the motherland, for Stalin,' rather than for themselves or each other, or for genuine freedom." He picked up a triangle and out tumbled a photograph of a sweetly smiling boy with round eyeglasses and the gleaming hair of youth. The contrapuntal dissonance between the ritual display of stentorian speakers, gold-embroidered flags, and decorated military men on the screen a few feet away and the tremulous passion that infused Mikhail Gefter's commemorative project resonated in my brain.[2]

Many were happy to be swept along by the ludicrous torrent of newspaper and journal articles, television and radio programs, posters, postcards, paintings, slogans, leaflets, *znachki,* plays, and poems—especially war veterans, who were heaped with honors for the occasion. Every veteran was supposed to receive a gift and a fortieth anniversary medal (actually, the Union of Veterans' inefficient administration missed some, who later complained vociferously in the press). Some people, including a number of my closest longtime soul mates, were so deeply offended by the kitsch that they would have nothing to do with the holiday.

Others, like Gefter, had managed to make Victory Day their own. He had received his new medal but had stuck it in a box together with his others. He would never strut around showing them off as did so many of his compatriots. And yet he observed the holiday. In the Gefter household, May 9 was usually a day given over to family and the company of wartime friends. On the fortieth, Mikhail was not well enough to receive groups of visitors, but as he and I sifted through his classmates' letters and portraits, we were repeatedly interrupted by telephone callers conveying holiday greetings. In addition he had received a stack of Victory Day letters and cards, including one crayoned by his granddaughter. He read me a letter from a wartime friend, now a mathematician in the Siberian city of Tomsk. It was reflective, even profound, the way ordinary letters sometimes used to be in our own country in past decades. "All this talk of triumph reminds me even more of that constant sickening fear we lived with, fear not only of the enemy, but of our own war administration, and fear for all humanity. I feel a similar tremor now as I wonder, is the world now threatened by a new Hitler?" The reference was to Ronald Reagan, who had long been portrayed in the Soviet press as a trigger-happy communist basher.

Ira, my tipsy lunch partner of the previous day, had been right. Victory Day *was* the only real, official holiday. It was *both* the tool of propagandists touting its triumphs and a memorial day for millions of relatives and friends of the war dead. The Victory Day anniversary was both a sham—with its managers seeking to manipulate popular emotion inspired by a genuinely traumatic past experience in order to mobilize public energies in support of the Party and state, a time for the inescapable barrage of self-serving hype—and a day for families to lay flowers on the graves of their loved ones or to leave a bouquet at their local war memorial. It was a time for official speeches fueling the battle against Reagan's politics and declaring the 1945 victory over Germany an almost exclusively Soviet affair, demonstrating the superiority of socialism over capitalism. And it was a day for reveling in the camaraderie of elderly veterans united with their old buddies in thousands of informal meeting places throughout the land.

For the evening of May 8 I had bought two tickets to *the* commemorative concert held in the Bolshoi Theater, but none of my Soviet friends were willing to sacrifice their principles and aesthetic standards to accompany me. To an outsider, totalitarian kitsch may be revealing, titilating, entertaining. But when you are part of the target population, the experience is tedious at best and, at worst, genuinely upsetting. In the end, my friends felt sorry for me, and someone's aunt, whom I had once met seven years earlier, volunteered to come to the concert, as it turned out, because she wanted me to convey a message to her émigré cousin in Newton, Massachusetts.

The concert was a motley musical mix that started off with orchestral pieces by Beethoven (why begin with German music, I wondered?) and Shostakovich to give the evening a proper solemnity, and then moved on to the more "popular" part of the program. Fat women and fat men with voluptuous voices sang some hauntingly beautiful wartime melodies. The most erotic number was a ballet called "Red Banner," which featured a woman in a sexy, gauzy, red fluttery costume who was tossed around by graceful men in khaki leotards. The biggest applause went to an elderly but still vigorous baritone who belted out "The Souls of Veterans Do Not Grow Old." Indeed, the evening was a kind of senior citizens' jubilee, the magnificent hall filled with benign-looking, balding, bemedaled veterans and their similarly decorated spouses.

Throughout the Soviet Union, for a few days in May, millions of old folks, typically unhappy and unwanted dependents living with their grown children, shook off their troubles, donned their medals, and tried to turn themselves into objects of popular respect and even admiration. The sighing, grumbling, embittered, and often despondent old people I had been used to seeing in Moscow shop queues and trolleybuses were serene and sometimes buoyant as they strolled proudly in groups, accepting the congratulations of their younger compatriots.

Den Pobedy

Victory Day, 1985! I was jolted out of sleep at 6:30 in the morning by the sound of a major commotion outside the ample windows of my hotel room. World War II tanks—hundreds of them—were rumbling down Gorky Street toward Red Square. A gray thicket of clouds hardly detracted from the holiday atmosphere in Fiftieth-Anniversary-of-October Square outside the National Hotel. Food and holiday souvenirs were on sale at little stands like the kind I used to see on Central Park West on Thanksgiving morning before the big parade. The difference was that in Moscow the crowds were small—since the entire parade route was off-limits to most pedestrians—and instead of soft pretzels and Mickey Mouse balloons, I bought soft rolls and generic red holiday flags imprinted with yellow five-pointed stars and swirling fireworks.

Admission to viewing the parade in Red Square, which began at ten o'clock, was by invitation only. Our own ambassador, Arthur Hartman, was boycotting the event on orders from Ronald Reagan, who had gone from Bitburg to the beaches of Normandy to make his Victory Day statement. Like most everyone else, I watched the parade of veterans of front and labor, and contemporary troops, on television. The military hardware I saw, heard, and smelled while leaning out my hotel room window.

In an updated version of the grand tradition that used to send elaborately uniformed commanders in chief to review massed troops on horseback, Defense Minister S. L. Sokolov, his chest dripping with heavy metal, surveyed the fatherland's finest from an open convertible, shouting to and receiving greetings from each military group. Mikhail Gorbachev surveyed the procession from atop the Lenin Mausoleum, standing on the spot from which, on June 24, 1945, Generalissimo Stalin had observed the original victory parade. In contrast to the elaborately decked-out top brass, Mr. Gorbachev looked unassuming in a gray overcoat, gray print scarf, and soft gray fedora, the sort of outfit my father used to wear in New York in the fifties. The general secretary saluted occasionally; Minister Sokolov made the only speech, a short, punchy exaltation of the triumph, followed by a protracted display of the Victory Banner and gold-embroidered red flags from the Great Patriotic War.

The parade's highlight, which many viewers later reported to have enjoyed, was the cavalcade of World War II military machinery accompanied by men in period uniforms. Most of the machinery and costumes had come from the state film studio. When the hundreds of old-fashioned tanks massed beneath my window began to move into Red Square bellowing white smoke, the noise was deafening.

The parade ended with a banal exposition of current military hardware. "The Soviet people won a victory in the Great Patriotic War in the name of peace and life of earth," declared *Pravda* the next day. "Looking on the mighty modern weaponry passing through Red Square, you are once more assured: no one has the strength to overpower the leading workers' and peasants' state in the world!"

After the parade, veterans and well-wishers gathered, as they do every year on Victory Day, in front of the Bolshoi Theater. How rich in feeling and narrative were the faces of the old people, with their gnarled fingers wrapped around small bouquets of flowers! The tone of the gathering turned joyful as groups of veterans and their companions on the theater steps broke into song. Joining them in "Katiusha" (a prewar song that became popular during the war because of the famed rocket of the same name), I felt unaccountably close to those unknown men and women; my sister and I had sung that song together when we were young. Then the group shifted into the lilting song "Tovarishch Stalin," and I once again remembered who and what had been their wartime inspiration.

In the afternoon, veterans congregated in Moscow's parks with comrades from their wartime divisions. I spent some five hours at Gorky Park, together with hundreds of thousands of veterans and their families and friends. At the entrance to the park, handwritten posters, affixed to lamposts or held up by patient relatives, displayed old blurred photographs of unsmiling boys and begged for information about them in a search for their loved ones who were listed as missing in action.

Gorky Park was throbbing with life. A warm sun had dispelled the morning's cloud cover and projected lacy shadows through fragrant, newly leaving trees. "Ladies, please undress!" shouted a florid veteran to a group of women veterans strolling close by. "Today is Victory Day! Please undress!" he continued, with a twinkly smile, ostensibly (but not definitively) referring to only their outer garments.

Although women, including female veterans, made up a goodly portion of the crowd, the afternoon was dominated by men. Indeed, Victory Day was a decidedly male holiday. Attaching myself to a contingent from the division that had taken Berlin, I felt my feminist standards begin to erode (as they always did in the Soviet Union) when the men, led by a vigorous colonel with friendly features and a full head of gray hair, sang bawdy front-line songs. "Hey, gals! Where are you?" went the refrain of a song about a girl with remarkable "pinecones." The women in the group answered, giggling, "Here, here!" At the end of each song, the colonel waved his hand twice, then shouted, "three, four," and the men yelled out "*mo-lod-tsy!*" (fine fellows).

Ambling through another part of the park in the second half of the afternoon, the balmy spring air filled with music, balloons, laughter, and shouts from people of all ages, I came upon a wooden concert shell and large row of benches already filled to capacity. A few moments later uniformed boys with rifles saluted as the audience applauded military banners on parade. The proceedings resembled a Memorial Day celebration in an American small town, except that the veterans were feted with a fuller spirit than we ever exude at home. The audience stood and clapped in time to a marching band as the old guard marched onto the small stage. Graceless speeches were followed by a bland children's concert.

MINUTE OF SILENCE

The eternal flame at Moscow's Tomb of the Unknown Soldier filled the television screen with darting, pointed waves of orange and yellow. The click . . . click . . . click of a ticking metronome. Then a ghostly female chorus started humming the German composer Robert Schumann's "Träumerei," the oddly chosen theme melody of the official remembrance of the war dead. It was 6:50 in the evening, and I was watching "Minute of Silence," an elaborately contrived, quasi-religious ritual of mourning intended as the emotional climax of Victory Day.

In an all-knowing, compassionate basso that Americans are used to hearing in laxative ads, a mellow male voice began to intone a prose poem lament to the unknown soldier and the twenty million war dead. In 1985, twenty million was the official number of victims commemorated in the cult of the Great Patriotic War. That number would rise in the Gorbachev period. "Comrades, let the light of our grateful remembrance, the light of our love, and of our grief, now illuminate the names of our fallen warriors. Let us remember, twenty million of our lives were carried away by the war." The chorus kept on crooning the lyrical Schumann dirge in the background as the comforting voice continued for ten minutes to eulogize those who had given their lives for the defense of the fatherland. The timbre of the faceless voice was measured, mournful, but the words were manifestly calculated to instil a sense of pride—even glory—in the Red Army's victory. "In the victory marches of the great holiday, the voices of our heroes live on. Their lives continue from generation to generation. History will preserve the heroes' valiant deeds."

The wave of sopranos swelled thickly in the background. "The earth of many countries in Europe is drenched with the blood of the soldier-liberators, and a grateful humanity bows its head before them."

Nikolai Gogol had ended *Dead Souls* with his famed, messianic vision of Russia as a troika of galloping steeds tearing the wind to shreds as the world's nations step aside in awe. The "minute of silence" lament revealed the Soviet Union as a messiah that, by the spilling of its own blood, had delivered humankind. A self-proclaimed post-hoc messianism honed by self-sacrifice.

The sonorous voice now turned to the unknown soldier with a low, slow declamation of the epitaph engraved on his tomb: "Your name is unknown, your deed is immortal." The warmest, softest part of the poem humanized the soldier into a young father lifting his little son high into the air. "Or maybe he did not yet have a wife or son or daughter, but only a first love . . . "

The voice toughened a bit as it lauded the twelve hero cities of the Soviet Union.* Then, moving down the pecking order from Soviet soldiers, the poem praised the "inspiring word" of the Party, followed by Soviet partisans and underground resistance fighters, wartime laborers—women, old people, adolescents—and, in order, the finest sons of Yugoslavia, Poland, Czechoslovakia, Bulgaria, Albania, Hungary, and Romania. Only after the acknowledgment of Romania—whose forces had mostly fought on the wrong side—did the narrator enjoin his listeners to remember the soldiers of "England, America, France, all the countries of the anti-Hitler coalition." Each of the above groups was also ranked in order of the level of reverence due them. Thus the sagacious voice entreated us to "bow down low" before our dead Soviet comrades, to "pay our respects" to the memories of the war dead from the fraternal socialist countries, but merely to "remember duly" the dead soldiers of Europe and America.

> History will eternally sanctify those hurriedly scribbled yellowing sheets of paper reading, "I am going off to war. I ask to be considered a communist." That was both an oath and a commandment to us—to build communism. We are carrying into the future Lenin's banner, warmed by the blood of the revolutionary generations. Our victory is with us. Born in the spring of forty-five, it brought us the happiness of life.

Somebody had composed this televised ritual with great care. For immediately following the crescendo of accolades to the Party that

---

*Moscow, Leningrad, Odessa, Kiev, Minsk, Stalingrad, Sevastopol, Novorossiisk, Kerch, Tula, and, as of May 9, 1985, Smolensk and Murmansk.

would prompt a random Soviet listener instinctively to move into a well-practiced tune-out mode, the narrator's rich baritone uttered a phrase meant to go straight to the heart: "Let us bow our heads to the bright memory of the sons, fathers, husbands, brothers, sisters, comrades-in-arms, friends, comrades, dear ones who did not return from the war."

The last couple of minutes of the broadcast constituted the highest ritual in the entire liturgical calendar of Communist Party culture. "The minute of silence is upon us," tolled the bell-like baritone, the screen still showing the by now hypnotic tongues of flame. Suddenly I heard a clamor of pealing bells. What bells? The Kremlin church bells had been silent for decades. The sound was eerie, disembodied. Then the bells tolled seven times. "The minute of silence," intoned the invisible priest. After a minute's pause, a lone bell chimed out the haunting melody of "*Vy zhertvoiu pali*" (You Have Fallen Victim), an old Bolshevik funeral hymn. The narrator intoned his final incantation as though he were casting a spell: "ETERNAL GLORY TO THE HEROES WHO FELL IN THE STRUGGLE FOR THE FREEDOM AND INDEPENDENCE OF OUR MOTHERLAND!" An astonishing wave of organ music ended the ritual, filling my hotel room overlooking Gorky Street with the sounds of a Lutheran worship service. Why, I wondered, did the carefully composed liturgy climax with a fair imitation of "A Mighty Fortress Is Our God" when the music in a Russian Orthodox church is always a cappella? No doubt because the people who, in the 1960s, first composed the annual "Minute of Silence" were striving to convey an aura of sacredness without in any way simulating the rites of Russian Orthodoxy, which at the time (indeed, until the 1988 millennium of Russian Christianity) was officially spurned.

A TIME TO REMEMBER

Later that evening, after watching the splendid fireworks from a friend's balcony, I asked him to drive me as close to Red Square as possible, since the downtown area was closed to traffic for *narodnoe gulianie,* holiday strolling.

My friend let me off at a bridge that leads toward Red Square's Alexander Garden. Charmed by the unearthly beauty of the

Kremlin, which was bathed in a jewel-like sheen, I was simultaneously chilled by the presence of soldiers standing at stiff attention every ten paces along the length of the bridge. Were they there to keep order? Did the authorities fear that strolling citizens might run amok? Perhaps someone's sense of aesthetics dictated the silent display of force on the grounds that the ramrod-stiff soldiers would lend, as they did, a military splendor to the occasion.

As a woman who grew up in New York City, I instinctively fear street crowds; the streets harbor danger. Thus I loved the feeling of freedom from harm that, in the Brezhnev days, leavened my solitary research trips to Leningrad and Moscow. Predictably, that ease of movement has since been sharply curtailed by the precipitous crime rise that accompanied, first, the new freedoms ushered in by the Gorbachev phenomenon, and, subsequently, the chaos that set in with the demise of the Soviet Union. But in 1985 the old rules still operated, and I joined the stream of strollers crossing the bridge, luxuriating in the warmth of being part of a large and friendly group gathered in a major world capital at nighttime. We moved toward Red Square, where knots of celebrants chatted, laughed, sang, and danced until midnight, when normal traffic resumed.

The next day was beautifully bright, and early in the morning, at a subway station in the southeast edge of Moscow, I met my best friend, Valentin (Valia) Gefter, a computer programmer born, like me, within months of the victory. He and some of his pals had packed food; I had brought liquor from the hotel hard-currency shop. Sixteen of us (twelve adults, four children) boarded a bus and rode off to the country for a picnic. By mistake, a young man in our group had taken the seat of the ticket collector, a heavyset woman in her fifties. When she confronted him, he jumped up at once, and Valia, chuckling, explained, "He thought he had a right to that seat, because he's a veteran of the Great Patriotic War." "How dare you make such a joke!" she grumbled. Valia's friends tittered.

When in 1970 the Communist Party of the Soviet Union consecrated the hundredth anniversary of Lenin's birth, that affair was so inappropriately overblown it immediately spawned jokes. (Newlyweds were now to purchase beds for three, because "Lenin is always with us." A new brassiere, called "Lenin Hills," went on sale. And so on.) In 1985, although the Great Patriotic War theme was every bit as pervasive as Lenin's visage and slogans had been fifteen years earlier, I heard many complaints about the pomposity and tastelessness of the jubilee, but only one relevant joke—and it bombed. "Do you know about the *velikii podvig* (great deed) of the hero Pavlik Matrosov?" Valia queried impishly, after the ticket collector was out of range. We had come to the edge of a splendid birch forest. Valia's riddle had intentionally melded two officially acclaimed young heroes: Pavlik Morozov, the fourteen-year-old martyr was murdered in 1932 by enraged villagers after he had turned in his own father to the authorities for hoarding grain during the forced collectivization of the peasants; Aleksandr Matrosov, the most famed of all war heroes, saved his buddies and lost his own life at age eighteen by throwing his body over the gun port of an exploding enemy pillbox.

"Okay, Valia, tell us about Pavlik Matrosov," said his smiling wife, Lena, who apparently had not yet heard the joke. "He saved his comrades by casting his body over that of his father!" Valia answered, laughing.

"Matrosov isn't someone to laugh about," remarked Valia's colleague, Igor. "That's right," the others joined in.

I felt sorry for Valia, who looked embarrassed, but his friends were right. It was impossible to make fun of the lavish cult of the Great Patriotic War without in some way deriding the actual war experience. The horrific and in some ways majestic stories that came together as collective memory were solid pieces of the mosaic of lies and truth that for decades had made up the sustaining myth of the Great Patriotic War, a mosaic that served both to evoke the past and to cover up selected portions of it.

Books about Russians invariably mention their love of the land, their delight in simple outings in country, and rightly so. Pretentious declamations of love for the fatherland or motherland are statements of loyalty to a political system and nothing more. But the pleasure Russian people take in a romp in the woods—not to achieve physical fitness, not to monitor their efforts to cope in a natural environment, not to feel good about themselves, but simply to fill the lungs with clearer air and indulge the senses in the sights and sounds of trees and sky—is intense and sensuous. No wonder Walt Whitman is such a favorite among Russians!

Valia and his friends yanked me out of the crowded bus, and we tramped through muddy new grass toward the beckonoing whiteness of the birches. By midafternoon the silvery morning sun had turned into heavy gold. We had all walked and talked and kicked around a soccer ball and eaten salami, bread, and boiled potatoes punctuated with vodka. It was time to leave; Igor's daughter, a fair-haired, timid teenager, had to sing in a school Victory Day concert, an event she was not looking forward to, she told me, but had no choice. It was hard for me to relinquish the riches of the forest. Sitting on a low tree stump, I inhaled the gamy smell of the dark soil and, warmed by friends and vodka, thought of the moist Mother Earth that the Slavs had sanctified for millennia and that in the years just before my birth had consumed the rotting flesh of so many millions of boys, girls, men, and women.

STALINGRAD

Just outside of Volgograd is the Soldier's Field Memorial, featuring a large stone triangle covered with writing, a statue of a little girl holding a flower, and a carefully crafted, modernistic sculptural montage of pieces of wartime weaponry.

In the late 1970s, peasants farming that field came across an unopened letter that they had dug up along with helmets and remnants of weapons from the war. Its characteristic triangular shape instantly identified it as a letter sent from the front. When they opened it, some pieces of a dried flower tumbled out. It was written on September 18, 1942, at the beginning of the great Stalingrad battle, by one Major Dmitrii (Dima) Petrakov to his young daughter.

> My Black-eyed Mila,
> I am sending you a cornflower. . . . Imagine: the battle is going on, enemy shells are exploding all around, there are shell holes everywhere, and yet here was a flower growing. . . . Suddenly the next explosion came. . . . The cornflower was torn up. I picked it up and put it into the pocket of my field shirt. The flower had grown, stretched toward the sun, but was torn up by a wave of explosions. And had I not picked it up, it would have been trampled. Mila! Papa Dima will fight the fascists to the last drop of his blood, to his last breath, so that the fascists should not do to you what they have done to this flower. Whatever you do not understand, Mama will explain to you.

Little Mila, by then a middle-aged woman, was given her dead father's letter some thirty-five years after he had written it. Together with the local Party organization and a group of resident artists, she helped enshrine it in a special memorial for children. Its message had the perfect combination of drama and touching sentimentality that Russian adults used to think children would go for.

The statue of the little girl in the completed complex is, of course, Mila, and the marble triangle at her feet is her Papa Dima's letter. Across a small cement expanse rests the striking sculptural assemblage of weapons collected in that field and, behind it, a black marble slab displaying old helmets.

When I visited Soldier's Field a few days after Victory Day 1985, the trunk of a dead tree with twisted branches rising above the displayed helmets was entwined with red kerchiefs gaily fluttering in the warm breeze. Each slab and pedestal was strewn with wilting flowers. In every direction freshly plowed or grassy fields dotted with newly leaving trees stretched toward the horizon. A prominent local sculptor told me that it had become traditional for groups of Pioneers to bring flowers to the memorial on the days surrounding Victory Day. They always put a real flower into the hands of the statue. As a parting ritual each child removed his or her red neckerchief and tied it to the dead tree—a symbolic offering to the spirits of the war dead.

Only the previous day I had seen scores of Volgograd Pioneers in white shirts and red scarves visiting the famed memorial on Mamaev Hill. There the children were merely silent (or rather, whispering) observers of a stone spectacle. Unlike the understated Soldier's Field Memorial, there was nothing modest about the immense monument complex, which was the most celebrated of the flamboyant memorial ensembles constructed during Brezhnev's tenure as general secretary of the Central Committee.

Memorial ensembles—multifigured architectural and sculptural constructions intended to saturate the visitor with a carefully contrived cluster of impressions and emotions—were the cathedrals of the organized memorialization of the Great Patriotic War. Like cathedrals, they were sponsored by a large and powerful institution—in this case, the Communist Party of the Soviet Union.

Opened with great fanfare on the fiftieth anniversary of the revolution, in 1967, the Volgograd memorial bore all the hallmarks of totalitarian kitsch, including vast outer walls whose bas-reliefs told the story of the Stalingrad battle on a physical background that itself looked battle-scarred, a symbolic "Lake of Tears" mourning the hundreds of thousands of its Soviet victims, loudspeakers that played and replayed wartime radio broadcasts monitoring the progress of the battle, a gargantuan snarling motherland figure wielding an immense sword, and an eternal flame blazing up from a hand clasping a stone torch, like a submerged Statue of Liberty.

As with any pilgrimage site, the process of approaching the shrine was itself an important preparatory part of the visit. The ascent, past the ruined walls and toward the huge statue set up against a vast expanse of sky, was designed to generate an inner state that would inspire in the visitor sympathy for the harrowing ordeal that was Stalingrad, admiration for the valor of the Soviet soldiers, grief for the hundreds of thousands of Soviet lives lost, and gratitude for the victory to its organizer and inspirer, the Communist Party of the Soviet Union. Like millions of visitors before me, I laid a bouquet of flowers at a designated area not far from the base of the hand before circling the shrine room to the sound of Schumann's "Träumerei" echoing off the mosaic walls, which displayed the names of the Soviet victims of the battle.

This was my first visit to Volgograd, which I had presumed would be a depressing collection of shabby, high-rise apartment buidlings hastily thrown up in the fifties. Instead I found myself in an inviting urban environment constructed on an accessible, human scale. A long, elegant promenade along the Volga made the leisurely stroll— an impossibility in Moscow—a pleasant experience.

During my second evening in Volgograd I walked along that embankment with Georgii Fetisov, a successful sculptor of war memorials and other monumental statuary. He was a native of Volgograd and that morning had taken me to see the house in which he was born, and to meet his old mother, who still lived there. It was my first visit ever inside one of those countless rickety wooden houses with carved eaves left over from an earlier era, ramshackle houses without indoor plumbing that foreigners like me found charming but that native Russians were happy to replace with high-rise apartment buildings—until the new Russian nationalism of the

Gorbachev and Yeltsin era brought the traditional wooden house back into vogue (with plumbing, of course).

Fetisov's father had been killed in the final year of the war, and several faded photographs on a dusty shelf served as a kind of icon corner to his memory. I paid my respects to the solemn figure in the photographs and gave a small gift to his shriveled, toothless widow, who looked positively ancient. She had never seen a foreigner before. After this, Georgii considered me a friend. He was a man of ordinary education, seemingly good-hearted (despite the fact that his hero, whose likeness he had more than once lovingly sculpted, was Felix Dzerzhinskii, the first head of the Cheka, Lenin's secret police). Before going to visit his mother, Fetisov and I had spent the whole day together in his studio and at an exhibit of paintings dedicated to the fortieth anniversary of the victory.

As we meandered along the gracious Volga embankment, Georgii talked about America's apparent lack of feeling for the war experience, and I responded by telling him that as a Jew I had a personal stake in the war and its hapless victims.

"Oh yes," he said, "there were many Jews killed during the war."

"Many," I replied. And then, almost as an afterthought, I added: "do you know how many?"

"A great number—maybe one million?" he asked, looking at me inquisitively as the river glided by us in the twilight.

I stopped walking and looked directly at him. "Six million, six million Jews were killed," I said, raising my voice and attracting the attention of some passersby.

He seemed genuinely shocked. "I had no idea there were so many," he explained in an apologetic tone.

POLITICS OF VICTIMIZATION

I had long felt personally bitter about the refusal of the Soviet authorities to acknowledge the Holocaust or even the Nazi policy of Jewish genocide. How thoroughly must anti-Semitic sentiments have penetrated a culture that needed to prevent the entire Soviet population from knowing about the Jewish people's definitive ordeal! For surely the slaughter of six million of its members is—even more than the creation of the state of Israel—*the* unifying and defining event of modern Jewry. So was that it? Did anti–Semitism—the imperative to weaken and undercut whatever binds together the Jews of the world—explain that malignant silence about the Holocaust?

Yes and no. Anti-Semitism had long been a deeply engrained feature of Soviet life, especially in the Slavic republics. But I believe that in this case the main explanatory factor had to do with the psychological economy of suffering: from the point of view of official Soviet historiography, the Germans had meted out to all the Soviet peoples a most horrible fate; to have granted to the Jewish people an equal or even (in terms of this logic) higher status on the pecking order of martyred nationalities would have vitiated somewhat the Soviet claims on behalf of their own victimization, and was therefore impermissible.

The emotional and political dynamic was not unlike the heartrending arguments that for years surrounded the design of the United States Holocaust Memorial Museum in Washington, D.C. Should the memorial commemorate only Jewish victims? What about other groups singled out for genocide, such as the Roma, homosexuals, the mentally retarded? Those many proponents of the exclusivity of Jews as the object of memorialization resembled the Soviets in their insistence on maintaining their unique status as victims. The big difference, of course, was that the Jews in the discussion fully acknowledged that other peoples had been gassed, whereas the Soviets not only refused to memorialize Jewish Holocaust victims but also systematically covered up the truth about their fates.

Soviet historiography of the war was fundamentally mendacious, promoting a standardized version of the experience meant to celebrate the Communist Party's wartime successes and provide an inspirational image of exemplary unity and popular heroism. That image contained truths and lies and unforgivable blank spots: the Nazi-Soviet pact and its secret protocol that plotted the demise of the independent Baltic states and areas in Central Europe; Stalin's 1940 massacre of thousands of Polish officers in the Katyn Forest; the real extent of lend-lease; Soviet prisoners of war who were later incarcerated for the purported treason of surrendering to the enemy; and the millions of Soviet citizens whose wartime deaths were caused, directly or indirectly, by Stalin's brutal rule.

Deliberate distortions of history for political reasons, especially the history of the Soviet Union, were the trademark of Soviet historical writing almost since its inception. In particular, the official saga of the Great Patriotic War was filled with hyperbole and glaring omissions. At the same time, in complete contradistinction, under the banner of its prime slogan, "no one is forgotten, nothing is forgotten," the war cult claimed to recall every incident, every person, every moment of those 1,418 days and nights of war. Indeed, the official memorialization of the war was obsessively determined to tell the story of the war in the greatest possible detail. The cult's managers manifested a compulsion to display the names of the war dead on slabs and stone obelisks and walls, such as the mosaic walls of the grand memorial at Volgograd wherein are embedded thousands of names of Soviet soldiers who died in the Stalingrad battle. And yet that very compulsion was part of a massive effort to obliterate the real collective memory of the most horrific war in the history of humankind.

4

"NO SEA WITHOUT WATER, NO WAR WITHOUT BLOOD"

"No sea without water, no war without blood" is one of many Russian peasant proverbs that testify to the sober realism about war that centuries of brutality and warfare had implanted in the Russian popular mentality. "War is good to hear about, but hard to endure." "There is no such thing as a war without fatalities." During the better part of a millennium following the establishment of an empire based in the fortress city of Kiev, war was an almost constant feature in the east Slavic realm, which had few natural boundaries and was both particularly vulnerable to invasion and singularly impelled toward territorial expansion. By 1689 the Muscovite tsars ruled the largest country in the world, stretching from the border of Poland to the Pacific Ocean.

Hunters and gatherers that we are somewhere at the base of our brains, we are inclined to exalt those who protect or expand our territory. In addition, weapon-wielding warriors and their delegates sacralize themselves and their military actions to transfer military success outside the community into dominance within the group. Like virtually all other countries, Russia has a long history of sacred battles and wars. Indeed, the *Primary Chronicle,* or *Tale of Bygone Years,* that constituted an official chronicle for the rulers of medieval Russia is largely an inventory of glorified victories and lamented military losses. However, unlike some other courtly traditions that produced odes only to victorious wars, medieval Russia's greatest epic poem,

The Song of Igor's Campaign, immortalized a major Russian military defeat by the nomadic Turkic Kuman tribe in 1185. "And brothers, Kiev groaned in sorrow, and so did Chernigov in adversity; anguish spread flowing over the Russian land." Defeat was nurtured for the moral lessons it offered.[1]

In February 1931, almost eight centuries after Prince Igor's defeat by the Kumans, Joseph Stalin, like his medieval predecessors, drew upon past defeats. In this case, his goal was to mobilize popular energy for his campaign of intensive industrialization of the Soviet Union:

> One feature of the history of old Russia was the continual beatings she suffered because of her backwardness. She was beaten by the Mongol khans. She was beaten by Turkish beys. She was beaten by Swedish feudal lords. She was beaten by Polish and Lithuanian gentry. She was beaten by the British and French capitalists. She was beaten by Japanese barons. All beat her—because of her backwardness. . . . They beat her because to do so was profitable and could be done with impunity. . . . We are fifty or a hundred years behind the advanced countries. Either we do it or we shall go under.[2]

The consecration of the Great Patriotic War has its antecedents not only in Russia's centuries-old propensity to hallow wars against foreign invaders but also in the Soviet political culture that took shape in the more than two decades that preceded Operation Barbarossa. The social disintegration that characterized the turbulent years of revolution and subsequent Civil War (1918–21) gave rise to imagery of primal fantasy. It pictured the world in Manichaean terms of good versus evil, with titanic champions trouncing triple-headed hydras of counterrevolution. In those years before the standardized gray prose of Stalinist bureaucratese, many newspaper articles and letters to the editor crackled with colorful folkloric metaphors, and the dramatic poster art of the Civil War years writhed with fanciful representations of Red soldiers slaying dragons of imperialism or terrorizing top-hatted, rotund little capitalists of the Entente interventionists.

The cult of Lenin developed during his lifetime and was organized into a nationwide cluster of symbols and rituals in the two years following the leader's death in 1924. It was instrumental in making the transition from image to words, from the image-based propaganda of the early years of Bolshevik power, when a significant majority of the population was still illiterate, to a studied political exploitation of Russian logocentrism that characterized the eras of Stalin and his successors.

In the 1930s the Lenin cult was eclipsed by a more flamboyant cult of Stalin. These cults together formed the core of a sweeping attempt to remake the Soviet Union and imbue the populace with characteristics combining those of a German burgher and a nineteenth-century Russian terrorist. The Commissariat of Enlightenment (Education), Communist Party, Komsomol, and Pioneer propaganda organs and the Political Administration of the Red Army sought to transform the cautious, suspicious, risk-avoiding Russian peasant character formed by centuries of eking out a living under the inhospitable conditions of a northern climate into a "new Soviet man" and "new Soviet woman." These were self-disciplined, sober, thrifty, industrious, literate, and imbued with respect for high culture, humorless, loyal to their leaders, subservient to authority, and ready (indeed eager) to sacrifice everything for the cause.

The systematic celebration, through ritual and symbol, of a mythic world that eclipsed quotidian reality chipped away at the primeval scepticism of the Russian people. Using real people and real incidents Stalinism created popular heroes to embody some of the values that the Party sought to instil in the population.

Pavlik Morozov, the adolescent who during the dekulakization drive of the late twenties turned his own father in to the authorities for illegally hoarding grain and got himself killed by angry neighbors for this act of betrayal, was sanctified as a socialist martyr. The regime honored him with statues, and books hailed him as an exemplar of righteousness. He served as a nationally celebrated hero, especially to Pioneers, until the *perestroika* period. Another renowned hero of Stalinist times was Alexei Stakhanov, a miner from the period of the Second Five-Year Plan. This veritable John Henry worked so intensely that his output of coal far exceeded the expected quota, which—much to the chagrin of his fellow miners—then rose as a consequence of his famed exploits.

Making use of the organized Stalin worship of the time, the Party tried to rekindle the popular enthusiasm of the revolutionary period to spark the combined economic supergrowth and political central-ization that was the hallmark of Stalinist totalitarianism. Posters, newspaper engravings, photos, propaganda films, and touched-up newsreels specialized in showing groups of happy collective farmers, megamachines, factory chimneys spewing smoke, mighty dams con-quering the Soviet Union's great rivers, and the mustachioed visage of Stalin himself. Everything—the polity, economy, society, educa-tion, the arts, even the truth—was subordinated to strengthening the Soviet Union under the aegis of the Supreme Leader.

In the ten intervening years between Stalin's shrill warning about Russian backwardness and the German invasion of the Soviet Union, Russian peasants had lost the wary, suspicious, self-protective stance that had seen them through the best and worst of times for the better part of a millennium. They had been starved out of the village and driven onto collective farms in something like a reinstitution of serf-dom, forced into breakneck labor during the five-year plans, fright-ened into obedience by the Great Terror of the thirties, deprived of spiritual sustenance in the antireligious campaigns that destroyed thousands of churches and most parishes, and stultified by the hype about Soviet superiority and military invincibility spewed out by the gargantuan propaganda machine of the Communist Party during the heyday of the Stalin cult. By 1941 many young Russians, Belorus-sians, and Ukrainians had—like their German, British, and French counterparts in August 1914—turned into the kind of young men with a limited sense of their own vulnerability that could confidently throw themselves into battle, joyfully expecting quick victory in a contest of nations.[3]

Operation Barbarossa

Dawn, June 22, 1941. More than three million German troops, 3,350 tanks, 7,184 pieces of artillery, and over 2,000 aircraft were poised to invade the Soviet Union. Operation Barbarossa was under-way. With the Red Army utterly unprepared for the attack, German forces rolled through Soviet territory with devastating speed, wiping out most of the air force on the ground in the first few days, bomb-ing and shelling military installations and civilian targets, and captur-ing thousands of prisoners. The Germans seized the Baltic states,

Belorussia, Ukraine, and much of European Russia, imposing the kind of notorious occupation that the Nazis reserved for nationalities they intended to exterminate. By the second half of July, they had occupied a chunk of Soviet territory more than twice the size of France. Within a few months, Leningrad was surrounded in a blockade that was to last over two years and kill one million of the city's three million inhabitants. The Soviet Union had suffered the greatest military disaster in the history of modern warfare. It would take four years and at least thirty million Soviet lives to repel the German invaders.[4]

How tragic and ironic that although preparedness for war with the imperialist powers had purportedly justified the ordeals the Stalin regime had inflicted on the populace, when war did come, the country was woefully unready! The reasons for the Soviet Union's lack of readiness for the onslaught of June 1941 are inextricably bound up with Stalin and Stalinism: the 1937–39 purge of the armed forces that decimated the officer corps; the economic and social dislocation and devastation that resulted from the destructive policies of the thirties; Stalin's unwillingness to envision the possibility of a defensive war on Soviet soil and his misplaced trust in Hitler; the Stalinist system, which made the dictator supreme and legitimated even his most foolhardy decisions. There is evidence that Stalin and his cronies were convinced Germany would not attack the Soviet Union until Britain had been defeated, because Germany could not win a two-front war. At the very least, Stalin hoped that good behavior on his part might help delay the German invasion until the spring or summer of 1942.

Terrified of provoking Hitler into a premature attack, Stalin refused to take necessary precautions on his country's borders and rebuked for their "excess of zeal" military officers who did make such moves. On June 20, some thirty-six hours before Operation Barbarossa began, the commissar of defense invited bigwigs from the general staff to view a German propaganda film of the Balkan peoples warmly welcoming their Nazi occupiers.[5]

Although Stalin had chosen to deny, or at any rate, ignore the warnings of imminent invasion conveyed to him by his own intelligence as well as by Winston Churchill and other Western informants, the Soviet leadership had certainly known of the probability of

German attack. The populace, on the other hand, had been exposed to nothing but propaganda about the invincibility of the Red Army.

From the first moments after the attack, the civilian leadership moved into a slow-motion mode reflecting their incredulity and appalling disorganization. When, at 3:15 A.M. on June 22, the commissar of the navy telephoned Stalin to report that German airplanes were bombing Sevastopol and antiaircraft artillery had begun to fight back, he was unable to get through to the leader, even after several attempts. Commissar Admiral N. G. Kuznetsov finally reached Stalin's associate Georgii Malenkov and blurted out the news about the attack.

"Do you understand what you are reporting?" Malenkov answered gruffly.

"I understand and I report, taking full responsibility, that war has begun—" countered Kuznetsov.

Malenkov hung up on him.

"Later I learned that he did not believe me," Kuznetsov recalled. "He called Sevastopol to verify my report. The talk with Malenkov showed that the hope of avoiding war was alive even at a time when the attack had begun and blood was being spilled over enormous areas of our land."[6]

Back in Moscow, Stalin had, at three o'clock in the morning, just ended a meeting of the Politburo and gone to bed, incognizant of the fact that enemy airplanes had invaded Soviet territory. A knock on the door called him to the telephone. "General Zhukov is asking to speak to you on a matter that cannot wait!" said the officer on duty. "Stalin picked up the phone and listened as Zhukov briefly recounted the attacks by enemy aircraft on Kiev, Minsk, Sevastopol, Vilna, and elsewhere. Zhukov then said, 'Did you understand what I said, Comrade Stalin?' The dictator said nothing. Again Zhukov asked, 'Comrade Stalin, do you understand?' Stalin finally understood."[7]

WAR!

The motherland was invaded and the center did not hold. While Stalin consulted on a daily basis with the high command of the military and with his chief political leaders during the first week following the invasion, he suffered a brief paralytic loss of nerve at the end of the month, when the extent of the disaster was clear to him. Not until July 3 did he pull himself together enough to address his people by radio. It was, without a doubt, the most affecting speech of Stalin's quarter-century as Supreme Leader. After years of appearing as a distant, awesome, and often displeased father, now, in the nation's —and his own—greatest trial, Joseph Vissarionovich seemed entirely human, even vulnerable. He sounded tired, breathing heavily, and at moments one could hear him gulping water as he spoke. His opening words represented an unprecedented statement of his closeness to the people: "Comrades, citizens, brothers and sisters, fighters of our Army and Navy! I am speaking to you, my friends!"

"Brothers and sisters! My friends!" whispered Sintsov, a character in Konstantin Simonov's novel, *The Living and the Dead,* as he listened to the speech. "And suddenly he realized that for a long time now he had missed in all the tremendous and even great achievements of Stalin the very words he had spoken today: 'Brothers and sisters! My friends!' or rather the sentiments that were behind those words. Did it need the tragedy of war to bring out of him such words and sentiments?"[8]

Whatever feelings of affection for his people the dictator may have conveyed in that first speech, Stalin was soon himself again. He ordered the execution of Gen. Dmitrii Pavlov, who had been commander in chief of the western front, and his chiefs of staff and communication. In the middle of July he himself took the post of commissar of defense and three weeks later, on August 7, appointed himself commander in chief of the armed forces.

By 1941, when the war began, the general secretary had for many years ruled as an absolute dictator, making policy decisions completely on his own. He was master of life and death—especially death. Stalin had grown accustomed to wielding all the power and taking none of the responsibility when things went wrong. For example, on March 2, 1930, some months after launching the brutal drive to collectivize the peasantry, he published his "Dizzy with Success" speech, in which he blamed local officials for "excessive zeal" in carrying out what had been his own orders to force the rural population to give up their small private farms.

Once his country found itself involved in a defensive war, Stalin could no longer wield absolute power. For all the talk in the thirties about the invincible Red Army, for all the *shapkozakidatel'stvo,* or exuberant jingoism—the term literally means "cap-flinging"—Stalin had to take responsibility for the massive military debacle of 1941, and to tolerate the loss of political and social control it engendered. Of the many fears that had driven Stalin to cauterize the polity through purge and terror, one of the most profound—and least inexplicable—was his dread of having his authority undercut by military opposition. The grand finale of the Great Terror of the 1930s had been the purge of the army and navy, in which the NKVD (Stalin's secret police) murdered more than fifty thousand officers (including, according to some estimates, triple the number of Soviet generals killed by the Germans during the entire war). Throughout the war, despite all the propaganda about his genius as a military leader, Stalin had to rely on the expertise of his commanders, some of whom had begun the war with relatively low ranks (Marshal Rokossovskii had spent the purge years behind bars) and had risen to positions of authority not through sycophancy but by demonstrating genuine military aptitude.[9]

During the Great Patriotic War, as commander in chief, Stalin had to take responsibility both for the many defeats and for the senseless loss of life incurred in the victory. How many soldiers perished because their officers preferred to shoot them rather than allow them to be taken prisoner! How many more fell in attacks that military commanders timed solely to give the leader symbolic gifts of victory to mark Soviet holidays? Military actions scheduled to coincide with February 23 (Red Army Day) or May 1 or November 7 were sacrificial gifts to the leader, launched no matter what their cost in lives.

Long after the war was over, poet Iurii Belash mused about Stalin's wartime crimes:

We're attacking . . .
Every day—from morning on, for two weeks now—
We're attacking.
Oh my God! when will they end,
these stupid attacks on German machine guns
without artillery support? . . .
For a long time now it's clear to everyone—from soldier to battalion

commander—that we're laying down our people in vain,—
but somewhere there, in the rear, someone dull and cruel,
about whom even the battalion commander knows nothing,
every evening issues one and the same order:
"In Russia there are many people. In the morning take the hill!"[10]

As German tanks speedily rolled eastward in the summer of 1941, popular responses to the outbreak of a devastating war ranged from disbelief, to patriotic outrage and misplaced confidence in an immediate victory, to outright panic. In Moscow there was a rush on the banks and shops in a frantic effort to withdraw savings and stockpile food and paraffin. While some citizens eagerly volunteered to fight, others refused: "Hitler, Soviet power, they're all the same to me," declared a textile factory worker. Many conscripts showed up at their recruiting centers thoroughly inebriated. Komsomols tore up their Party cards to disassociate themselves from the Party in the eyes of the German invaders.[11]

At the same time, a dramatically large number of youngsters, like the flower of 1914 imbued with a romanticized vision of their army and insanely inappropriate expectations of success, willingly offered themselves up as cannon fodder in Stalin's ruthlessly run war. I am convinced there is no hyperbole in the many oral reminiscences I have collected from Soviet veterans who told me about their total dedication in marching off to fight. This was true not only of draftees but of the thousands of people not eligible to fight who went off to do so anyway—mostly the underaged and those physically unfit for service. They filled the ranks of the people's militias that got virtually no training and endured massive casualties. Young men and women left their loved ones ready to meet death with optimistic resolve.

In mid-October 1941, with the enemy threatening the capital, the Party and government began a speedy—indeed, somewhat panicky—evacuation eastward to the Urals. For the Soviet Union, the first five months of the war, until its costly success in the battle of Moscow in December 1941, was an unmitigated catastrophe. The prospect of a crushing defeat by Germany seemed likely until the end of the Stalingrad battle, in February 1943.

The historian Roy Medvedev, a tall, handsome, white-haired gentleman with a powerful voice and commanding presence, was hardly out of childhood when the Germans invaded. "In June 1941 I was fifteen years old. I had been brought up in the belief that our army was the strongest in the world. And suddenly everyone understood that we had been routed, utterly defeated. Everyone understood it even though the newspapers described enormous German losses. But the Germans kept on moving. They took Ukraine, they took the Donbas, they reached Moscow, they reached Leningrad. It was totally incomprehensible.

"My father had been arrested and shot in 1938. What remained was a female and thoroughly Jewish household. Through the Jewish grapevine we had heard that as soon as the Germans occupied a town, they immediately shot all the Jews. We were living in Rostov at the time. My grandmother, who was partially paralyzed, kept wailing that if the time came, we would all flee and leave her behind, so she kept exhorting us to all get out at once, before the inevitable German occupation, and join her daughter in [the Georgian city of] Tbilisi. This we did, and it was a good thing too, because in November the Nazis did take Rostov and kill all the Jews. Some of our remaining Rostov relatives were rich, and couldn't bring themselves to leave their fine homes. When the city was taken and they saw it was too late to leave, they all swallowed poison and killed themselves. Those of my Rostov relatives who did not commit suicide were killed by the Germans."

When Medvedev turned eighteen, he was drafted into the army, into a Caucasian regiment. "I went off to fight, I went off to die," he said.

"Arise, O Vast Land!"

The sacralization of the war with fascist Germany began almost immediately after the launching of Operation Barbarossa. Two days after the invasion, on June 23, an article titled "The Great Patriotic War of the Soviet People" appeared in *Pravda,* the Communist Party newspaper, thus providing for this war an epithet linking it directly to the first "Patriotic War," the one fought against Napoleon's *Grande Armée* in 1812.

On the same day, at the Belorusskii railroad station, troops bound for the front were feted by an orchestra, which played, among other things, "Sacred War." A beautiful military march, it quickly became (and remains to this day) the prime Russian hymn of the war. Both the haunting melody in a minor key and the words convey a combination of urgency, determination, and the hortatory appeal of an Old Testament prophecy. They also appeal to the strength inherent in the vastness of the Russian and Soviet lands and in the dormant might of its people.

Rise up, vast country,
Rise up to mortal battle
With the dark fascist power,
With the accursed horde!

Chorus:
   Let noble rage
   Boil up like a wave!
   A people's war is going on,
   A sacred war.

As two opposite poles,
So we differ from them.
We fight for light and peace,
They—for the kingdom of darkness.

"Sacred War," with its grand melody that keeps resolving itself and swelling out anew like ocean waves, calls to mind the scene in Sergei Eisenstein's film *Alexander Nevsky,* when the title character calls on Russia to rise up and cast out the Teutonic Knights, a crusading order that in 1242 had occupied Pskov and was headed for the wealthy, mercantile city of Novgorod. "Arise, O Russian people," intones an unseen chorus to a melody composed by Sergei Prokofiev, as the screen shows soldiers, workers, peasants, and merchants rushing out of their homes and stacking up at the blacksmith's to get armor and weapons, which he is donating to the cause.

Nevsky's military exploits had earned him an official canonization under the category of saintly princes, whom the Orthodox Church canonized for performing their earthly duties heroically. A few months after Hitler's armies invaded the Soviet Union, Joseph Stalin canonized Nevsky a second time. On November 7, 1941, the morning of the twenty-fourth anniversary of the October Revolution, Stalin made one of the most inspirational speeches of his entire career, a speech in which he conjured up images of some of old Russia's most famed military heroes: Alexander Nevsky, Muscovite prince Dmitrii Donskoi, who battled the Tatars in 1380, Aleksandr Suvorov, the hero of Catherine the Great's wars of territorial expansion, and Mikhail Kutuzov, the great general of the patriotic war against Napoleon.

> Comrades, Red Army and Red Navy men, officers and political workers, men and women partisans! The whole world is looking upon you as the power capable of destroying the German invader robber hordes! The enslaved peoples of Europe are looking upon you as their liberators. A great liberating mission stands before you. Be worthy of this great mission! The war you are waging is a war of liberation, a just war. May you be inspired in this war by the courageous figures of our great ancestors, Alexander Nevsky, Dmitrii Donskoi, Kuzma Minin, and Dmitrii Pozharskii, Aleksandr Suvorov, Mikhail Kutuzov![12]

If any of his listeners caught the irony of Stalin the Georgian invoking Russian legendary princes and generals in his heavily accented Russian, they doubtless kept their thoughts to themselves.

After decades of spurning the prerevolutionary Russian past in favor of the exploits of socialism, Stalin and the wartime propaganda machine had turned to Russia's legendary warriors and tsarist generals and even heroes of old Russian culture to mobilize the spirits of the Soviet people. The Stalin cult continued to thrive, and propaganda in praise of socialism remained a prime focus in the wartime press. At the same time, however, the theme of Russian national pride and valor was added to the repertory of printed and visual propaganda.[13]

The government opened up churches and allowed people to worship freely for the first time since the mid-twenties. In 1943, Metropolitan Sergius was installed as patriarch, a post that had remained vacant since the death of Patriarch Tikhon in 1925. (U. S. Ambassador George Kennan, who together with other foreign dignitaries witnessed that installation, said that after decades of persecution the church hierarchy had so few ecclesial vestments, these had to be borrowed from the Moscow Art Theater!) Stalin, who as a boy had been trained for the priesthood, understood very well that Communist Party pap alone was too insipid to inspire a people who were being pushed to their very limits. But the mighty weight of history and the millennium-old devotion to the god of Orthodoxy could provide the Russian people with the sustenance they needed to pull through the ordeal of war with an intact sense of nationhood.

In this time of crisis, with Stalin fearful that the occupation might fan the fires of national separatism, newspaper articles emphasized the fraternity of Soviet peoples. "A United, Powerful Soviet Union" was the name of an article published in 1943 on the day after Stalin's birthday. It lauded the unity of the peoples of the USSR and ended with the opening quatrain of the national anthem whose words were written—and chosen by Stalin himself—during the course of 1943. A half-century later they would resound with a sad and hollow ring:

Unshakeable union of free republics
Has been united by Great Rus'.
Long live the country founded by the peoples' will,
United, mighty Soviet Union![14]

FREEDOM IN WAR

The war brought devastation, mass hysteria, grief, and death, but in the first two years it also brought a measure of freedom from Stalinist totalitarian intrusion. The Leningrad poet Olga Berggolts's 1942 poem "February Diary" effectively depicts this paradox:

In filth, in gloom, in hunger, in sorrow,
When death trailed along behind us like a shadow,
We used to be so happy,
Inhaled such a tempestuous freedom,
That our grandchildren would have envied us.[15]

The historian Mikhail Gefter remembered vividly the liberating atmosphere of the early war period. "I was twenty-three when the war began, and I remember how paradoxically, even though 1941 and 1942 were the blackest years of the war, they were also the freest." Gazing at me through his big glasses, he raised his finger for emphasis. "This was a period of *spontaneous de-Stalinization*. We were in full crisis. Stalin's totalitarian system had fallen apart in the face of the invasion and occupation. People were suddenly forced to make their own decisions, to take responsibility for themselves. Events pressed us into becoming truly independent human beings. But by 1943, after Stalingrad, the war machine had been more or less consolidated, and with it, Stalinism once more revived. Strange as it may sound, 1941 was more of a liberation than was 1945." As evidence, Gefter showed me a frontline letter written by his university classmate, Liova Seichan, on July 9, 1941: "I'm just a typical hussar! There are no ranks, no discipline to speak of . . . I live as I always dreamed I could." Liova died in 1944.

To illustrate the nature of wartime de-Stalinization, Gefter recalled a wonderful short story by the popular writer Vasilii Shukshin. In it, the manager of a collective farm remembers one and only one time in his life when he was fully and responsibly human. He was twelve years old and went with his father and baby brother to a horse farm. Suddenly the baby took sick and his father ordered him to fetch a doctor from the nearest town. He leaped onto a horse and raced for help, his heart pounding with the realization that something of paramount importance—his brother's life—depended on him alone. He felt excited, responsible, alive. He reached the physician and his brother was saved. After that, he only did what he was told. They said, "Join the Komsomol!" He did. He was told to get a job, join the Party, fight in the war. All these things, he did. But those unique feelings Gefter associated with 1941–42—the sense of initiative, of self-reliance within the drama of crisis—never returned.

"I belong to that generation of people who in 1941 went to war directly from high school," recalled Lazar Lazarev, an elderly literary critic with a specialty in war literature. His mobile face expressed a gentle good humor, wisdom, and enormous fatigue. The fourth and fifth fingers of his right hand were missing—a legacy of the war. With the remaining three he chain-smoked the Marlboros I had (with some misgivings) brought as a gift. "In school we had all believed the myths about the all-powerful Supreme Leader. The military catastrophe of 1941–42 forced us for the first time to question Stalin, and threw us back onto our own resources. So for many of us, those first two years of the war coincided with a spontaneous de-Stalinization, a true emancipation. We felt that everything depended on us personally, and that gave us an extraordinary feeling of freedom." In a 1991 article on the war theme in literature, Lazarev quoted the novelist Vasil' Bykov, who wrote that during the war "[we] realized our strength and understood what we were capable of."[16]

The power of the unvarnished truth that characterized the early months of the war is perhaps most brilliantly conveyed in a poem published by Julia Neiman in 1956:

1941
Those Moscow days . . . The avalanche of war . . .
Uncounted losses! Setbacks and defeats!
Yet, comrades of that year, tell the whole truth:
Bright as a torch it flamed, that shining year!
Like crumbling plaster, subterfuge flaked off,
And causes were laid bare, effects revealed;
And through the blackout and the camouflage
We saw our comrades' faces—undisguised.
The dubious yardsticks that we measured by—
Forms, questionnaires, long service, rank and age—
Were cast aside and now we measured true:
Our yardsticks in that year were valor, faith.

And we who lived and saw these things still hold
Fresh in the memory, and sacred still,
The watches, rooftops, and barrage balloons,
The explosive chaos that was Moscow then,
The buildings in their camouflage attire,
The symphony of air raids and all-clears—
For then at last seemed real
Our pride as citizens, pure-shining pride.[17]

THE OCCUPATION

Many of the areas occupied in the first weeks and months after Operation Barbarossa had endured a rather mild German occupation a quarter-century earlier, during World War I. But in World War II the German rule of Belorussia, Ukraine, and a large swath of Russia proper was unimaginably harsh. Most people who were well enough informed to expect the deportation and slaughter of Jews that in fact did come were shocked to learn that Slavs were almost as low as Jews on the Nazi racial pecking order. Russian prisoners of war were kept in conditions unheard of in the history of modern warfare; they were fed starvation rations and in many cases housed in open-air camps even in winter. The civilian population likewise suffered unprecedented hardships, tribulations at least as grim as those inflicted by Stalin's policies in the previous decade.

The Jews, of course, were the first targets of the organized occupation. Rounded up into ghettos, almost all of them were either transported to concentration camps or shot in enormous groups after digging their own mass graves. To save bullets, the Germans sometimes buried the Jews alive. The responses of their gentile neighbors ran the full gamut of human behavior, from the heroic self-sacrifice of those who hid Jews in their homes at the risk of their own lives, to the barbaric sadism of people who were glad to betray their Jewish compatriots to the Gestapo. On September 29 and 30, 1941, 33,371 Kievan Jews were transported to the wooded ravine of Babi Yar just outside Kiev. There they were stripped naked, shot with machine guns, and fell or were thrown into the ravine. In all during the fall of 1941, about ninety thousand Kievan Jews and ten thousand non-Jews were killed at Babi Yar in the first mass genocide the Germans carried out on Soviet soil.

Until September 29, 1941, the first day of the massacre, no one had known for sure what the Germans were planning to do with all the Jews who were being rounded up. "I could not, of course, miss such a rare spectacle as the deportation of the Jews from Kiev," wrote novelist Anatoli Kuznetsov, who in 1941 was a child living in Kiev. "As soon as it was light I was out on the street.

"When I got home I found my grandfather standing in the middle of the courtyard, straining to hear some shooting that was going on somewhere. He raised his finger.

"'Do you know what?' he said with horror in his voice. 'They're not deporting 'em. They're *shooting* 'em.'

"Then, for the first time, I realized what was happening.

"From Babi Yar came quite distinctly the sound of regular bursts of machine-gun fire: ta-ta-ta, ta-ta . . . "[18]

Before long, Slavs too found themselves the victims of both racism taken to its extreme and a thorough, ideologically based hatred of communism. Millions were deported to German factories to work as slaves. The Germans tortured and murdered civilians at the slightest pretext. As for rape—there was no need for any pretext. While World War II was hell for just about everyone involved, the German occupation of the Soviet Union bore little resemblance to that of the countries of Western Europe. Hitler's war in the east was a war of extermination. His plan was to destroy the Union of Soviet Socialist Republics, kill all the communists, and reduce the surviving native population to a menial labor force in the service of vast numbers of future German colonists.

In the 1970s, Belorussian writer Ales Adamovich published a collection of devastating accounts of the occupation of Belorussia, in interview form. He later used those interviews as the basis for a film, *Idi i smotri* (*Come and See*), directed by Elem Klimov and released in 1989.[19]

Together with the central character, a fourteen-year-old boy (the author's approximate age when the war began), we watch in horror as the Germans—together with a few *Polizei* (*politsai* in Russian), indigenous collaborators—drive the entire population of a village, consisting mostly of women, children, and old folks (the young and middle-aged men are off fighting) into a large, empty barn. They torch the barn and then the rest of the village. We hear the terrified screams of the victims and the roar of the fire, and watch numbly as a horribly disfigured lone survivor of another such ordeal describes it in a ghostly voice as he lies dying. The Germans meted out this fate to some 630 Belorussian villages.

I first met Ales Adamovich, a deputy in the Soviet parliament and the celebrated author of many novels and screenplays, in the summer of 1990. "Human beings just aren't equipped to handle something so devastating as the annihilation of their entire village," he explained in his soft-spoken voice. "It turns out that one of the most common reactions to such intense trauma was sleep. You would enter a hut and see three or four children dead on the floor, much of the rest of the village in flames, and the children's mother sound asleep." In all some two and one-half million people, about one-quarter of Belorussia's total population, were killed during the Second World War.

THE BLOCKADE

For some nine hundred days beginning in September 1941, Leningrad was besieged by the Germans. Hitler intended to starve the population and destroy the city—raze it, like ancient Troy. He did not achieve his goal, but the civilian population was put through an ordeal unprecedented in the history of warfare. In all, of more than two and one-half million inhabitants, well over six hundred thousand died of starvation, cold, and accompanying diseases. Including deaths from enemy shelling and bombing and battle casualties, the death toll was about one million.[20]

The privations and suffering were horrific. The disastrous effects of the blockade were compounded by mistakes the Leningrad administration made early in the war, such as waiting too long to begin rationing and failing to evacuate the city's children when it was still possible (the siege trapped four hundred thousand children in the city). The possession of a ration card was a matter of life and death, although many who owned these cards died anyway.

A Leningrad librarian in her fifties recalled the death of her mother from starvation in the bitterly cold December of 1941. She was a little girl of six, now left alone with an eight-year-old sister. The bewildered little girls turned to their neighbors for help and received two instructions. First, they were to wrap their mother's body in a sheet and hide it between the storm and inside windows of their apartment, where it would surely not begin to decompose before spring. Second, they were to keep their mother's death a secret. In this way, they were told, they could use her ration card to supplement their pitiful diet and at the same time protect themselves from being eaten by starving neighbors who might be tempted to take advantage of their vulnerability.[21]

People ate dogs, cats, petroleum jelly, carpenter's glue, sheep's gut

jelly, and (rarely) each other. By November 1941, there was no food
or heating fuel or light or transport, and yet day after day weary
Leningraders walked to and from their long hours of labor in war-
related industries. They worked until they had no strength left even
to pull the frozen little corpses of their children on sleds to common
graves. People would die suddenly at work, at home, on the street—
anywhere, at any time.

The diary of a twelve-year-old girl, Tania Savicheva, records the
demise of her family:

> Zhenia died on December 28, at 12:30 P.M., 1941
> Grandma died on January 25, at 3 P.M., 1942
> Leka died on March 17, at 5 A.M., 1942
> Uncle Vasia died on April 13, at 2 A.M., 1942
> Uncle Liosha, May 10, 4 P.M. 1942
> Mama, May 13, 7:30 A.M., 1942
> Everyone is dead.
> Only Tania is alive.[22]

Tania Savicheva did not survive the war.

BLACK SUMMER OF '42

The "black summer" of 1942 in many ways marked the most pro-
foundly discouraging period of the war. Leningraders had suffered
through the first and worst winter of the blockade, which would
continue until January 1944. In June 1942 the German Army was
solidly established within eighty miles of Moscow. The Party and
government were in full evacuation. During the course of June and
July, the Germans advanced into significant chunks of southern
Russia as the Red Army lost Kerch, Kharkov, and finally the Crimean
naval port of Sevastopol. At the end of June, a few days before the fall
of Sevastopol, the Germans launched a major offensive around
Voronezh. They met with enormous Soviet resistance and failed to
take that city, but by the end of July they had taken Novocherkassk
and Rostov and were ready to invade the Caucasus.

The loss of Rostov on July 28 came as a profound blow to the
country at large and was particularly frightening because accounts of

it in the press were accompanied by intimations that some Red Army units, including their officers, had fled in a panic before the powerful German forces. The fall of Rostov signaled the beginning of the end of the spontaneous de-Stalinization that had characterized the first year of the war and the reassertion of a certain measure of Stalinist terror in order for the Party and government to gain more control over the army and the rear. The code words of the new order were "iron discipline." The goal: to make Red Army soldiers and officers fear their superiors more than the enemy, to prevent panic and defeatism in the country as a whole, and to instil within the armed forces a new professionalism based on technical expertise.[23]

On July 30, 1942, blaming the loss of Rostov on the cowardice of Soviet troops, Stalin issued his now infamous "Not a step back" order. Anyone retreating without orders would be shot by military police. Officers whose units fell apart would be transferred into *shtrafnye bataliony* (punishment battalions) to face certain death. These battalions consisted of political prisoners and were routinely sent on suicide missions. As *Pravda* explained on July 30:

> "Soviet soldiers! Not a step back!"—such is the call of your country. . . . Our Soviet country is large and rich, but there is nothing worse than to imagine that you can . . . yield even an inch of ground, or abandon this or that town without fighting to the last drop of blood.

The army newspaper, *Krasnaia zvezda* (*Red Star*), reminded its readers that "now is not the time when a coward or traitor can rely on mercy. Every officer and political worker can, with the powers given him by the State, see to it that the very idea of retreating without orders becomes impossible." Meaning: officers and commissars may shoot suspected cowards and traitors. And in fact, executions within the army became commonplace while, at the same time, a propaganda campaign stressed the importance of military discipline, bravery, and total loyalty.[24]

It was now clear to both military personnel and civilians that to the Stalinist leadership, surrendering to the Germans was unacceptable under any circumstances. Better to die than to fall into the hands of the enemy. The groundwork was laid for Stalin's postwar practice of incarcerating Soviet prisoners of war for the crime of having surrendered to the enemy—a fate meted out to hundreds of thousands of unfortunates.

How did the army and citizenry react to the privations and horrors of war? Among Russians, a people disinclined to moderation even under ordinary circumstances, the war and all its tribulations brought out the most extreme kinds of behavior: extraordinary courage, shameful betrayal, untold suffering, endurance, self-sacrifice, brutality, passion. For sheer drama it is hard to find another period in history to match it.

A portion of the Soviet citizenry demonstrated extraordinary acts of heroism, while others joined the *polizei,* turning traitor to their own army and people, some with a vengeance, helping the Nazi occupiers to terrorize and torture the populace.

The cruelty some Soviet people meted out to their neighbors is hard to explain; human brutality, fortunately, is not something we expect to find as a matter of course, even though Maxim Gorky would have said that in the Russian case such behavior was perfectly in character. "Russians have a predilection for brutality in the same way, let us say, that Englishmen have a sense of humor," he wrote in a bitter reflection in 1922, following the end of the traumatic Civil War that broke out in Russia less than one year after the Bolshevik revolution.[25]

It was a harrowing ordeal, characterized by atrocities on both sides. Surely the nightmarish first two decades of Soviet history following that war had done much to craze a beleaguered populace. In those bleak years Soviet people forced other Soviet people onto collective farms at gunpoint, shot *kulaks* (prosperous peasants) and middle peasants, starved out entire villages of recalcitrant peasants, interrogated Party comrades, frequently with the use of torture, brought false charges against neighbors and colleagues leading to their certain arrest, sentenced one another to long years in jail or forced labor camps, and shot one another in the dread courtyards of Soviet prisons.

Considering, for example, how World War I had brutalized Italian and German soldiers, and the significant role this played in the emergence of strong fascist movements in those two countries, it is likely that the protracted agony of the Soviet experience in the Civil War should help explain the harsh excesses of collectivization and the purge and terror, and that these in turn could have produced the callousness toward one another that portions of the Soviet populace displayed in the Second World War.

That tragic history readied the people of the Soviet Union for the requisite feelings of loathing toward the German enemy that would become so important in their eventual victory in the war.

Holy Hatred

The wartime press and radio were enormously effective in sustaining the spirits of both front and rear, and instilling in soldiers and civilians alike a complex of emotions: love of country, hatred of the enemy, pride in the Red Army and navy, and faith in ultimate victory.

In the initial year of the war Ilya Ehrenburg was one of the first publicists to equate German officers and men, fascists and Germans, and to help inspire in the populace a burning hatred that, by the terrible summer of 1942, had become the accepted Stalinist position. "I knew that my duty lay in showing the true face of the fascist soldier who, with an excellent fountain pen, recorded in a neat diary bloodthirsty, superstitious nonsense about his racial superiority, evil and ferocious things that would have shamed a primitive savage," Ehrenburg later wrote in his memoirs. "In the past there were sadists and marauders to be found in any army, for war is no school of morality. But what Hitler did was to incite into committing mass atrocities not only SS and Gestapo men but the whole of his army, binding millions of Germans together by complicity in crime. I recall a sandy-haired, amiable-looking German; before the war he had worked in Dusseldorf where he had a family; he had thrown a Russian baby into a well because he suffered from insomnia, had taken several sleeping-tablets and the child had prevented him from falling asleep."[26]

Ehrenburg's newspaper articles in the army newspaper, *Krasnaia zvezda (Red Star)*, and the poems of Konstantin Simonov and of Aleksei Surkov, reflected and helped shape the popular mood during some of the worst moments of the war. *Krasnaia zvezda* published Surkov's famous "I Hate" in August 1942:

My heart has become hard as stone,
My cause for complaint is great.
With these very hands
I have lifted the corpses of little ones.

. . . .

I hate them deeply
For those agonized sleepless hours
And because the fire of war
Has turned my hair white before its time.

Their drunken laughter dims my reason.
And with these hands of mine
I want to strangle every one of them.[27]

During the black summer of 1942 the authorities let loose a propaganda campaign of hate and vengeance to mobilize the populace
and support the call for "iron discipline" and self-sacrifice—and
threat of punishment from above—embodied in the post-Rostov
reforms of late July 1942. "May holy hatred become our chief, our
only feeling," urged *Pravda* on July 11. "This hatred combines a
burning love of your country, anxiety for your family and children,
and an unshakable will for victory."[28]

For Russians, who cherish poetry like no other art form, for
whom poems provide the deepest spiritual solace, surely the most
effective expression of the "hate the Germans" mood of that summer
was published in *Krasnaia zvezda* in July 1942. It was Konstantin
Simonov's poem "Kill Him!"

If you cherish your mother,
Who fed you at her breast,
From which the milk has long since gone,
And on which your cheek may rest;

If you cannot bear the thought,
That the fascist standing near her,
Beat her wrinkled cheeks,
Winding her braids around his hand;

If you do not want the fascist to trample
On your father's wartime portrait,
In front of your mother's
Very face. . . .

Then kill at least one!
Then kill him quickly!
As many times as you see him,
That many times should you kill him![29]

Poster art was particularly effective in arousing the powerful com-bination of disdain for and rage at the enemy. Hitler, a runty creature with a combination of human and bestial characteristics, has torn through the Soviet-German nonaggression treaty and now cowers before a powerful representative of the Red Army who is thrusting a bayonet into his pointy little head. An enraged mother clutches her terrified son as they both watch the approach of a German bayonet; Madonna and Child are illuminated by the white beam of a search-light, and the only color in the poster is the red blood on the bayo-net's tip and the red letters of the caption: "Red Army Soldier, SAVE US!" Against the background of a village in flames, a dazed young woman calls for revenge as she holds her dead daughter in her arms, a disproportionately enormous right hand grasping the little wounded head that still drips blood.[30]

Wartime posters also underscored the courage and success of the Red Army: A gigantic soldier replete with helmet, cape, and rifle stands tall atop the windswept Kremlin wall and, with glaring eyes and open mouth, shouts at the viewer to defend Moscow. Of all Soviet wartime posters, surely the best known was Iraklii Toidze's 1941 version of "Uncle Sam Wants YOU!" Large red letters across the top spell out "RODINA-MAT ZOVET!" (The Motherland Is Calling!). A fully proportioned woman clothed completely in red, her long scarf fluttering in the winds of determination and her huge left hand raised in a gesture of confident leadership, displays with her right hand an unfurled scroll bearing the Red Army oath. Her mature, attractive face conveys both calm and a sense of urgency. Behind her, like the rays of a rising sun, is a fan of bayonets.[31]

SAINTS AND MARTYRS

In order to inspire the populace to give their all to the war effort and not lose heart despite the Germans' continuing slaughter of civilians, wartime newspapers abounded with stories of heroic feats and with assurances that Soviet heroes were and would continue to be feted and remembered. "In songs, pictures, works of art, monuments, in the names of brigades, collective farms, and streets we cherish the memories of the deeds of our valiant fighters and heroes. This will be our pride-filled military honor-roll, which will be cherished by many generations of Soviet people. . . . The patriotic war will leave among our people an imperishable memorial of glory. And on the memorial will be inscribed the names of all those to whom the motherland is obliged for her future victory!" promised *Izvestiia* in 1942.[32]

A mythic, heroic war was embodied in the idealized personae of the youthful war heroes and heroines enshrined during the war as martyrs and moral exemplars in newspaper stories, poems, plays, movies, and paintings. They would later become the saints of the cult of the Great Patriotic War. The first of these was Capt. Nikolai Gastello, an airplane pilot who earned his immortality on the fifth day of the war by flying his shelled, burning aircraft into a cluster of enemy fuel tank trucks, killing himself and a slew of Germans in a fiery inferno. The legendary "Panfilovtsy" were a twenty-eight-man antitank unit who fought to the death to prevent the Germans from reaching Moscow in November 1941. The *politruk* (political instructor) among them purportedly said to the soldiers, "Russia is big, but there is no place to retreat to, because Moscow is behind us," and then after several hours of fierce fighting, flung himself under an enemy tank together with some hand grenades.[33]

And there was Zoya, the Joan of Arc of the Great Patriotic War. Zoya Kosmodemianskaia was a teenaged Komsomolka from Moscow who joined the partisans. In November 1941 she allegedly torched a stable of German horses and was caught, tortured, and publicly hanged. Some two weeks later, during the battle of Moscow, the Soviet Union's first counteroffensive, a *Pravda* reporter discovered her frozen body and wrote a story that marked the beginning of her secular canonization. Her vita quickly caught on as an inspirational tale and she became a national symbol of exemplary courage and self-sacrifice. For every Zoya and Panfilov there were thousands of equally deserving but unsung heroines and heroes. But for a people reared for centuries on the lives of Russian saints—whose icono-graphic likenesses graced the icon corners in homes of all Russian Orthodox believers—and a people who for decades had seen communist ideals embodied in the idealized personae of Lenin and Stalin, there was a strong pull toward the reverence of exemplary individuals.

In the 1942 color drawing, "The Interrogation of Zoya," by Kukryniksy, the acronym for a famed trio of cartoon poster artists, the young girl's vulnerability is emphasized by the effective use of light: in a darkened room, splotches of light pick out the angular, evil faces of the enemy leaning toward and leering at the short-haired Zoya, whose fair skin and little white undershirt form the brightest part of the sketch, because they are illumined by a candle held close to her by a German who is about to sear her flesh with it. Light and warmth, usually positive symbols, have been perverted into instruments of torture. Zoya Kosmodemianskaia's life and martyrdom eventually became the subject of a play and, in 1944, a feature film, *Zoya*.

The movie, directed by Lev Arnshtam, makes no pretense of being anything but an idealized story of the making of a secular saint. It largely takes the form of a narrative flashback as the tortured Zoya recalls her life story. She was born on January 21, 1924, the day of Lenin's death. The first prime embodiment of the Soviet spirit dies, and on the same day, another one is born to take his place. We see documentary footage of Lenin's lying in state, and a cut to a crying baby wriggling on a set of scales. In the film, Zoya is a happy, loved child whose parents teach her about courage and self-sacrifice. She, of course, becomes an outstanding student and a dedicated Komsomol member who puts her civic loyalty above her personal devotion to her boyfriend. When the war comes her father leaves at once for the front and Zoya volunteers for partisan work behind enemy lines. She worries only about her dear mother's tears.

In the village of Petrishchevo, Zoya is captured and tortured for information but keeps silent, and when she is finally taken out to be hanged, she strides barefoot through the snow to the sound of a dramatically waxing score, valorous and beautiful in her torn white shift. As the noose is slipped around her graceful neck, she shouts out words of encouragement to the enraptured villagers whom the

Germans have herded out to watch the execution. Her last words: *"Stalin pridet!"* ("Stalin will come!"). The film heroine can die only after having predicted the Second Coming of Joseph Stalin.

The real Zoya Kosmodemianskaia had had a tragic home life that propelled her toward suicide. Her father and grandfather had both been shot in the Stalinist terror of the thirties. After their deaths the girl had come under the influence of a devoutly communist uncle, and she became a zealous member of the Komsomol. In order to clear her late husband's name, Zoya's mother pushed her daughter toward self-sacrifice and heroism. She supported Zoya's wish to join the Komsomol partisan group, even though at this early stage of the war, effective partisan activity was impossible, particularly in the area in which she was stationed, some ninety kilometers from Moscow. The forest there was sparse and the terrain flat. There was no cover for partisans and no opportunity for them to accomplish anything except to turn themselves into exemplars of heroism by getting killed. During the war Arnshtam actually accused Aleksandr Shelepin, who was then secretary of the Moscow committee of the Komsomol, of sending the flower of youth on suicide missions. Once Zoya died, her mother campaigned constantly to have her turned into a national heroine and in 1944 goaded Zoya's under-age brother into the war. He died within the year.[34]

Eighteen-year-old Aleksandr Matrosov, who was immortalized as a symbol of ideal military valor, was said to have shielded his comrades from death by flinging his body over an exploding enemy pillbox gun port. The story of his death inspired other similar suicides of men who were moved to emulate his heroism.

Although he was not referring specifically to Matrosov's deed, Ilya Ehrenburg in his memoirs explained something about its timeless appeal: "Gradually we began to be less impressed by stories of snipers who had accounted for fifty Germans and of infantrymen who had destroyed five tanks with 'Molotov Cocktails'; one can learn to take even extraordinary valour for granted. But there was one thing that never failed deeply to move me and all those whom I came across: self-sacrifice, the death of the soldier who gives up his life voluntarily to save his comrade. This is something you can never take for granted; each time it stops your breath, seems a miracle, and no matter how difficult things are, your confidence in life is restored."[35]

Numberless unknown, unnamed heroines and heroes gave themselves to their cause, their country, and their people. Some eight hundred thousand Soviet girls and women voluntarily joined the active war effort both in the more traditional roles of cooks and medics and serving in a full range of military duties as gunners, snipers, tank drivers, parachutists, tank commanders, and bombers. Those who were not at the front dug ditches or worked in munitions factories, on railroads, in mines. They produced all the country's food.[36]

One of those hundreds of thousands of unsung heroines was a girl named Liza. Liza Shamshykova had just graduated from the history faculty of Moscow State University with a concentration in nineteenth-century Russia when the war began. Right away she volunteered for nurse's training. Liza's mother saw her daughter for the last time in August 1941. "She told me that as soon as she finished her training course [in a Moscow hospital], she would ask to be transferred to the front-line," the mother later recalled in an open letter to Liza's classmates. "And when I return, I shall definitely study to be a doctor," continued Liza. "What joy, what satisfaction there is in helping a suffering, wounded soldier!" Her mother was suffused with enormous pride in her daughter but at the same time was overtaken by the painful feeling that she was seeing her daughter for the last time. "Liza dear, and what if you don't return? What if you die?" the mother had asked. In her letter she reported her daughter's textbook—but purportedly genuine—response: "Who will go to where it is dangerous, who will help the wounded there, if not we Party members? I consider this my duty."

In December 1941 a full battle was raging in the village of Besedino. A fellow nurse recalled the day of Shamshykova's death, December 27. Liza, now commander of her medical station, was bandaging the wounded under fire of enemy machine guns. "The enemy burst into counter-attack and our troops were slowly retreating. 'Get out quickly,' someone shouted to Liza. But how could she leave? Heavily wounded soldiers were all around her; she wouldn't abandon them. She heard a foreign language being spoken, but continued her work. A German officer kicked her with the tip of his boot. Liza got up, flushing. 'I am a nurse,' she said in German, 'the wounded need my help.' The officer issued a command to his soldiers, who dragged Liza and the wounded to a shed. Shots rang out. . . . The last to fall was a young girl in a Red Army greatcoat."[37]

As far as Stalin was concerned, an ideal Soviet hero was much better dead than alive. Death was, of course, far preferable to imprisonment. Besides, death was the perfect conclusion to a heroic feat, because it allowed the hero to sacrifice to the motherland the most valuable thing in his possession, his life. Dead heroes were also useful in that they could not interfere with the myths concocted about them, let alone spoil them in some embarrassing manner, and they could not be, furthermore, in a position to claim some form of reward after the war was over.

Despite the genuine heroics of a Matrosov or a Shamshykova, surely the most widely beloved of wartime personages was the most ordinary one, a fictional figure called Vasia Tiorkin, who was the central character in Aleksandr Tvardovsky's epic poem that bore his name. The subtitle was "A Book About a Soldier," and it was published in newspaper and journal installments from 1942 to 1945. Tiorkin was a comic figure and an antihero, simple, mundane, organically bonded to the Russian land:

Face half-buried in his arm,
Flat out on his stomach,
Tiorkin settles, snug and warm,
On a grassy hummock.

Damp his heavy greatcoat feels.
Fine rain drizzling lightly;
Sky for roof and trees for walls,
Tree-roots hurting slightly.

But he never gives a sign
That he's feeling restless.
You would think him bedded down
On a feather mattress.

Then he gives his coat a hitch,
Since his back feels colder;
Silently, he starts to bitch,
Just like any soldier.

On the damp ground lying prone,
Very tired and weary,
Just as in his bed at home
Sleeps my gallant hero.

Tiorkin snores. There's no more to it.
He just takes things as they come.
"I belong, and well I know it.
Russia needs me. Here I am!"[38]

The Russian love of poetry and historic inclination to develop strong relationships with fictional characters made Tiorkin a believable antipode to the Aleksandr Matrosovs of the wartime press. He was unpretentious, cheerful, funny, truly an Everyman the common soldier could love and try to emulate.

FROM STALINGRAD TO BERLIN

From mid-July until early September 1942, despite fierce Soviet resistance, German and Romanian forces advanced toward and encircled the city that bore Stalin's name. The legendary battle inside the city was unimaginably destructive. Street by street, house by house, sometimes room by room, the fighting consumed the city and hundreds of thousands of soldiers and civilian defenders. In the heart of the city not one house was left untouched.

"Anyone who has been here will never forget it," wrote Konstantin Simonov, the journalist, poet, and novelist, in his report on the battle for *Krasnaia zvezda*. "When, many years later we begin to think about it and our lips pronounce the word 'war,' Stalingrad will rise before our eyes, the flashes of rockets and the glow of fires, and the heavy, endless thunder of bombing will again resound in our ears. We shall again experience the suffocating smell of burning, we shall hear the dry rumble of roofing iron which has been burned right through."[39]

Stalingrad had all the hallmarks of a twentieth-century epic battle: a massive attack by the invader; two armies ready to fight to the death; enormous casualties on both sides; the senseless slaughter of tens of thousands of trapped children and women; scorching heat followed by bitter cold, ceaseless shelling, dead bodies toppling into a mighty river; and finally, at a monstrous cost in lives, a rout of the enemy, resulting in an astounding volte-face in the military balance. The famed Soviet counteroffensive began on November 19 and ended with a complete encirclement of the Germans and the subsequent surrender of Field Marshal Paulus and some forty thousand German officers and soldiers on February 2, 1943. In all, over one million soldiers and civilians—Soviets, Germans, Romanians—lost their lives at Stalingrad.

At Stalingrad Soviet forces had stopped the German eastward advance. After Stalingrad, the Defense Council could start dreaming of an eventual march on Berlin. The summer 1943 battle of Kursk, in which almost a million Soviet soldiers and more than a half-million Germans clashed, was a massive battle that included six thousand tanks and four thousand aircraft, from which the Soviet side emerged victorious. After Kursk the defeat of Germany seemed assured.

"We speak of *deep* night, *deep* autumn; when I think back to the year 1943 I feel like saying: deep war," wrote Ilya Ehrenburg. "Peace had been put out of mind by then and was unimaginable. In that year everything changed: the liberation of our country from the invaders began. Early in July the Germans tried to pass over to the offensive in the Kursk bulge. First they were halted and then thrown back. A fortnight later, near Karachev, I saw a signpost: '1209 miles to Berlin'. This was in the very heart of Russia and the Germans were still holding Orel, but some ready wit had calculated the distance his battalion would still have to cover."[40]

At the end of January 1944 the Leningrad siege was officially lifted. With partisan activity at its height, the Red Army pushed westward to reestablish Soviet power in enemy-occupied areas, including those lands Stalin had seized in 1939–40 under the terms of the Molotov-Ribbentrop pact—eastern Poland, the Baltic states, Bessarabia, northern Bukovina—and to replace German with Soviet domination over much of Eastern Europe.

Wartime War Memorials

In the spring of 1942, with Hitler's armies still advancing, the Moscow and Leningrad branches of the USSR Union of Architects organized the first competition for the design of a monument commemorating the Great Patriotic War. An exhibit of the entries included more than fifty sketches of monuments to the defenders of Moscow and to heroic Leningrad.[41]

As the war progressed, the impulse to memorialize both its victims and heroes grew stronger. In 1943 the Moscow organization of the Union of Architects ran a contest for the best design for a "pantheon to the heroes of the Patriotic War." Similar competitions, often with public exhibits of the entries, continued to be held throughout the rest of the war. Doubtless it was at once inspiring and comforting to wartime artists to put their creative energies toward the shaping of shrines and tombs and other symbolic edifices celebrating the heroic efforts of their fallen brothers and sisters.

Many of their creations are fanciful and stirring. Probably the most moving are the simplest conceptions, such as a 1943 design of a necropolis of fallen fighters, consisting of rough-hewn wooden constructions displaying five-pointed stars or hammers and sickles, often under traditional little roofs of the sort one sees in Russian peasant homes. A similar design for a memorial atop a mass grave called for a grassy mound capped with a large, five-pointed star made of unpainted timber. In fact, the original memorials to World War II were simply grave markers; gradually the concept evolved to include larger and grander schemes.

Inspired by the immediacy of the war, and freed from the shackles of real financial and other practical constraints, sculptors, artists, and architects concocted fanciful triumphal arches, vast columned pantheons, museums and monument ensembles whose scale and complexity of design make St. Basil's Cathedral look like a dull and simple architectural creation by comparison. Their intent was to arouse the emotions of large numbers of people. [42]

My own favorite wartime design was for a memorial and museum to the defenders of Moscow drawn in 1943. Situated on a grassy hill at a distance from the center of the city, its broad white steps lead into a conical tower out of a European fairy tale. Surely the most sumptuous of wartime designs was a vision of a museum of the Great Patriotic War situated in Red Square, as an extension of the GUM department store. The perspective of the artist's drawing resembles an eighteenth-century Venetian painting; fluffy white clouds against a brilliant blue sky set off the massive arched entryway to the museum, which, as pictured, would have blended harmoniously into Red Square.[43]

Perhaps the most dramatic of these wartime designs was Andrei Burov's 1944 plan for a museum and memorial to the defense of Stalingrad. The main monument, entitled "Stalingrad Epic," is a gigantic, elaborately carved ziggurat that one would expect to find on some Mesopotamian plateau. It was to be crowned with an eternal flame. The museum, called a "Temple of Glory," was to be an elaborate white-and-gilt structure topped with a dome and golden cupola.[44]

WHO WON THE WAR?

"At the time, the success of the Red Army in the war appeared absolutely as incomprehensible as had been our defeat in the first months of the war," observed the historian Roy Medvedev as he mused on his wartime impressions as a twenty-year-old soldier in 1945. "The Germans were everywhere, deep in the heart of Russia. It was clear that we were defeated: the Germans were near Moscow; they had encircled Leningrad; they ranged along the Volga; they had moved into the Caucasus. And then suddenly the totally unfathomable began to happen: we began to counterattack; our army became more and more powerful; we developed mighty tanks, airplanes; the Germans began to lose control of the skies; in every battle they seemed to grow weaker and weaker, while our five- or six-million man army, battle-scarred, no longer afraid of anything, now much more skilled and better-equipped than the German soldiers, themselves came to Germany and, and . . . " Medvedev stopped the fluent monologue that had been rolling out in a mellifluous baritone and waved his fingers in the air as though he were trying to pull out the right word. "Nothing could stop them. They swept away everything in their path!"

Medvedev's account of his youthful perceptions of the victory skirted the tragedy of the last months, weeks, and even the last days of the war—the temporary reversals, the tens of thousands of needless deaths incurred out of sheer stupidity or callous calculation. For example, on April 27 Soviet and American Allied troops joined up on the Elbe River at Torgau and split the German forces. But Stalin had insisted that the Red Army and only the Red Army should take Berlin. And so it did, by "storm," meaning that tens of thousands of Soviet soldiers lost their lives unnecessarily. In all, the Soviet Union suffered some three hundred thousand casualties in the Battle of Berlin.

Despite everything, despite even Stalin, the Red Army did triumph, like some wounded phoenix arising from the bones and rubble of its own devastated country. How and why did the Soviet Union win and Germany lose?

The contemporary Soviet press maintained that Stalin, the Communist Party, the Red Army, and the great Soviet people (especially those who had died in the effort), in that order, had won the war, together with a little help from their friends to the west. On the other hand, less than two decades after the war's end, German generals-turned-memoirists largely attributed their army's failure in the Soviet war to what the historian Michael Cherniavsky called "Corporal Hitler, General Winter and the Russian Peasant." Those German accounts, wrote Cherniavsky, offered two answers to the painful question of Germany's defeat and the Soviet victory: "Russian 'qualities' and Hitler's mistakes. The Russian 'qualities' are three in number: the Russian climate, chiefly symbolized by General Winter, who always comes in earlier than expected and is always more severe than any preceding one on record; inexhaustible manpower reserves which, when finally mobilized, overwhem the Germans; and the primitiveness of Russian communications, of Russian army organization, and of the Russian himself as a human being . . . even when surrounded the Russian soldier went on fighting with the soulless indifference of Asiatic man."

Hitler's alleged mistakes included a five-week delay in the orginal planned launching of Operation Barbarossa, his insistence on holding Stalingrad at all costs, his failed summer 1943 offensive at Kursk, and, above all, his having stuck his army with a two-front war against the warnings of his own generals. So much for "Corporal Hitler."[45]

Leo Tolstoy, who wove his philosophy of history into the rich tapestry of *War and Peace,* probably would have posed the question in terms of free will versus inevitability. "The war came about because it was bound to come about," he wrote of the Russian war against Napoleon. "Millions of men, renouncing their human feelings and their common sense, had to march from west to east to slay their fellows, just as some centuries previously hordes of men had moved from east to west, slaying their fellows. . . . We are forced to fall back on fatalism to explain the irrational events of history (that is to say, events the intelligence of which we do not see). The more we strive to account for such events in history rationally, the more irrational and incomprehensible do they become to us."[46]

Tolstoy is a hard act to follow. But rather than throw up my hands at the idea of finding any rational explanation for the war and its outcome, I would gently suggest that the Soviet victory in the war with Germany was just as likely to have been caused largely by factors and events unknown to scholars, as by those we know about.

In fact, Germany, and that includes the general staff, must itself bear responsibility for a senseless war. "In short, the task undertaken was too vast," was the succinct bottom line offered by General Heusinger, who had planned the 1941 Russian operations. The Germans lost because they were fighting for fascism, and that meant they were out to destroy bolshevism and the Soviet Union, together with its cities, its culture, and many of its people—and their actions as an occupying power reflected those aims. As a consequence they lost whatever support of the indigenous population they might have garnered had they treated the Soviet people as a civilian population in a conventional war, rather than as *Untermenschen*.[47]

In the first months of the war, when none of this was as yet clear, many Soviet people did in fact welcome the Germans as potential liberators from Stalinism. But by and large their backing of the enemy fell away when they saw their homes plundered and their fellow villagers murdered. There is, of course, no way to know how many of the Soviet citizens who did continue to collaborate with the enemy after the first months of the war did so by conviction and how many by necessity. The post hoc explanation invariably was, "we did whatever we had to in order to avoid starvation," which sounds plausible enough.

The highest-ranking anti-Stalinist supporter of the German Army was Gen. Andrei Vlasov, who had been instrumental in the defense of Moscow in the first year of the war. In 1942 the Germans captured him and exploited him as a propaganda tool until early 1945, when they let him form two divisions of the anti-Stalinist Armed Forces of the Committee for the Liberation of the Peoples of

Russia. Its members were mostly Soviet prisoners of war. In the end, Vlasov was captured and hanged, the form of capital punishment meted out to traitors. He remains a mysterious figure, a flamboyant giant of a man who genuinely believed that Stalin was destroying Russia and had to be gotten rid of by military means. Portrayed as an arch-villain until the demise of the Soviet Union, his career (like everything else having to do with the Stalin years) was reevaluated in the heady days of *perestroika*.[48]

For three years following Operation Barbarossa the eastern front— with the exception of some active fighting in Italy in 1943—was the only theater of war in Europe. Although the Union of Soviet Socialist Republics had allies, the populace had the understandable impression that they alone were fighting the Germans. In Soviet eyes the British—incorrigible capitalists who could never be trusted anyway— were occupied with their own air war. The United States was synonymous with hundreds of Studebaker trucks, Spam, and dried eggs, which we had sent over under the lend-lease arrangement. Spam everyone loved, and many drivers of "Studebekkers" regarded their trucks as adored wartime companions.

The dried eggs were more difficult to deal with. Lela Gefter, who spent the war in Moscow, recalls mixing the egg powder with water in varying proportions and coming out with almost inedible pastes of different consistencies. One day during the war she came across a published newspaper interview with a United States embassy attaché in which he informed the readers how to make American dried eggs palatable. "It turned out," Lela said, laughing, "that we were supposed to combine the egg powder with an equal amount of *cream!* Can you imagine that? The Americans thought we had *cream* to drink! When I read that interview I realized that they didn't understand anything about what the war was like for us."

Almost since the beginning of the shaky wartime alliance, Stalin had been urging Winston Churchill and Franklin D. Roosevelt to open up a second European front and take some of the pressure off the Soviet Union. By June 6, 1944, when the famed allied landing on the Normandy beaches finally materialized, victory over Germany was already well in sight. The Teheran Conference of November 1943 had virtually assured the Soviet leader a major voice in determining the postwar European order. Stalingrad, Kursk, the staggering Soviet wartime losses, and Stalin's own canny diplomacy had given his country the status of a major global power—and that of a *national* power as opposed to the internationalism of prewar communism. Indeed on May 22, 1943, the Presidium of the Executive Committee of the Comintern (Communist International) proclaimed the dissolution of that world communist organization.

Doubtless this move succeeded in its goal of impressing the United States and Britain. On the eve of his departure to the November 1943 allied conference at Teheran, Roosevelt reportedly remarked to former ambassador William Bullitt: "I have just a hunch that Stalin doesn't want anything but security for his country, and I think that if I give him everything I possibly can and ask nothing from him in return, *noblesse oblige,* he won't try to annex anything and will work toward a world of democracy and peace."[49]

The American president had made a terrible mistake in judgment. Indeed, as victory approached, even before the Red Army had had a chance to leech itself onto Eastern Europe, the Stalinist apparatus had turned toward the repression and control of a populace that had already suffered indescribable ordeals. The Gulag continued to suck in new inmates, and in 1943–44, together with the liberation of many areas from German occupation, the regime deported entire peoples, some of whose members Stalin had suspected of collaboration with the German occupiers. Crimean Tatars, Chechen, Ingush, Kurds, and Kalmyks were only some of the peoples sent by the tens of thousands from their homelands in the Crimea, the north Caucasus, Georgia, and other areas. Those deportees who survived their long and terrible journeys eastward were herded into "special settlements," detention camps with hard conditions of life and work. Only representatives of the smaller nationalities suffered these deportations. Although plenty of Ukrainians and Russians had in fact collaborated with the Nazis, "technical reasons," meaning the fact that they existed in the tens of millions, prevented the forced exile of enormous masses of them.[50]

VICTORY!

The fall of Berlin! How many odes, paintings, reminiscences, plays, films have celebrated this mythic moment of triumph and retribution! The fighting was fierce; German resistance was surprisingly strong. A photograph that was to become a prime artifact of the war cult was snapped by a photojournalist on April 30. It shows two Russian soldiers on the roof of the shell-riddled Reichstag building hoisting up the banner of the 150th infantry division of the Third Army—the fighting force that took Berlin. Upon the banner itself was ultimately conferred the status of the most sacred relic of the victory of the Soviet people in the Great Patriotic War.

Although the vanquished capitulated to the victors on the afternoon of May 8, Muscovites learned the news only early the next morning. At 2:10 A.M. on May 9, Radio Moscow aired the long-awaited announcement that Germany had surrendered unconditionally, and that the war was over. Together with the announcement of the victory, the Presidium of the Supreme Soviet declared May 9 a nationwide festival day, a victory day holiday.[51]

In Moscow, immediately after the broadcast, people poured into the streets to celebrate. Others, manifesting years of political conditioning that stressed the importance of meetings in the workplace, and eager to seek one another out, made their way to factories and institutes before the sun was up, to hear and make impromptu speeches. Throughout that warm, sunny day a spontaneously generated energy gripped the capital. Crowding onto the streets, strangers hugged and kissed each other in joy. They pressed flowers and candy into the hands of uniformed soldiers and officers. Ilya Ehrenburg immersed himself in the street crowds:

> A little girl pushed a bunch of snowdrops into a sailor's hand, but when he tried to kiss her she gave a tiny hoot of laughter and ran away. "Eternal memory to the dead," an old man said in a loud voice. A major on crutches raised his hand to his cap in a salute while the old man explained: "It's the wife who begged me to say it. She's in bed with a chill. Sergeant Berezovsky of the Guards. Mentioned twice by Comrade Stalin." Someone remarked: "Well, now he'll soon be home again." The old man shook his head: "He died a hero's death on 18th April. His commanding officer wrote to us. My wife said to me: 'Tell people about it.'"[52]

United States Ambassador George Kennan recalled that shortly after ten o'clock in the morning, an enormous throng of young people surged over to the American embassy and "settled down to demonstrate before the embassy building feelings that were obviously ones of almost delirious friendship." The crowd quickly swelled and stayed on cheering and celebrating, until well into the evening. "If any of us ventured out into the street," wrote Kennan, "he was immediately seized, tossed enthusiastically into the air, and passed on friendly hands over the heads of the crowd, to be lost, eventually, in a confused orgy of good feeling somewhere on its outer fringes."[53]

"That evening," wrote Ehrenburg, "there could not have been a single table in our country where the people gathered round it were not conscious of an empty place. Tvardovsky later put it into words: 'To the thunder of guns, for the first time we bade farewell to all who had died in the war, the way the living say farewell to the dead.'"[54]

The sky over Moscow was slashed by gigantic white rays of light from huge projectors, and at ten o'clock in the evening the city shook to a one-thousand-gun salute and a spectacular display of fireworks. Some two to three million people had gathered in and around Red Square. No one had told Muscovites to assemble in the heart of their ancient city. They simply streamed into the center by the tens of thousands, in their country's first spontaneous mass demonstration of collective emotion, at any rate, since Lenin's death in 1924.

GATHERING CLOUDS

At nine o'clock in the evening Stalin's voice came over the loudspeakers in Red Square and all over the city. Its timbre had none of the softness of his famed speech of July 3, 1941, when he had called the people "brothers, sisters, friends." Now he sounded tough and remote as he spoke briefly of the glory of victory. "Comrades! Compatriots! The great day of the victory over Germany is upon us," he began. Generalissimo Stalin laid out the news about the Wehrmacht's capitulations first in Rheims on May 7, then Berlin on May 8, and added that one group of German forces in Czechoslovakia had not yet yielded. He said that the Soviet people's enormous sacrifices and tribulations had paid off, but he uttered no words of gratitude or even compassion.[55]

On May 9 and 10 the press was filled with articles about the victory, most of them emotional, even rhapsodic. There was minimal mention about the need to remember the war dead and more emphasis on their unforgettable heroism than on the tragedy of the loss. No casualty figures were published during these days. Every article praised Stalin and thanked him for leading the Party and people to the victory, which was already being presented as a vindication of the Communist Party, the Red Army, and the socialist system.

The impassioned people cheering and singing and dancing in the streets on May 9 may have had little idea what the victory really meant to the leader whom they lauded and applauded with such evident enthusiasm. For the astute observer, indications were readily in evidence. On May 9, *Krasnaia zvezda* ran an article whose concluding section contained the following paragraph: "Victory! For You we fought for almost four years, *and now we will never give you up for anything, for anyone.* You are the offspring of our unprecedented struggle. You are the gate to our bright future. You are the eternal pride of our mighty, invincible Red Army" (emphasis added).

Holding on to a victory meant that the Red Army would never fully yield the lands it had liberated with its own blood. And, in fact, the Soviet Army did not begin to give up most of those territories until 1989, at which time some veterans would complain that Mikhail Gorbachev had thrown away the victory for which so many had sacrificed so much.

On May 24 at a Kremlin banquet in honor of the commanding officers of the Red Army, Stalin raised his glass and offered a toast:

> Our government has made many mistakes. We had some desperate moments in 1941–42 when our army was in retreat, forced to abandon our native villages and cities in Ukraine, Belorussia, Moldavia, the Leningrad region, the Baltic territories, the Karelo-Finnish republic, abandoning them because there was no other way out. Some other nation might well have said to its rulers: You have not fulfilled our expectations, go away, we shall set up another government, which will conclude peace with Germany and will secure us quiet.[56]

This statement may well reveal something about Stalin's concerns at the war's end. He knew that tens of millions of his subjects expected to be rewarded for their trials with better, happier, freer lives. He also knew that if the Soviet Union were to become that which the Western powers seemed to think it already was—a mighty global power—he would have to continue much the same kind of rule the populace had endured in the 1930s.

Stalin also was acquainted with enough Russian history to know something about the causal relationship between war and the demand for internal reform in his country. Those young military officers who had returned to Russia after pursuing Napoleon to Paris later gave birth to the 1825 Decembrist movement, which sought to prevent Nicholas I from taking the throne after the death of his brother Alexander. The Crimean War was followed by the emancipation of the serfs and other reforms in the 1860s. Revolution in 1905 that turned autocratic Russia into a parliamentary monarchy erupted directly after Russia's defeat in the Russo-Japanese War. And the Romanov emperor's inability to handle the vast problems raised by Russia's entry into World War I helped lead directly to the February and October Revolutions of 1917. (To continue the pattern, the USSR's ten-year entanglement in Afghanistan was surely a precipitating factor in the *perestroika* phenomenon of the late 1980s.)

All these wars had given those who had fought in them, especially junior officers, a sense of entitlement, of self-respect, of independence that inevitably led to demands for change. In Stalin's eyes, the wartime reliance on individual initiative was utterly incompatible with his continued or, rather, renewed totalitarian control of the country. The resurgence of the Stalinist *apparat* was his main domestic goal in the spring of 1945. To that end he drew up a series of draconian control measures, including the immediate incarceration of released prisoners of war. And he planned a ritual parade to celebrate the new order.

VICTORY PARADE

June 24, 1945. The Kremlin clock chimed ten times, marking the beginning of the carefully orchestrated official ritual celebrating the triumphant end to the war: the Victory Parade. Under a light rain, squadrons of frontline soldiers and officers massed in perfect squares. To the sound of martial music, deputy to the supreme commander in chief, Marshal Georgii Konstantinovich Zhukov, rode out of the Spasskii Gates on a white steed to meet the parade together with its commander, Marshal Konstantin Konstantinovich Rokossovskii, astride a black charger. Zhukov and Rokossovskii made the rounds of the troops; Zhukov yelled out ritualized greetings, and each of the divisions responded with the phrase, "Health to the Comrade Marshal!" followed by a long "*Ura!*" (Hurrah!).

Joseph Stalin, who was not particularly adept on horseback, chose to review the parade in full military regalia from the safety of the tribunal atop the Lenin Mausoleum in Red Square. Next to him stood Viacheslav Molotov, Klimentii Voroshilov, Lazar Kaganovich, Anastas Mikoyan, Andrei Zhdanov, Nikita Khrushchev, Lavrentii Beria, and others.

After riding past all the massed troops, Zhukov dismounted, ascended the steps to the mausoleum tribunal, and delivered the Victory Parade address. He spoke of the army's undying confidence in the victory that Stalin had foreseen, which had been achieved because of the socialist system and the wise leadership of the Party and Soviet government. "And we triumphed because we were led to victory by our great leader and brilliant commander, Marshal of the Soviet Union—Stalin!" Zhukov proclaimed the eternal glory of the Red Army: "Henceforth and forever our victorious Red Army shall enter world history as *armiia osvoboditel'nitsa* [army-deliverer], covered with an unfading halo of glory." Zhukov also spoke in quasi-religious terms of those who had been martyred in the cause. "For our victory over German imperialism we paid a heavy sacrifice. In fierce battles many of our fighting friends—the best sons and daughters of our nation—fell to their heroic deaths. Today, this day of great ceremony, let us pay our respects to their sacred memory and pronounce: 'Eternal glory to the heroes who fell in battle for our Soviet Homeland!'"[57]

To the accompaniment of a large military orchestra, a lengthy procession of troops from army and naval divisions, arranged in the chronological order of their major wartime battles from 1941 to 1945, followed Zhukov's speech. Suddenly the music stopped. After a silence, a long drum roll resounded through Red Square. And then, according to *Pravda*, came "an unforgettable, deeply symbolic tableau." Two hundred Soviet soldiers, each bearing a German fascist banner attached to a swastika-bearing wrought-iron pole, rushed forward simultaneously and flung those banners at the foot of the Lenin Mausoleum.

That gesture was dramatic, primal, atavistic. Triumphant warriors were demonstrating to all the viewers that the Nazis had been completely vanquished by their conquerors. And those warriors were laying trophies at the feet of their leader and at the tomb of their Founding Father.

5

AFTER THE WAR WAS OVER

The June 1945 parade was weeks away from the American bombings of Hiroshima and Nagasaki and the end of the war. The United States was still a Soviet ally, and by previous agreement Stalin was bound to enter the war against Japan on August 9, three months after Germany's defeat. But the chill of the Cold War to come was already in evidence. After President Roosevelt's death on April 12, 1945, Stalin's conflict with Mr. Roosevelt over the borders of Poland and Germany, the future government of Poland, the power configurations in the new United Nations, and a host of other issues carried over into the rapidly deteriorating relationship with President Harry Truman.

By the end of 1945 the Cold War was on in earnest, and the Red Army had replaced the Wehrmacht in a gigantic swath of territory "from Stettin in the Baltic to Trieste on the Black Sea," as Winston Churchill put it in the famed "Iron Curtain" speech he delivered in Fulton, Missouri, in February 1946. Paradoxically the four-year period from 1945 to 1949, which marked the United States monopoly of the atomic bomb, coincided with the most dramatically successful era in the history of Soviet foreign policy. This was due, in part, to the fact that the United States grossly overestimated the postwar strength of the Soviet Union, which, like imperial Russia in 1812, projected the image of an invincible superpower that had played the major role in saving Europe from the armies of a maniacal dictator. In the Western countries the general assumption in the second half of the 1940s was that the Soviet Union was such a powerful and aggressive adversary, only the threat of an American nuclear attack prevented the Soviet Army from continuing its westward roll begun after the 1943 Stalingrad victory. In reality, in the postwar years the victorious Soviet Union was at least as devastated and impoverished as Germany and Japan.

Back in the USSR, the transition from wartime to postwar society was unimaginably difficult, in no way resembling the "return to normalcy" that people invariably long for when a war is over. Out of a total population of approximately one hundred ninety million, at least thirty million people had died in four years. Over seventeen hundred towns and more than seventy thousand villages had been destroyed, as well as thousands of factories and tens of thousands of miles of railroad track and roads. In the cities, more than half the housing had been demolished and much of the rest of it was in terrible repair, as were the heating, sewage, and other systems vital to the functioning of urban areas. In industry, most of the achievements of the Second and Third Five-Year Plans of the thirties had been reversed, with industry in a state of ruin almost, but not quite, as complete as the breakdown that followed the tumultuous 1914–21 period.[1]

In the years immediately following the war's end, food cultivation was in a disastrous state. The year 1946 saw drought in much of the Soviet Union, and the harvest was even poorer than in the last year of the war. Rationing remained in effect until 1947 and food prices tripled. Despite widespread famine, forced deliveries of grain, milk, and meat to the state made it seem "as if Stalin was determined to make the peasants pay for postwar reconstruction," wrote the economist Alec Nove.[2]

Draconian labor practices filled out the pathetically shrunken labor force with labor conscripts and convicts of every description. Once again the Gulag welcomed new victims by the tens of thousands: prewar convicts serving out their original sentences or additional ones that had been slapped on for good measure; war prisoners and slave laborers released from German factories; those who had committed some transgression during the war and were left free to fight to the end, only to be picked up as soon as the war was over.

Inhabitants of the Soviet Union experienced migrations of millions of their numbers in movements not seen in Europe since the fourteenth century's traumatic dislocations caused by the black death. Prisoners of war and slave laborers working in Germany were repatriated—often against their will—and usually transferred to domestic internment camps. Entire peoples, accused of collaboration with the enemy, continued to be deported to remote geographical locations. Vast territories to the west acquired during the war—Latvia, Lithuania, Estonia, Carpatho-Ukraine, western Belorussia (formerly eastern Poland), and Moldavia—were populated by hundreds of thousands of Russians and Ukrainians and outfitted with Soviet-style institutions and policies—planned economies, rigid Communist Party and police controls, and collectivized agriculture.

Some portion of the Soviet people evidenced an atrophy or paralysis of some basic aspects of human decency. In his memoir of growing up in Leningrad after the war, Joseph Brodsky described an incident showing this very kind of malfunction:

> I remember, for instance, how in 1945 my mother and I were waiting for a train at some railway station near Leningrad. The war was just over, twenty million Russians were decaying in makeshift graves across the continent, and the rest, dispersed by war, were returning to their homes or what was left of their homes. The railway station was a picture of primeval chaos. People were besieging the cattle trains like mad insects; they were climbing on the roofs of cars, squeezing between them, and so on. For some reason, my eye caught sight of an old, bald, crippled man with a wooden leg, who was trying to get into car after car, but each time was pushed away by the people who were already hanging on the footboards. The train started to move and the old man hopped along. At one point he managed to grab a handle of one of the cars, and then I saw a woman in the doorway lift a kettle and pour boiling water straight on the old man's bald crown. The man fell—the Brownian movement of a thousand legs swallowed him and I lost sight of him.[3]

IVAN, I HARDLY KNEW YOU

Postwar medical facilities were pitifully deficient in providing care and medicine for the millions of sick and wounded. Demobilized Soviet soldiers—unlike those of their Allied counterparts who reaped rewards and privileges and went off to university on GI bills—received for their years of military service little more than the barest necessities for their trip home from the front and a negligible salary.[4]

Amputees, cripples, and paraplegics took up positions on street corners and in outdoor markets, hawking whatever they could find to earn a bit of money—usually loose cigarettes—without resorting to outright begging. Suddenly, some two years after the end of the war, they disappeared from view. Stalin had evidently decided that the presence of those mutilated war victims was upsetting to people, and that they should no longer be in evidence to remind the public of the horror of the past war. They were rounded up off the streets of the larger cities and sent off to special colonies in the far north to live out the rest of their days.

An official silence enshrouded those war invalids until 1982, when the author Yuri Nagibin published a short story about them called "Patience." Anna, a microbiologist from Leningrad, goes with her family to make a tourist visit to the northern island of Bogoiar. (Bogoiar is the fictitious name of Valaam, an island north of Leningrad that Nagibin himself visited. There he was shocked to see the aging paraplegics he later described in the story.) Anna is a middle-aged woman with a husband she has never loved, a man whom she married because he was the best friend of her deceased beloved, Pasha, whom she had lost in the war, and his rival for her attention. At the Bogoiar quay she sees middle-aged and elderly cripples missing arms and legs, selling roots from the forest. She remembers that the old monastery on the island was supposed to have been a shelter for invalids of the war.

In one of those cripples, a half-man with a handsome face, broad chest, and no legs, she recognizes Pasha. His only means of locomotion were homemade wooden iron-shaped blocks with handles with which he walked on his hands. Although it was a fourteen-kilometer round-trip walk from the monastery to the boat dock, Pasha had met every tourist ship that had come to the island in the more than three decades he had lived there, in the hopes that Anna might be among the passengers. The rest of this powerful story plays out the pained interaction between the reunited lovers. In the end, Anna pleads with Pasha to allow her to remain with him on Bogoiar; his pride prevents him from giving his consent. She boards the ship to return to Leningrad with her family, then is impelled to swim back to the island to rejoin him, and in the process drowns. He, unknowing, continues his daily vigil of walking on his hands to wait on the quay for her return, just as he had been doing for more than thirty years.

Nagibin's Pasha had many counterparts in real life. "It is bitter to remember the soulless attitude toward invalids that reigned in government institutions after the war," wrote literary critic Lazar Lazarev in an article marking the fiftieth anniversary of the beginning of the war in 1991. "Beggarly pensions forced cripples to make their way from car to car on trains, asking for handouts (I remember a poor wretch with no hands who held in his clenched teeth a cap into which people threw coins)." Lazarev also recalled the pitiful home-hewn prosthetic devices on wheels that cripples made for themselves because government-issued prostheses were either unavailable or of unusable quality.[5]

NEW TIMES, NEW VALUES

After the war the Stalinist system reasserted its control over an exhausted and fractionated society by means not only of the *knut* but also the *piroshki*. The "Big Deal" is a term the literary critic Vera Dunham gave to the concordat struck between the Stalin regime and its aspiring middle-class managers in the postwar years that helps explain the success of Stalinist post-traumatic social controls and the incongruous embourgeoisement of middle-level society within the framework of totalitarian terror. Her splendid book, *In Stalin's Time: Middleclass Values in Soviet Fiction,* examined novels, plays, and poems from the decade before Stalin's death in order to explore the values championed by their authors.[6]

The chaotic circumstances of war had willy-nilly created pockets of cultural freedom as areas formerly under tight control were left to govern themselves, while in Moscow, dapper attachés of Allied governments mingled with Soviet citizens. When the war was over, the Big Deal exchanged that freedom for the rewards of careerism.

Middlebrow literature began to put forward new ideals that had no possibility of realization. "Material craving engulfed power society from top to bottom. Coiffures, cosmetics, perfume, clothes—the trappings of enhanced femininity—gained social significance. They, too, began to represent the new public good. In real life, however, they were no more than a hope, and it is as such that they entered fiction."[7]

Kulturnost, a phalanx of assumptions and rules about proper social conduct that in the twenties and thirties had applied mostly to physical hygiene and the most elementary kind of courtesy, was expanded after the war into a far more inclusive program designed to replace the disorder of wartime with proscribed social norms.

Self-sacrificial wartime heroes were rapidly demoted. This was no time to rest on one's laurels, much less to expect rewards. The only postwar hero was Hero Number One, and he was not inclined to make room for any competition. Military heroism per se faded from the novel, which moved its focus from feats of valor to the practical business of economic and social reconstruction.

THE ART OF WAR

Just as Stalin had found it necessary to clear the streets of cripples whom he saw as ugly vestiges of the war, so paintings on the war theme dating from his last years tended to prettify wartime episodes. *Victory* (1948) is a vast panorama of the entrance to the Berlin Reichstag building at the moment of victory. The expansive set of steps is littered with rubble and the bodies of soldiers (indistinct, but they must all be German to be consonant with the logic of the painting), columns and walls riddled with shell and bullet holes, while exuberant Red Army men jubilantly raise their arms and toss helmets into an atmosphere smoky from celebratory rifle shots. Another often reproduced scene in this genre is *Rest After Battle* (1951), a silly rendition of about thirty men relaxing together in the snow-covered clearing of a pine forest. They are probably singing, and every single one of them is either grinning or laughing.

Norman Rockwell might have come out with a smile of recognition had he been shown the most widely known painting from the entire postwar era, *Letter from the Front* (1947). In a classic idyll of a

Russian small-town courtyard drenched with sunlight, a woman, a slightly wounded young soldier, and three gorgeous, well-fed children revel in the happy tidings evidently contained in a letter read aloud by a red-headed Rockwellesque little tyke in a baseball cap, a letter evidently sent from the front by his dad. The inherent message of this wonderfully successful painting: with confidence and love, the rear awaited the frontline soldiers to return so they could recreate their happy lives together.

Postwar monuments, like monumental art more generally, were political statements par excellence. Most blatant were those many monuments that were quickly erected on foreign soil as tributes to Red Army casualties in Germany, Austria, and Eastern Europe. "We spilled *our* blood to free your country from fascism, therefore you are indebted to *us*," ran the implied message. Obelisks, pyramids, columns, and other classic architectural forms of homage—some of them bedecked with sculptures—were hurriedly erected in Poland, Czechoslovakia, Romania, Germany. The great classic of the group, completed in 1949, marked the center of a major memorial complex in East Berlin's Treptower Park. A towering Soviet soldier with classic Russian features clasps in one hand a beautiful little German girl rescued from the flames of Berlin, while his other hand wields a lowered sword. His booted foot crushes a swastika. Within newly acquired Soviet territories to the west of the 1939 borders, similar imperatives dictated the construction of monuments to Soviet fighters who died "liberating" those areas.

In the Soviet Union proper, a number of modest monuments went up, but they were slow in coming. In Stalingrad the newly rebuilt central square, known as Square of the Fallen Fighters, was graced with—what else?—a monument to Comrade Stalin.[8]

As eager as Stalin might have been to play down the status of war heroes, his administration could not realistically place a taboo on the theme of the war as it had on the purge and terror of the thirties, over which there reigned a malignant silence. Besides, the idea was not to turn the war into a nonevent but rather to shape its public memory to suit the needs of the regime. The Great Patriotic War should serve as a stirring, but safely distant, reminder of the success of the socialist system and its Supreme Leader.

STAR IN THE EAST

The cover of the December 1949 issue of the picture magazine, *Ogonek,* showed the winter night sky over the Kremlin. A bright portrait of Stalin shone in the heavens, suspended from a blimp and illumined by carefully aimed projector lights. The occasion was Stalin's seventieth birthday, December 21, 1949, which was in some ways the climactic moment in the entire history of the Stalin cult, replete with effulgent, laudatory speeches, the conferring of medals upon Stalin, the unveiling of new statues and monuments, a profusion of gushing odes, and gaggles of little Pioneers bestowing poems, songs, and flowers upon their beloved leader.

Stalin, characteristically, could not allow his ravaged empire to make the transition from war to peace, from power to superpower, from defensive victim of capitalist encirclement to aggressive leader of a world communist bloc, without brutal, hate-filled campaigns that made the last eight years of Stalin's life among the most horrific of his quarter-century rule. These included the so-called Leningrad Affair, a 1946 purge of top Leningrad Party officials; the *Zhdanovshchina,* or "Zhdanov Times," after Andrei Zhdanov, Leningrad Party boss and Stalin's ideologue-and-crony-in-chief, who cracked down on the most creative Soviet writers and intellectuals; the nationalist "anticosmopolitan" campaign against Jews, which coincided with the creation of Israel in 1948 and took on massive proportions, as persons of Jewish origin were booted out of universities, institutes, and other places of work and study to make room for Party loyalists of non-Jewish—mostly Russian—descent.

In the last years of his life, Stalin reckoned with some of the officers in the armed services whose very existence had made his life so miserable during the war. Some, like Marshal Zhukov and Admiral Kuznetsov, were demoted; Marshal Rokossovskii was dispatched westward as overlord of Poland; other marshals and admirals, including some of those who had worked most closely with Zhukov, ended up in prison or labor camp.

The generalissimo also moved to dispose of the war as well, or at least to whittle it down into a size and shape he could control. Military Order #270 (of August 16, 1941), which equated being taken prisoner with treason and stipulated that the families of prisoners of war would suffer dire consequences, and Military Order #227 (of July 28, 1942), popularly known as "not one step back," which created punishment battalions and established within military divisions special units to shoot anyone who retreated without orders, had been read aloud to all troops at the time of issuance and on other occasions when necessary. After the war, it was forbidden to print or even refer to these orders, which were first published only in 1988. Stalin wanted his country to curtail talk about the war, to move past the ordeal and on to the tasks of economic reconstruction and the waging of the Cold War against the capitalist nations.[9]

DAYS OF VICTORY IN THE YEARS OF TURMOIL

Like the first anniversary of the October Revolution in 1918, which was celebrated with parades, floats, and a dramatic reenactment of the seizure of the Petrograd Winter Palace, Victory Day 1946 was a holiday that combined official management with popular enthusiasm. Giant portraits of Stalin and his wartime military commanders draped the sides of buildings in Moscow, Leningrad, and other cities, setting off the red bunting and decorations that were held over from the May Day celebration. People gathered in squares and parks to congratulate bemedaled veterans, to listen to street musicians and orchestras, and to revel in the thrill of victory. Some modest rituals commemorated the day, including speeches by veterans, organized relay races, and concerts. In Moscow, the Museum of the Red Army invited guests to meet with participants in the storm of Berlin near the display case containing the Victory Banner that had flown over the Reichstag the previous spring. In the evening *narodnoe gulianie* (public strolling) brought more people out onto the brightly lit streets after a festive meal. And at night, in the republic capitals and hero cities, fireworks blazed across the spring sky.

Just about a week earlier, on the May 1 holiday, the generalissimo had issued an order that demonstrated his desire to diminish the public attention paid to the war: "The Armed Forces of the Soviet Union . . . fulfilled their duty toward the Motherland in the Great Patriotic War. *Now before our armed forces stands a no less important task*—to vigilantly guard our hard-won peace and the creative labor of the Soviet people. . . . "[10]

The message was clear: the war with fascist Germany was over, a cold war was on, and it was time for the country to mobilize its energies for the daunting task of economic reconstruction. Already in 1946 the press carried articles setting the desired postwar tone. "One Year Later," published in *Pravda* on May 10, 1946, told of a former soldier who returned from the front to run a collective farm. His sense of duty had impelled him to fight, and now that same patriotism inspired him to labor for his country.

The Supreme Leader let it be known that this was not the time for military commanders to publish memoirs about the war. In his book, *A Lifelong Cause,* Marshal Aleksandr Vasilevskii reflected on an incident that occurred not long after the war's end. The Military Publishing House had accepted for publication two memoirs, one on the storm of Berlin and the other called *From Stalingrad to Vienna.* Stalin rejected both volumes, explaining that "it was too early to be writing memoirs so soon after these great events, at a time when passions were still too much aroused, and thus the memoirs would not have the required objectivity." The literary critic and war veteran Lazar Lazarev, who cited this passage in an article on the trajectory of Russian literature about the war, observed that "Stalin's attitude not only prevented the publication of memoirs but also stopped people from even picking up their pens, because everyone understood at once that it was not subjectivism which Stalin feared, but the truth." Lazarev added that not just military memoirists but historians were muzzled as well and denied access to archives pertaining to the war. "Historians quickly understood that their job was to embroider prepared patterns using beautiful materials to delight the eye, not to conduct research into facts."[11]

In 1947 Stalin stepped up his efforts to leave the war aside; he demoted Victory Day from a state holiday to a regular working day. From 1947 until 1965, when Victory Day was reinstated as a holiday, its annual commemoration was largely informal, with meetings of veterans, visits to cemeteries, and public strolling. The one festive ritual the authorities retained was nighttime fireworks in the hero cities and republic capitals.

By 1949 and 1950 the tenets of mature Cold War propaganda had thoroughly saturated the official stance on the war. The wartime enemy was no longer called fascism but imperialism. In these years the press contended that not only had the Soviet Union alone saved the world, defeating imperialism and the forces of reaction, but that throughout the war, its so-called allies, the United States and Britain, had maintained an active collusion with the enemy. These "friends" had not only delayed opening a second front but had also conducted secret negotiations with the Germans. From a genuine holiday in 1945 and 1946, Victory Day had turned into yet another channel for the mobilization of popular efforts in the service of the state—plus fireworks.[12]

DEATH OF A DEITY

An anecdote that, for obvious reasons, circulated around Moscow only after Stalin's death told of an old woman who, early in the winter of 1953, took to making a daily stop at her neighborhood newspaper kiosk. She would glance at the first page of *Pravda,* then shake her head with a sigh and trudge away. After several weeks of witnessing this same scene, one day the newspaper seller asked, "Are you looking for something in *Pravda* that you can't find?"

"An obituary," replied the old woman.

"But obituaries aren't printed on the first page of *Pravda,*" countered the man behind the glass.

"This one will be . . . " murmured the woman, with a smile.

In the end, Stalin was partly done in by the system he himself had created. In the recesses of his apartment, which no one dared enter without being summoned, the seventy-three-year-old dictator lay undiscovered for hours on the floor in his pajamas, the victim of a massive stroke. Within a few days—on March 5, 1953—he was dead.

Stalin's death is one of my earliest political memories, along with the election of President Eisenhower. I came home from my third-grade class and to my astonishment found my family, including aunts and uncles, noisily celebrating at the dinner table in the middle of the afternoon. When I asked what was going on, my father, chewing some herring and rye bread, pointed to the center of the dining table, on which the *New York Post* was propped up by a big bottle of Smirnoff vodka. The three-word headline took up the entire page: STALIN IS DEAD!

"'At nine-fifty in the evening . . . ' The medical bulletins spoke of leucocytes, of collapse, of intermittent arrhythmia. We had long lost sight of the fact that Stalin was mortal," recalled the writer Ilya Ehrenburg. "He had become an all-powerful and remote deity. And now the deity had died of a cerebral haemorrhage. It seemed incredible."

It did seem incredible. The old woman at the newspaper kiosk notwithstanding, for many people, political life without Stalin was unimaginable. Even a personage as sophisticated as Ehrenburg "could not see the future of the country as other than bound up with what was daily called 'the wisdom of our leader of genius.'"[13]

Stalin's death evoked a public outburst of grief and hysteria. To prevent panic, the streets of downtown Moscow were lined with trucks. Of the hundreds of thousands of people who had thronged the streets of Moscow to bid farewell to their leader, hundreds were crushed to death, their bodies "hurtled against the trucks by the crowd, and their heads smashed," as the poet Yevgenii Yevtushenko recalled in his *A Precocious Autobiography*.[14]

Someone once noted that in death, as in life, Stalin continued to take victims, like an ancient Egyptian pharaoh pulling his slaves down with him into the netherworld. Stalin only went as far as Red Square, where he joined his embalmed predecessor in the Lenin Mausoleum.

DEMOTION OF A DEITY

No new Stalin could possibly have been waiting in the wings to assume the role of successor-dictator. The Supreme Leader could not have tolerated the presence either of such a figure or even of a regular succession procedure. His death of necessity spurred a jockeying for power that temporarily resulted in the more or less collective leadership of Nikita Khrushchev, Georgii Malenkov, Nikolai Bulganin, and Lavrentii Beria. Beria was shot in December 1953, and Khrushchev, formerly head of the Communist Party of the Ukrainian Soviet Socialist Republic, assumed the post of Party head, which he renamed First (as opposed to General) Secretary of the Central Committee of the Communist Party of the Soviet Union.

Nikita Sergeevich Khrushchev, who during the Brezhnev era was reviled for his "hare-brained schemes" such as the ecologically disastrous attempt to cultivate vast virgin lands in the east, and who died in 1971 in obscure retirement, achieved posthumous recognition in the Gorbachev years for his famed—although limited—de-Stalinization campaign.

Stalin's successor had to find some way to disassociate himself from the ugliest aspects of Stalinism and to utter some sort of statement that would, at the very least, allow him to release from the Gulag its millions of innocent victims, some of whom had been languishing there since the thirties. Otherwise Khrushchev would have had to assume the burden of attempting to maintain Stalin's system intact, with all its political, economic, and moral consequences.

Khrushchev went public in his struggle with Stalin's ghost early in 1956, when the first secretary delivered his famed "Special Report to the Twentieth Congress of the Communist Party of the Soviet Union." He spoke before a closed session of the Party's Central Committee and expected his "secret speech" to go no further. But it was leaked abroad and immediately Western radio transmitted the document back into the Soviet Union, where it made a profound impression.

In the speech, which Khrushchev spent hours reading before a roomful of stunned Central Committee members, he attacked Stalin's "cult of personality," an umbrella phrase that embraced the dictator's personal vanity, active cruelty, his unwillingness to share power, and his abuse of the vast power he had contrived and connived to accumulate. Khrushchev included gory details about the purge of the Party—the arrests, threats, torture, shootings.

He also tackled the subject of Joseph Stalin and the Great Patriotic War. The first salvo was aimed at Stalin's postwar propensity to take all the credit for the victory and no responsibility for the defeat that preceded it. "When we look at many of our novels, films and historical 'scientific studies,' the role of Stalin in the Patriotic War appears to be entirely improbable. Stalin had foreseen everything. The Soviet Army, on the basis of a strategic plan prepared by Stalin long before, used the tactics of so-called 'active defense,' i.e., tactics which, as we know, allowed the Germans to come up to Moscow and Stalingrad. Using such tactics, the Soviet Army, supposedly thanks only to Stalin's genius, turned to the offensive and subdued the enemy."

The first secretary then hurled at his predecessor a list of damning accusations: Stalin had willfully ignored warnings about the impending attack by Germany in June 1941; fearful of taking any action that Hitler might seize on as a provocation to attack, he had deliberately avoided a timely mobilization of men and matériel, which would have greatly minimized loss of life; Stalin had exhibited a callousness toward the value of the lives of Soviet officers and men. Khrushchev condemned the 1937–41 purge of the armed forces that left the country pitifully short of officers and "undermined military discipline, because for several years officers of all ranks and even soldiers in the party and Komsomol cells were taught to 'unmask' their superiors as hidden enemies." According to the stenographic account of the meeting, this last comment produced "movement in the hall."

Once the war began, continued Khrushchev, Stalin for a long time "ceased to do anything whatever" until his lieutenants brought him back to work. After that, his demeanor was characterized by "nervousness and hysteria," and, implies Khrushchev, by cowardice as well. "During the whole Patriotic War, he never visited any section of the front or any liberated city except for one short ride on the Mozhaisk highway during a stabilized situation at the front. To this incident were dedicated many literary works full of fantasies of all sorts and so many paintings." Khrushchev went on to denounce Stalin for clumsily interfering in military operations, with terrible results. He recounted an incident in which Stalin chose to ignore important information that Khrushchev himself tried to make available to him, and issued inept orders. "Consequently we lost hundreds of thousands of our soldiers. This is Stalin's military 'genius'; this is what it cost us. (Movement in the hall)."

With great indignation Khrushchev moved his attack to the postwar period, censuring Stalin's "downgrading" of so many of his wartime commanders (singling out Marshal Zhukov, who at the time was Khrushchev's special political ally). With lively sarcasm he turned to the 1949 film *Fall of Berlin*. "Here only Stalin acts; he issues orders in the hall in which there are many empty chairs and only one man approaches him and reports something to him—that is Poskrebyshev, his loyal shield-bearer. (Laughter in the hall)." Aleksandr Poskrebyshev was Stalin's personal secretary, who vanished just after Stalin died.

In challenging the Stalinist version of the Great Patriotic War legend, Khrushchev offered his own variant: "Not Stalin, but the Party as a whole, the Soviet government, our heroic Army, its talented leaders and brave soldiers, the whole Soviet nation—these are the ones who assured the victory in the Great Patriotic War. (Tempestuous and prolonged applause)." Workers, peasants, members of the intelligentsia, women, youths, soldiers, officers, and political workers were the real heroes of the war. "The magnificent and heroic deeds of hundreds of millions of people . . . will live for centuries and millennia in the memory of thankful humanity." That populist statement earned "thunderous" applause. However, the one immediately following it evoked "thunderous and prolonged" applause, which gave evidence to the true loyalties of Khrushchev's audience: the Party comes first.

> The main role and the main credit for the victorious ending of the war belongs to our Communist Party, to the armed forces of the Soviet Union, and to the tens of millions of Soviet people raised by the party.

Khrushchev reserved for his last assault on Stalin's wartime conduct the subject of the 1943–44 deportations of entire populations of nations, some of whose members had aroused Stalin's suspicions. The first secretary named the Kalmyks, Chechen, Ingush, and Balkar peoples. "The Ukrainians avoided meeting this fate," he joked, "only because there were too many of them and there was no place to deport them. Otherwise he would have deported them also. (Laughter and animation in the hall)." Khrushchev had been born and raised in Ukraine.[15]

After 1956, Joseph Stalin's dethronement continued in many aspects of political and social life. Statues and busts of the leader vanished together with the formerly ubiquitous portraits, posters, and published obeisances. Stalingrad was renamed Volgograd. And one night in October 1961, workers acting on a decision taken at the Twenty-second Party Congress removed the dictator's embalmed remains from the mausoleum in Red Square and buried them in a grave just outside that political shrine.

OUT OF THE DEEP FREEZE

The change in Soviet life that followed Khrushchev's Twentieth Congress speech was profound, palpable, pervasive. For the first time in Russian history, the leader of that country evinced some modicum of trust in the populace. A miner's son who had learned to read and write only as an adult, Nikita Sergeevich sought to recharge the Communist Party and the nation with real popular initiative, and to this end was ready to lift some of the strict controls that had for decades dominated social and spiritual life. Limited foreign travel, the first academic and cultural exchanges (does anyone still remember an impresario named Sol Hurok, who brought to the United States the Moiseev folk dancers and other Soviet phenomena of that era?), and a relaxation of some of the more draconian censorship strictures in literature, the arts (with the dramatic exception of abstract art, which Khrushchev could not abide), and even the social sciences characterized this period known as the "thaw." Between 1956 and 1960, some five million to eight million inmates of the Soviet Union's vast network of prisons and labor camps were released from captivity.

During the Khrushchev years, Victory Day, May 9, still a working day, continued to be marked annually with meetings in schools and workplaces, informal gatherings of veterans and well-wishers in city parks, and, after dark, fireworks. A cult of the Great Patriotic War—an organized system of symbols and rituals driven by political imperatives determined by its managers—was in its formative stage. Some aspects of the symbolic matrix—like the basic plot of the war and the Victory Banner as the cult's central symbol—had been fixed. Others—such as Stalin's role in the war—were in flux.

The war against fascist Germany, which for the better part of a decade after its conclusion had been squelched as a topic of inquiry and public celebration, now became a focus of attention for many members of the intelligentsia. This was only natural, suggested the critic Lazar Lazarev, for "the deep source, the spiritual soil of the 20th Party Congress, which for a long time appeared to many to have come out of the blue, derived from the spontaneous, unconscious de-Stalinization of the first period of the war."[16]

A wave of wartime memoirs appeared in print—by officers, partisans, workers in armaments factories, even former prisoners of war, who under Stalin had considered themselves lucky if they had managed to avoid incarceration in their own country's camps and prisons. At the same time, some writers who had themselves fought in the war as soldiers and junior officers eagerly published their works, many of which were autobiographical and lyrical, and focused on serious moral questions. These were writers who had "seen sweat and blood on their tunics," as the poet Aleksandr Tvardovskii had put it. Their subject was the wartime realities of real human beings. The authors in this group, Grigorii Baklanov, Iurii Bondarev, Vasilii Bykov, Ales Adamovich, Bulat Okudzhava, and the story writer Viacheslav Kondratiev (whose works began to appear in 1978), for all the differences among their literary works, observed Lazar Lazarev, "all shared the conviction that the war was won by the *people,* that it was the people who had borne on their shoulders the whole burden, all the terrible consequences of Stalin's policies."[17]

My own favorite wartime novel of the thaw period, Konstantin Simonov's splendid opus, *The Living and the Dead,* throbs with terrible truths. There is nothing falsely heroic about the hero, Fiodor Serpilin, "one of those men whom life can break but never bend." The object of "outrageous and stupid charges," he was arrested in 1937, interrogated by the infamous Nikolai Yezhov, the head of the secret police during the most gruesome period of the purge, incarcerated for four years of a ten-year sentence, and released just in time to rush off to the front.

Simonov boldly tackles some of the most painful wartime issues that had been strictly excluded from public discourse: the extermination, on the very eve of the war, of an effective officer corps and the consequent depletion of the capabilities of the Soviet armed forces; the chaos and disarray that overwhelmed the country with the outbreak of war, especially in the western zones, which experienced Barbarossa as a devastating surprise (the main character through whose eyes the story is told is a journalist who finds himself on holiday in the Crimea when war breaks out and tries to make his way back to Grodno to his infant daughter, and to join the military newspaper for which he works, only to become a combat officer in the most desperate of circumstances); the shocking incompetence of military officers whose inept decisions cost untold numbers of innocent young lives. Possibly the most chilling portions of this powerful story depict the one-sided war that went on *within* the armed forces, with officers from the "Special Branch" interrogating as potential enemies the exhausted, courageous men who had been through the living hell of escaping the German encirclement.[18]

THE NEW FACE OF WAR

Some of the great films of the thaw period grappled with the theme of the war. Mikhail Kalatozov's film *The Cranes are Flying* (1957) with its dramatically geometric cinematography, is reminiscent of Soviet constructivist art of the twenties, all triangles and sharp contrasts of light and shadow. After her fiancé leaves for the front, the film's heroine, Veronika, allows herself to be seduced by his cousin, a no-good pianist who (we later find out) had bought himself a deferment from military service. Veronika, however, is not at all the witch she would have been made out to be—as a stereotyped adulterous wife of the good frontline soldier—had this plot line informed a movie made a few years before, or after. In fact, she is presented sympathetically, as genuinely confused by the stressful events of the war, in particular, by the death of her parents in an early bombing raid at the beginning of the war.

Surely the most artistically refined war movie of the thaw period is Andrei Tarkovskii's *Ivan's Childhood* (released in the United States as *My Name Is Ivan*). Made in 1962, the movie centers around the wartime career of Ivan, a twelve-year-old boy whose mother was shot by the Germans. The child becomes consumed by rage and joins the army as a spy behind enemy lines. The film is unsparing in its depiction of the devastation to the human spirit wrought by war. Young Ivan, crazed in his thirst for revenge, is only one of a number of deranged characters in the movie. Ivan is a peculiar hero; brave and smart, he impresses the viewer most strongly as simply a disturbed child. Tarkovskii invites the viewer to ponder on the war as unmitigated tragedy. Even shots of the Berlin Reichstag building, the site of so many triumphant movie scenes and paintings, focus on an officer's discovery in the ruins of that building of a photograph of Ivan, who had been executed by the Nazis.

Like cinema, painting in the Khrushchev years tended to depict the war more truthfully than in Stalin's time. Most striking is *For His Native Land,* painted in 1958 by A. P. Krasnov. A dead soldier has sunk face down near a birch tree into the long, weedy grass of a Russian village as a battle rages in the distance. At first glance the charging Russian soldiers are hard to make out because their colors and contours blend with the overgrown countryside, and the eye is drawn to the dead man. In battle scenes painted in the Stalin era the dead were incidental unless they were ceremoniously laid out as objects of worship. The slain soldier in Krasnov's painting has fallen onto the land for which he gave his life, and his utter powerlessness is modified only by the rifle his right hand still clutches, its lifeless finger reaching toward the trigger. *For His Native Land* represents the new face of the war in the thaw period: the fundamental truth about the Great Patriotic War was not that soldiers tore into battle for Stalin and the motherland, but that millions of young men with large, strong hands died, their faces nestled in the pungent Russian land.

LIFE AND FATE

There were, of course, limits to the degree of honesty permissible even at the height of the thaw. Vasilii Grossman, a writer who during the war had been a correspondent for *Red Star* and had later authored *For a Just Cause,* a fictional work about Stalingrad published in the journal *Novy mir* (*New World*) in 1952, finished in 1960 a major novel of the war, which he called *Zhizn' i sud'ba* (*Life and Fate*). He submitted it for publication in the journal *Znamia* (*Banner*), whose editors passed the manuscript on to the Cultural Section of the Communist Party's Central Committee. After some time, the author was notified that his novel had been ruled anti-Soviet, and in February 1961, KGB officers raided Grossman's apartment with the aim of confiscating every copy of the manuscript. They even seized used typewriter ribbons and pieces of carbon paper. (The only other work to have engendered such a thoroughgoing confiscation was Aleksandr Solzhenitsyn's *The Gulag Archipelago.*) Grossman countered with a letter to Nikita Khrushchev requesting that *Life and Fate* be published, but all he received was the promise of a meeting with Mikhail Suslov, the Party's chief guardian of ideology. When Suslov and Grossman met, the ideologist told the writer that his novel could not be published for another two or three hundred years![19]

Vasilii Grossman died of cancer in September 1964—a month before Khrushchev's ouster—in poverty, in physical pain, and depressed by the belief that his magnum opus would never be published. In fact, in the 1970s, the dissident writer Vladimir Voinovich (according to his own admission in a 1984 speech) smuggled a microfilmed copy of *Life and Fate* to the West, where it was first published in 1980. Only in January 1988, in the heady throes of the *glasnost* period of Russian cultural history, did *Life and Fate* first appear in the Soviet Union.

It is as much *the* novel of Russia in the German war as Tolstoy's *War and Peace* is *the* novel of the first Patriotic War. A massive work, alive with brilliantly rendered characters, *Life and Fate* could in fact never have been published in the old Soviet Union, even if Suslov had been replaced by someone less orthodox.

The main action of the novel revolves around the battle of Stalingrad, but the fundamental issues it discusses are at once universal and sharply political. In this ponderously written, powerful book, its plots and subplots larded with philosophical perorations à la Tolstoy, Grossman takes on the ultimate questions of life and death, love and loss, freedom and enslavement. He exposes the Stalinist system in all its crass brutality, its willingness to sacrifice countless lives for the sake of retaining control. We witness the relative autonomy of individual initiative in 1941–42 crushed by the heavy boot of Stalinist administration during and after the Stalingrad battle. Grossman equates communism with fascism. "When people are to be slaughtered en masse, the local population is not immediately gripped by a bloodthirsty hatred of the old men, women and children who are to be destroyed . . . it is necessary to stir up feelings of real hatred and revulsion. . . . It was in such an atmosphere that the Germans carried out the extermination of the Ukrainian and Byelorussian Jews. And at an earlier date, in the same regions, Stalin himself had mobilized the fury of the masses, whipping it up to the point of frenzy during the campaigns to liquidate the kulaks as a class and during the extermination of Trotskyist-Bukharinite degenerates and saboteurs." A moving passage about the fundamental human yearning for freedom was followed by referrals to the Warsaw ghetto uprising and a revolt in Treblinka extermination camp, and also to outbreaks in the Gulag after the death of Stalin. Totalitarianism left and right are one and the same.[20]

Life and Fate also confronts the "Jewish question," a taboo subject with two major prongs: the Holocaust and Soviet anti-Semitism. As a wartime journalist Grossman himself had witnessed the liberation of a number of Nazi death camps and in 1944 had published a journal article, "The Hell of Treblinka." One of the first reports of a death camp published anywhere in Europe, Grossman's essay incorporated interviews with survivors of the 1943 Treblinka revolt and with *Sonderkommandos,* camp inmates who engaged in some of the grisliest tasks of mass destruction. He was also coauthor, together with Ilya Ehrenburg, of *The Black Book,* a documentary compilation of eyewitness testimonies detailing Nazi atrocities against Jews.[21]

Grossman also expressed some of his thoughts about anti-Semitism in *Life and Fate:*

> Anti-Semitism can take many forms—from a mocking, contemptuous ill-will to murderous pogroms. Even Oleinichuk, the peasant fighter for freedom who was imprisoned in Schlüsselburg, somehow expressed his hatred for serfdom as a hatred for Poles and Yids. Even a genius like Dostoevsky saw a Jewish usurer where he should have seen the pitiless eyes of a Russian serf-owner, industrialist or contractor. . . .
>
> In totalitarian countries, where society as such no longer exists, there can arise State anti-Semitism. . . .
>
> The first stage of State anti-Semitism is discrimination: the State limits the areas in which Jews can live, the choice of professions open to them, their right to occupy important positions, their access to higher education, and so on.
>
> The second stage is wholesale destruction.

The implication was clear: Fascist Germany represented a totalitarian country at the second stage of State anti-Semitism; the Soviet Union was as yet at the first stage.

Grossman brilliantly linked freedom and life, enslavement and death. "When a person dies, they cross over from the realm of freedom to the realm of slavery. Life is freedom, and dying is a gradual denying of freedom." And love is a veritable Hercules wrestling death down in an agony of defeat.[22]

Maternal love of sons runs as a powerful river through *Life and Fate.* In a devastating scene a woman cares for and talks to her dead son, her potent love challenging the reality of death. In another, Anna, an elderly Jewish physician trapped within occupied territory and certain to die soon, writes to her grown son a poignant farewell letter. She describes terrible things. The Jews are rounded up, segregated, terrorized. Worst of all are the painful betrayals, acts of shameless collusion on the part of her Russian compatriots. After the Germans had entered the town and driven past her home in a truck, shouting *"Juden kaput!"* a neighbor muttered, "Well, that's the end of the Jews. Thank God for that!"

"How can I finish this letter?" Anna asks. "Where can I find the strength, my son? Are there words capable of expressing my love for you? I kiss you, your eyes, your forehead, your hair. Remember that your mother's love is always with you, in grief and in happiness, no one has the strength to destroy it."[23]

The world of *Life and Fate* includes a little Jewish boy named David. He is six years old, not much younger than my son Nicholas. Grossman skillfully relates David's terrible fate from the child's perspective. When I reread that section of the book or even think about David, I see one of my son's beautiful grade-school classmates. Sometimes the inescapable image of my own Nicholas fixes itself in my mind, and to reassure myself, I imagine I am licking him all over with a huge tongue, like a lioness.

David's mother had taken him to his grandmother's for the summer. She stayed with him there for five days and then left to go to work. The little son was so desperate to keep his mother from leaving that he threw his arms around her neck and hugged and hugged her and would not let her go, until she jokingly pleaded with him, "You'll strangle me like that, you silly. There are lots and lots of cheap strawberries here, and in two months time I'll come back and fetch you." But the war begins and David's grandmother abandons him to some other relatives. His only constant companion is a little cocoon that he keeps in a matchbox in his pocket.

In the end little David finds himself in a death camp, fingering the matchbox for comfort and befriended by a childless woman doctor of fifty, who accompanies him through the ultimate ordeal. The account of his death is particularly heartrending because Grossman tells it through the child's eyes. The fear, the sweat, the screams, the crowds, the nausea from the lethal gas filling the bathhouse, all these are softened, muted, in a choreographed, slow-motion dance of death.

David watched the door close: gently, smoothly, as though drawn by a magnet, the steel door drew closer to its steel frame. Finally they became one.

High up, behind a rectangular metal grating in the wall, David saw something stir. It looked like a grey rat, but he realized it was a fan beginning to turn. He sensed a faint, rather sweet smell.

The shuffling quieted down; all you could hear were occasional screams, groans and barely audible words. . . .

The half-dead boy was still breathing, but the air he took in only drove life away. His head was turning from side to side; he still wanted to see. . . . He had taken only a few steps in the world. He had seen the prints of children's bare heels on hot, dusty earth, his mother lived in Moscow, the moon looked down and people's eyes looked up at it from below. . . . This world . . . where there was milk in the morning and frogs he could get to dance by holding their front feet—this world still preoccupied him. . . .

All this time David was being clasped by strong warm hands. He didn't feel his eyes go dark, his heart become empty, his mind grow dull and blind. He had been killed; he no longer existed.[24]

(After rereading this passage I steal downstairs from my study and softly walk into my own son's bedroom. Nicholas is sleeping on his back, his right hand hugging a stuffed Mickey Mouse, his heavy head sunk into the center of the pillowcase, right on top of the Mickey Mouse design, so that big, black round ears project on either side of his tousled hair. I never want to let him out of my sight.)

COMMON GROUND

"Why do you keep calling it 'Masha's apartment'?" Nicholas, then six, said with a little laugh some two weeks after my sister's funeral. "That place isn't Masha's home anymore. Masha's home is the grave-yard."

Along with the rest of the family, my little boy had tossed a branch of white lilacs onto the lowered pine coffin within which Masha's body, her closed eyelids sprinkled with earth from Jerusalem, lay sewn, according to Jewish tradition, into a handmade linen shroud. Then, with some help, he had thrust a heavy shovel into a mound of mostly frozen earth, and a shovelful of it clattered down on the coffin. Our mother, too, her head wrapped in a Russian shawl, shoveled a portion of earth into her daughter's grave.

After everyone gathered had participated in this ritual, a few of us continued the work of burying my sister. In the cemetery it was cold and the snow was deep; New York had just begun digging out from a big blizzard. The hard work helped. I could still *do* something for her. I could settle her into, as Nicholas rightly had called it, her home.

In the great siege of Leningrad the million people who died had not been enclosed into fragrant pine coffins and lovingly covered up with earth by devoted family and friends. They had been wrapped in sheets and dragged to corpse depots, and then eventually transported to the city's cemeteries. The Serafimovskoe cemetery had received the remains of something under a quarter-million siege victims, and the Piskarevskoe cemetery became home to about a half-million. But these "homes" were unsightly mass graves filled with jumbled, unidentified bones.

As early as 1945, plans were laid to transform the Piskarevskoe cemetery into a memorial complex honoring those who perished in the blockade, or as the victims were later called, "the defenders of Leningrad." Read *Blockade Diary,* the wrenching record of misery written by Elena Kochina, a blockade survivor. In what way did she defend Leningrad? Like most of her fellow sufferers, she lived from day to day obsessed with the 125 grams of bread that she and her daughter each received as a daily ration. And she worked at preventing her crazed husband from stealing their child's food. Not only defenders but also babies and old folks and alcoholics and thieves and turncoats and "goners" ended up in those enormous mass graves in Leningrad's burial grounds. And each of them is worthy of respect.

By 1948, an architectural design for the Piskarevskoe Cemetery Memorial was in place, and it was agreed that the dominant symbol of the ensemble would be a motherland statue. However, the following year the murky "Leningrad Affair," a purge of Leningrad Party and government notables, put a halt to those plans, which were taken up seriously only in 1956. According to the architects, who the following year published an article about the project, the symbolic heart of the enterprise was to be an eternal flame, "symbolizing the triumph of eternal life for which the heroic defenders of the city of Lenin fell." A six-meter-high bronze statue of a woman personifying the motherland offered a garland of oak leaves in her outstretched arms, "as though wreathing with laurels those who gave their lives for their native land, for Leningrad." After four solid years of work, the Piskarevskoe Memorial Cemetery opened to the public on May 9, 1960.[25]

Most of the hundreds of thousands of siege victims had gone from communal apartments to mass graves, vast grassy areas punctuated by granite slabs marking the year of their death. Russians have never had much luck in getting private space.

BABI YAR

In the fall of 1961, poet Yevgenii Yevtushenko's friend Anatoli Kuznetsov took him to see Babi Yar. Kuznetsov, a writer, had grown up in Kiev and remembered seeing the grisly remains of human bones that had been bleached and torched. He related his family's wartime experiences to Yevtushenko, who told him that he should write a novel about them.

"But who would publish it?" asked Kuznetsov.

"Write it anyway," insisted the poet. That night, shaken by the visit to the grassy ravine, Yevtushenko sat down and wrote the celebrated poem, "Babi Yar."

> Over Babi Yar
> there are no memorials.
> The steep hillside like a rough inscription.
> I am frightened.
> Today I am as old as the Jewish race.
> I seem to myself a Jew at this moment. . . .
> Over Babi Yar
> rustle of the wild grass.
> The trees look threatening, look like judges.
> And everything is one silent cry. . . .
> When the last anti-Semite on the earth
> is buried forever
> let the Internationale ring out.

No Jewish blood runs among my blood,
but I am as bitterly and hardly hated
by every anti-Semite
as if I were a Jew. By this
I am a Russian.[26]

"The visit to Babi Yar filled me with shame," Yevtushenko recalled to me in a telephone interview. "Shame can be a very fruitful feeling. I was ashamed at my country's anti-Semitism, ashamed that the atrocity had not been marked by any sort of proper memorial." He immediately began reading his poem at public gatherings to enthusiastic audiences, and, despite official reluctance, managed to get it published in *Literaturnaia gazeta* on September 19, 1961, an issue that sold out entirely within a few minutes of its appearance in the newspaper kiosks.

Yevtushenko told me that when Kuznetsov read "Babi Yar," he agreed to write his novel. In the course of our telephone conversation the poet also revealed that Dmitrii Shostakovich had telephoned him and asked whether he might be permitted to set it to music. When Yevtushenko assented, adding that he was honored, Shostakovich replied, "Good, because I have already written the music." The result is his famed Thirteenth Symphony. When it was completed, the composer invited the poet to hear it and played the symphony on the piano, singing all the solos by himself.

In December 1962, after only two performances of the symphony, Yevtushenko and Shostakovich were ordered to change the text of two stanzas if the symphony were not to be banned altogether. In the fall of 1961 a lengthy diatribe by D. Starikov had attacked the poem, accusing the poet of nationalism and of failing to pay homage to the Russian triumph over fascism. The critic was particularly angered by Yevtushenko's identification of ancient Hebrews with Soviet Jews. In January 1963, in response to official pressure and with considerable reluctance, he supplanted some lines in which he envisioned himself as an ancient Hebrew in Egypt and as Christ on the cross with:

I stand here as if by a well
That gives me faith in our brotherhood.
Here lie Russians and Ukrainians;
They lie with Jews in a common grave.

Another addition responded to the charge that the poem had short-changed the Russian war effort:

I think of Russia's exploit
When it barred the way to fascism with its own body;
To the tiniest little drop
Russia is dear to me in its whole substance and fate.

In March 1963, Khrushchev made a speech in which he fulminated against Yevtushenko's "Babi Yar." "The poem represents things as if only Jews were the victims of the fascist atrocities, whereas, of course, the Hitlerite butchers murdered many Russians, Ukrainians and Soviet people of other nationalities." In Khrushchev's cosmology, to admit the reality of the Holocaust—the Nazi genocide of the Jewish people—meant to deprive the larger Soviet polity of its status as supervictim, par excellence, which was touted as a major source of legitimacy.

The Soviet authorities' cover-up of the real nature of the massacres at Babi Yar had begun toward the end of the war. In January 1942, Foreign Minister Viacheslav Molotov signed a note addressed to all governments, deploring the German killing of 52,000 people in Kiev, and maintaining that the victims were "unarmed and defenseless Jewish working people." But by March 1944, an Extraordinary State Commission for the Investigation of Nazi Atrocities in Kiev talked about "thousands of peaceful Soviet citizens" killed by the Nazis; it had already become taboo to suggest that the fate of the Jews had been harsher than that of other Soviet peoples. After the war, Ilya Ehrenburg, among others, lobbied for the construction of a monument at Babi Yar, but the Ukrainian Communist Party Central Committee, headed by Nikita Khrushchev, turned down the proposal. Indeed, in 1957, when Khrushchev was already first secretary of the Communist Party of the Soviet Union, and more monuments to the war dead were going up, with a major memorial planned for Kiev proper, a decision was made not only to refrain from building a monument at Babi Yar but to raze the area and erect on the site a sports stadium and a dam. Despite published objections by a number of intellectuals, including the noted war novelist Victor Nekrasov, construction of the dam began in 1960.[27]

On Monday, March 13, 1961, the dam broke. Anatoli Kuznetsov described the event in the uncensored version of his novel *Babi Yar.* "At 8:45 in the morning there was a frightful roar, and a wall of liquid mud thirty feet high poured out of the mouth of Babi Yar. . . . Whole crowds of people were swallowed up instantly in the wave of mud. People sitting in trams and in their cars perished, presumably without having time to grasp what had happened. . . The number of people who perished was never, of course, stated." People in Kiev warned that Babi Yar was taking revenge.

Anatoli Kuznetsov was born in Kiev of a Russian father and a Ukrainian mother. His young adolescence coincided with the German occupation of Kiev and all its attendant horrors. "The first version [of the book] was written when I was only fourteen. In those days, when I was just a hungry, frightened little boy, I used to write down in a thick, home-made notebook everything I saw and heard and knew about Babi Yar as soon as it happened. I had no idea why I was doing it; it seemed to me something I had to do, so that nothing should be forgotten."

Not long after Leonid Brezhnev and Alexei Kosygin had relieved Nikita Khrushchev of his job, Kuznetsov submitted a completed draft of *Babi Yar* to the journal *Iunost* (*Youth*). As he tells the story, "it was returned to me immediately with the advice not to show it to anybody else until I had removed all the 'anti-Soviet stuff' from it." The author cleaned up his manuscript, deleting some controversial sections, including the description of the 1961 dam disaster. Even this version was unacceptable to the editors, but Kuznetsov refused to make further cuts and instead demanded the return of his manuscript. When the editor refused, the author, playing out a grade-B drama, snatched the goods out of his hands, ran away with it, and ripped it up. *Youth,* however, had retained a copy of the manuscript that its editors submitted to heavy censorship and then published in October 1966 (Kuznetsov in the end agreed to the publication because he could not afford to return the advance).[28]

The author subsequently restored and expanded his original manuscript and, fearful that it would be confiscated in his home, which was frequently searched, he photographed and then buried it. In 1969 Kuznetsov defected to the West while on a trip to London. He had with him the filmed manuscript, which was published in full in

English translation in a remarkable edition that demarcates those sections that appeared in *Youth,* those that had been censored, and those that he had added between 1967 and 1969, when he expanded the book.[29]

"Relentless" is the adjective some of my students used to describe *Babi Yar* the one time I assigned it in my Russian history course. No humor, no leavening of any sort relieves the first-person tale of human brutality, of extraordinary suffering. Kuznetsov's source for the recounting of what actually happened at Babi Yar was Dina Mironovna Pronicheva, an actress at the Kiev puppet theater who had managed to avoid a bullet and then escape from the ravine by pretending she had been shot with all the others.

"This book contains nothing but the truth." That is the opening line of *Babi Yar.* But much of that truth had been deemed unacceptable for publication, and very likely had the editors of *Youth* waited until after the June 1967 Six-Day War, with its subsequent intensification of official Soviet anti-Semitism, the novel would never have been published in the Soviet Union at all, at any rate, not until the Gorbachev era.

What had the censors cut out of Kuznetsov's tale? Which truths had they deemed too seditious for the eyes of Soviet readers? The offending portions fall into several categories: all references to anti-Soviet, anti-Bolshevik sentiments expressed by any citizen of the Soviet Union, including those who welcomed the German occupiers, hoping for a better life; all manifestations of anti-Semitism by some of the local Ukrainian and Russian populace, who were glad to get rid of the Jews, stole from them as they were being driven off, taunted them, and turned over to the Nazis Jewish children who were trying to seek refuge in hidden places; the September 1941 destruction of the Kreshchatik, the downtown center of Kiev and center of the Nazi occupation forces, which had been bombed and burned by the NKVD (secret police) but publicly blamed on the Germans; the NKVD demolition of the ancient Kiev-Pechersk Monastery; all descriptions of Soviet soldiers hiding from the Germans, destroying their uniforms, giving in and giving up, acting in anything other than a two-dimensionally heroic way; all perorations that point out similarities between German fascism and Soviet communism, including even a passage that observes how since both of their flags were red, they resembled one another when the wind was not blowing; all lines of prose that expressed sadness about the difficulties of Soviet life; the story of the 1961 collapse of the dam in Babi Yar.

In 1976 a memorial was finally constructed, although it was put up at a spot almost a mile away from the site of the killings of Babi Yar, where the Germans had attempted to hide the evidence of the carnage by burning up a vast number of corpses. It depicts eleven bronze figures in tortured motion, a kind of latter-day Laocoön. The inscription on the monument makes no mention of the fact that most of the victims of the Babi Yar atrocities had been Jews.

By the time it was constructed, the country was deep into the "stagnation" for which Mikhail Gorbachev later made Brezhnev infamous. A full-blown cult of the Great Patriotic War trumpeted a nationwide celebration of a tinsel-covered triumph of the Forces of Good over the Forces of Darkness and with ringing pride declared that "no one is forgotten, nothing is forgotten."

6

"NO ONE IS FORGOTTEN, NOTHING IS FORGOTTEN"

Every year when I go to Russia, I always go to church. I purchase a smooth tan taper and, breathing in the sharply sweet smell of incense, listen to the haunting chants of the priest and choir while I scan the church for an icon that beckons me. After settling on one, usually a mother of God with child, I walk over to the rings of candleholders before it, and, touching my taper's wick to an already burning one, I silently say a prayer for my loved ones back home. Then I press my candle into a vacant depression; more often than not, some older woman shakes her kerchiefed head disapprovingly and reinserts my candle in a manner more to her liking. Being Jewish does not prevent me from fully participating in this ritual. Lighting candles before a holy icon is how one worships in Russia. The flame illuminates the image and summons the spirit it represents.

In the home of the Russian Orthodox believer a red candle glows in the icon corner, expressing the household's devotion to the spirit embodied in the images of some beloved saints or the *bogomater* (mother of God). In a traditional peasant hut of old Russia, the icon corner was placed diagonally across from the hearth, the precise spot where, in pre-Christian, Slavic pagan belief, the souls of a household's ancestors were presumed to reside. The natural syncretism of Russian Christianity incorporated elements of older pagan practices and beliefs and made ancestor worship an important component of saint cults. Saints were adored forefathers who had sacrificed themselves for the sake of future generations. And the great foremother was the *bogomater*, who was venerated not as virgin, not as queen of heaven, but as mother. To light a candle for the saints was to enter into spiritual discourse with the protective spirits of the past.

SACRED FIRE

With sacred flame playing such a significant role in traditional Russian worship, a role at once public and intimate, it is no wonder that fire was brought into Soviet civic practice early on in the development of communist, secular, spiritual ritual geared toward mass mobilization. The eternally blazing torch that in 1920 graced the newly erected memorial to the fallen martyrs on Petrograd's Field of Mars was a perfect metaphor: similar enough to a lit candle to summon up popular feelings of venerational worship, it also reverberated with heroic images of Greek athletes and Olympic games, with their auras of magical male strength and international competition. Yellow and orange tongues of fire, leaping unevenly in constant motion as they hungrily consume oxygen, giving off heat and light, dangerous to touch, absorbing to watch—they symbolize life in all its dissonant complexity.

But although fire is always and everywhere both largely the same and filled with ever-changing, flickering differences, in Soviet culture the life it purported to embody was not universal but particular. The eternal flame on the Field of Mars was specific to the martyrs of 1917, relaying to future generations the might of the cause for which they had given their lives.

Soviet political culture—which waged war on traditional religion and at the same time aimed to capture the hearts of a disparate populace whose history had inclined it toward a thorough distrust of all government—was hard-pressed to find effective sources of devotional sentiment to the nation and its political system. The ever-glowing flame served as a prime symbol of the sacral, since its timelessness could be understood by all.

On May 9, 1960, a survivor of the wartime blockade touched a torch to the eternal flame on the Field of Mars. That blazing beacon was then transported across the city to the Piskarevskoe cemetery and used to light the eternal flame at the new memorial construction.

The revolutionary martyrs had conveyed their fighting spirit to the next generation of Leningraders, who in turn had defended their city during the war and were now passing on their greatness of soul to future generations.[1]

On May 8, 1967, at 9:45 in the morning, an armored carrier bearing precious cargo appeared in the vicinity of Red Square and pulled up near the recently constructed Tomb of the Unknown Soldier. Leonid Ilich Brezhnev, well into his third year as general secretary of the Central Committee of the Communist Party of the Soviet Union, headed the delegation of notables on hand to greet the vehicle, which had made the 650-kilometer journey from Leningrad, stopping on the way in many towns and villages to receive silent homage from local honor guards and residents. Now, at the edge of Moscow's Alexander Garden, it had come to its final destination.

In December 1966, to mark the twenty-fifth anniversary of the Battle of Moscow, the remains of an unknown soldier had been conveyed from a mass grave forty-one kilometers outside of Moscow, scene of the Soviet Union's first successful counteroffensive against the Germans in December 1941, and buried with full military honors near the Kremlin wall. The relics were lowered into an underground vault to the strains of Chopin's funeral march, the Western world's best-known classical dirge.

The Tomb of the Unknown Soldier—a spare, square monument of polished red stone decorated with a modest bronze sculpture of a military banner topped with a soldier's helmet—was unveiled on May 8, 1967, together with a row of six marble blocks honoring the "hero-cities"—Leningrad, Kiev, Volgograd, Sevastopol, Odessa, and the Brest Fortress. In the words of *Ivzestiia,* those blocks were to house "sacred earth from the hero-cities, drenched with the blood of the Motherland's courageous sons and daughters in the years of the Great Patriotic War." The inscription near the tomb was simple and strong: "To Those Who Fell for the Motherland, 1941–1945." Sometime later, huge, gilded letters were attached to the gleaming marble just in front of the stark bronze star, spelling out a message directly aimed at the unidentified human remains and using the familiar form of address: "YOUR NAME IS UNKNOWN, YOUR DEED IS IMMORTAL."

The armored transport had brought to Moscow two consecrated objects: an urn filled with earth from Leningrad's Piskarevskoe cemetery and the eternal flame from Leningrad's Field of Mars. The sacred fire that for almost a half-century had blazed out in solemn homage to a heavenly host of revolutionary martyrs was now to be transmitted to the Tomb of the Unknown Soldier, in a symbolic incorporation of the Great Patriotic War into the Soviet Union's foundation saga, a mythic history of the glorious Soviet socialist state, whose prime creator had been the idealized Lenin.

The ceremony began with a speech by the first secretary of the Moscow Committee of the Communist Party of the Soviet Union, N. G. Yegorichev. His prose was more than just purple. In effusive, sentimental language full of descriptions of grieving widows and devoted comrades-in-arms, the speaker laid out a carefully constructed system of meaning that constituted the spiritual core of the by then highly developed cult of the Great Patriotic War. It is symbolic, he said, that "the Fire of glory" to be lit today at the Tomb of the Unknown Soldier has come from "the city that bears the name of the great Lenin, from the sacred field of Mars where the fallen warriors of the revolution, the heroes of October, repose." "This fire," he continued, "somehow transfers across an entire half-century the undimmed flame of October, illuminating the stages of the great path taken by the Soviet people under the leadership of the Leninist party." Now the October fire would continue its inspirational work through the spirits of the immortal heroes of the second great trial and triumph—the Great Patriotic War. "It is as if the soldiers of the revolution and the soldiers of the Great Patriotic War have closed ranks into one immortal rank, illuminated by the Eternal flame of glory, lit by the living in honor of the fallen who will always live."

Overblown language did not even attempt to disguise the political agenda of the speech. "Heroes do not die," pronounced Yegorichev; they live on to serve successive generations as exemplars of "wholehearted courage and patriotism, fidelity to military duty, steadfast devotion to the Communist Party, to the socialist Fatherland. They were victorious, they achieved immortality." The underlying message: war heroes served their country in life, in death, and in life after death. Consequently, surviving generations who live not in fascist enslavement but in freedom have incurred certain obligations. Those whose loved ones died in the war will regard the unknown soldier's tomb with a prescribed affect, namely, "with profound grief and radiant pride," and all successive generations are morally bound to emulate the martyrs' valor and their devotion to country and Party.

As thousands of Muscovites stood witness under bright sunshine, Hero of the Soviet Union A. Maresiev approached the armored carrier, lit a torch from the sacred fire borne by the vehicle, and, accompanied by a deputation of military dignitaries from Leningrad, handed the flaming torch to General Secretary Leonid Brezhnev. Brezhnev leaned over and brought its fiery tip to the center of the bronze five-pointed star splayed onto the shiny black marble platform before the unknown soldier's tomb. Instantly the flame began its eternal leap into the atmosphere of downtown Moscow.

A triple artillery salute was followed by the playing of the national anthem. Then delegations from the hero cities deposited in their respective granite cubes small vessels containing earth from their territories. Leningrad's bit of soil from the Piskarevskoe cemetery was conveyed from the armored carrier by its honor guard. And then, over the course of many hours, delegations and individuals filed by to lay wreaths and bouquets of flowers.

Homo Sovieticus

With Leonid Brezhnev and Alexei Kosygin firmly in place as heads of the Party and government, respectively, a new era of tight control on the domestic front had set in, coupled with an adventurous foreign policy and the start of an enormous military buildup, which consumed a vast proportion of the national budget. The age of the *apparatchik* was at hand and remained in force for Brezhnev's eighteen-year tenure in office. In the early 1970s, Brezhnev's sphere of authority came to encompass, in addition to his long-standing Party bailiwick, governmental rule that had previously been the province of Kosygin.

Bureaucratic dominance and incompetence, corruption as a way of life, the gradual disaffection and alienation of the populace, the emergence of a beleaguered, indeed, tormented dissident movement—all of these characterized the "era of stagnation." De-Stalinization stopped and with it the disclosures about the crimes of the Stalin years. Busts and statues of Stalin were not reintroduced into the public sphere, but neither were criticisms of the leader. (In 1978, I spent several weeks doing research in Moscow's Museum of the Revolution. One day I followed an archivist through the bowels of the museum building as she was trying to locate for me a special collection of posters from the Civil War period. She swung open the door of a dark, basement storeroom, turned on the light, and we both gasped as we saw its contents: Staliniana of all sorts, mostly busts, statues, and large oil paintings, in a variety of standard poses, with and without pipe. The archivist muttered some Russian equivalent of "oops!" hurriedly switched off the light, and shut the door. Was the museum holding on to that stuff because of its importance in the history of Soviet political culture, or because Somebody Upstairs was waiting for a revival of Stalinism? In those days I was young and too embarrassed to ask that question of my scholarly hosts.)

In October 1967, the half-century mark of Soviet socialism was commemorated with an orgy of ceremonious speeches celebrating its world-shaking achievements. In 1967 the Soviet Union was enjoying enormous international prestige, or at rate, influence, particularly in the first half of the year, before the humiliating defeat of its allies in the Six-Day War. China—the Soviet Union's only serious rival within the communist camp—was in the self-destructive throes of the cultural revolution, and the United States was deeply mired in Vietnam.

Despite their status as rulers of a feared nuclear superpower, the Communist Party of the Soviet Union and the Soviet government had been searching for sources of legitimacy that could mobilize the loyalties and energies of an increasingly disaffected, alienated, and alcohol-prone youth. Men of the 1940s had, of course, been almost entirely wiped out, and with them the last of the peasantry of old Russia, which had succumbed to forced collectivization and man-made famine, the Great Terror, and finally, World War II.

A new breed of Soviet citizen was taking shape. Postwar Soviet youth, particularly after de-Stalinization, tended to be slow to trust anyone representing political authority; reluctant to labor, particularly for meager rewards; and equally remote from the folk religion of their grandparents as from the revolutionary zealotry of their parents.

During the long stagnation period beginning in the sixties, tens of millions of young people expended their energies on splitting their lives in two: holding down a respectable job while at the same time bringing in money *na levo* (on the side); cultivating an officially acceptable persona wildly divergent from the private individual behind the mask; pretending loyalties and beliefs for the sake of career advancement; learning how to deceive and how to tolerate being deceived by others.

In his renowned *The Lonely Crowd,* first published in 1950, the American sociologist David Riesman wrote about the transformation of American character from the "inner-directed" type that had pre-vailed in the nineteenth century—self-sufficient, self-monitoring, with all the integrity of a gyroscope spinning on its axis. The emerging character type coming to predominate in the years after the end of World War II resembled not so much a gyroscope as a radar in constant rotation as it scanned for the contours of objects and persons in the environment. This was the "other-directed" person that I was brought up to emulate in the fifties, finely tuned to the responses of those around me, more inclined toward gaining approval than toward self-actualization. "The other-directed child is taught at school to take his place in a society where the concern of the group is less with what it produces than with its internal group relations, its morale."[2]

An analogous process of character transformation was taking place in the Soviet Union under entirely different circumstances. A fractionated culture of insularity, self-protectiveness, and an unsettling sense of estrangement that sociologists used to call "anomie" was replacing the revolutionary and postrevolutionary culture that had valued self-sacrifice, devotion to a cause, communality, faith in, or at least respect for, or at the *very* least, fear of, political authority. The process of this social change was varied and uneven. Some of the characterological changes already had been in evidence toward the end of Stalin's rule. But who was going to risk the Supreme Leader's displeasure by pointing out to the aging Stalin that the society was ailing?[3]

Nikita Khrushchev's Secret Speech at the Twentieth Party Congress and, indeed, the broad sweep of de-Stalinization had contributed greatly to the breakup of the older social polity. Societal disintegration rapidly followed both the public disclosures of some of Stalin's crimes against the Party and, at least as important, the reintegration into society of the Gulag's millions of inmates released in the late fifties.

When Leonid Brezhnev and Alexei Kosygin assumed power in 1964, the political and social system had not yet succeeded in making the transition to some kind of post-Stalinist ethic. Stalinism had ended with Stalin, but without him—and without the kind of ongoing cult of the dead leader's memory that had held the system together after Lenin's death in 1924—even social cohesion was difficult to maintain.

The new leaders, bureaucrats par excellence, set about trying to orchestrate a vast program of public *displays* of loyalty, expecting, no doubt, that these would somehow lead to real popular sentiments of devotion to the regime, its values, and its goals. Aware that the revolution of 1917 was a distant memory whose fiftieth anniversary celebration in 1967 was a swan song, and the cult of Lenin a hollow shell that had visibly crumbled after the jubilee centennial of his birth in 1970, the authorities focused on the Great Patriotic War. In its idealized form, the war had everything: violence, drama, martyrdom, success, and a chic global status.

While the 1960s had been in many ways a time of triumph in the Soviet Union, menacing changes were in the air. The 1968 "Prague Spring," Alexander Dubcek's attempt to wrest control of Czechoslovak communism away from the Big Bad Men who had dominated it for almost a quarter-century, so threatened the Kremlin that on August 21 Soviet tanks rolled in to restore the old order, which in a number of ways was being undermined in Europe. The growth of an international youth culture shaped by the Beatles, the Rolling Stones, new tastes in dress and leisure time activities, the American civil rights movement, the progressively unpopular Vietnam War (to name a few major influences) had led to the increasing politicization of European youth, particularly in France. Could the Union of Soviet Socialist Republics maintain its role as a global superpower and at the same time shield itself from the threat implied in the new youth culture without introducing some even more damaging "cultural revolution" like the one going on in China?

The "upbringing of the young" took on an unprecedented significance to those who strove to keep the old order intact. "Military-
patriotic upbringing" and an expanded, organized cult of the Great
Patriotic War were launched to rein in the populace and keep it
moving (or at least marching in place) on the right path. It was a
kind of countercampaign against the international youth culture and
some of the major forces impelling change in much of the western
hemisphere. And the main hook to draw in the young was to be
shame.

Shame. An old-fashioned inner response that in many places in the
West had long since ceased to function as a source of social control
but continued to resonate in Russia. Shame is a community-based
complex of emotions: we feel shame before others. Its more modern
analogue, guilt, is more self-contained: we feel guilt within
ourselves.[4]

With its rituals tying children and adolescents to aging veterans,
the Brezhnev regime tried to shame young people into feeling
respect for their elders or, as a minimum goal, into behaving obedi-
ently in their presence. The twenty million alleged martyrs had, after
all, given up their lives so that successive generations might flourish
in a world free of fascism. And, for better or for worse, the tiresome
veterans who came to school to repeat the stories of their exemplary
exploits and who expected bouquets of flowers on Victory Day had
given of themselves as well. The idealized war experience was a
reservoir of national suffering to be tapped and tapped again to
mobilize loyalty, maintain order, and achieve a semblance of energy
to counter the growing nationwide apathy and loss of popular
resilience of spirit.

GLORY TO THE VICTOR-PEOPLE! LONG LIVE COMMUNISM!

From 1965 on, the Great Patriotic War continued its transformation
from a national trauma of monumental proportions into a sacrosanct
cluster of heroic exploits that had once and for all proven the superiority of communism over capitalism. In 1990 I spoke with the literary critic Lazar Lazarev about the Brezhnev administration's considered decision to resurrect the Great Patriotic War, exploiting it to
serve political ends. "Those of us who had fought in the war

thought, at first, that at last the war was getting the attention it merited," he said. "But in fact that attention was purely an official attempt to turn the war into a show made up of concocted legends."

Lazarev's observation was exactly right. In the quarter-century that began with Leonid Brezhnev's accession to Party rule in 1964 and ended at the close of the 1980s with the devastating collapse of the system he had inherited from Stalin, the Communist Party created nothing less than a full-blown cult of the Great Patriotic War, including a panoply of saints, sacred relics, and rigid master narrative of the war endured by millions of tired tourists held captive by their Intourist guides at the most famous of the Soviet Union's tens of thousands of war memorials. What visitor to the Soviet Union does not remember the goose-stepping adolescents—especially the girls in short skirts and braided hair decorated with huge organza bows—wielding automatic rifles while serving as honor guards of those memorials' eternal flames?

The master narrative's basic plot: collectivization and rapid industrialization under the First and Second Five-Year Plans prepared our country for war, and despite an overpowering surprise attack by the fascist beast and its inhuman wartime practices, despite the loss of twenty million valiant martyrs to the cause, our country, under the leadership of the Communist Party headed by Comrade Stalin, arose as one united front and expelled the enemy from our own territory and that of Eastern Europe, thus saving Europe—and the world—from fascist enslavement.

The authorities would not tolerate significant deviations from this story. Since they deemed it no longer appropriate to prevent the publication of memoirs, as had been done in Stalin's time, their strategy of control depended on stringent censorship. "Not a word could be published about the catastrophic defeats of 1941 or the real reasons they occurred," wrote Lazar Lazarev, "nor was a whisper permitted about the astonishing fact that three times as many officers in the Soviet army and navy high commands died in the Stalinist purges of 1937–38 as were killed by Nazi bullets and bombs throughout the war."

The Ministry of Defense took over the determination of how the Great Patriotic War would be remembered. The publication of war memoirs under the sponsorship of the Academy of Sciences was stopped, and all such works were now referred to the Military Publishing House. All other war-related manuscripts had to meet the approval of a special commission of the Main Political Administration of the Defense Ministry. No deviations from the master narrative were permitted.[5]

The most notorious test case of this principle was the furor surrounding the historian Aleksandr Nekrich's manuscript, *22 June 1941*. Dr. Nekrich, who died in Cambridge, Massachusetts, in the summer of 1993, had fought at Stalingrad. In the spring of 1964, just months before Nikita Khrushchev's ouster, Nekrich completed a book about the German invasion, on the first page of which he raised questions about the alleged "suddenness" of Barbarossa, an important part of the canon about 1941, because it helped explain the Red Army's disastrous defeat in the first months of the war. The rest of the book discussed the background of the military debacle of 1941–42. The manuscript was subjected to a brutal censorship by the KGB, and the "Nekrich Affair" escalated into scandal that cost the author of *22 June 1941* his job and his membership in the Communist Party.[6]

The cult narrative fixed the number of wartime losses at the legendary figure of twenty million. Stalin's original 1946 assessment of seven million to eight million dead was for a time in the 1950s replaced by a figure of seventeen million. In 1961 Nikita Khrushchev first offered the number twenty million, which was reiterated four years later in the sixth and last volume of the official *History of the Great Patriotic War of the Soviet Union, 1941–1945.*[7]

Like world Jewry's appeal to the six million Holocaust victims, the Soviet Union's purported twenty million war dead came to represent a set store of redemptive suffering that the Brezhnev regime called upon again and again as evidence of the country's unique position in world history. Say the words "six million" to any Jew and he or she can fill in the rest of the phrase. During the two decades of the high war cult, 1965–85, "twenty million" served as a ritualized epithet that signified the war martyrology.

The big push in the creation of the war cult had come in May 1965 with the jubilee observance of the twentieth anniversary of the victory over fascism. For the first time since the immediate postwar period, Victory Day was declared a holiday, a real holiday marked by a day off from work and not, like Lenin's birthday, by a *subbotnik* during which people were expected to provide the state with an unpaid day of labor. Victory Day was sacred time, implying the annual presence of the collective spirits of the war dead and the renewed might of their descendants. In addition to sacred time, requisite components of the war cult would be sacred space and sacral objects.

HOME OF THE HOLY OF HOLIES

On May 8, 1965, the Central Museum of the Armed Forces of the USSR staged a grand opening of its new quarters on Commune Square. Far more space was devoted to the Great Patriotic War than to any other single chapter of Soviet military history. Just as the Central Lenin Museum in Red Square had laid out in perfect detail every contour of the legendary Lenin, from his boyhood report cards down to the precious bullet hole in the jacket he had worn on August 30, 1918, when he was injured in an assassination attempt, so the new Central Armed Forces Museum displayed a carefully selected array of objects designed to demonstrate precisely how the war was to be remembered. Those nine large halls devoted to the war remained fundamentally unchanged for a quarter-century, until Mikhail Gorbachev's *perestroika* campaign forced a flurry of activity in the guise of reconception.

In 1989, when *glasnost* was only barely glimmering in the military, I spent some days working in that museum. The best thing about working with the Soviet Army was that it was an institution in which efficiency was the norm. The food in the cafeterias was good and cheap, the verbal intercourse was polite to a fault, and I was never kept waiting (nor, I might add, was I ever left alone in a library study).

As an exchange scholar I was looked after by a host, Colonel Aleksandr Fedorovich Shvechkov, deputy academic director of the museum. He was a tall, dull-looking fellow of forty-five with a large, round, humorless face, short brown hair, blue eyes, and big gaps between his slightly protruding teeth. Like everyone else I worked with in the army, he insisted on calling me by my name and patronymic, Nina Pavlovna, even though I told him that Americans do not, strictly speaking, have patronymics. He cheerfully took me through the exhibit, murmuring about plans to make changes to conform to "new thinking."

He himself preferred the old thinking, it was plain to see, and wished the nuseum to remain just as it had been when it opened in 1965. The purpose of the Central Armed Forces Museum, Col. Shvechkov told me in his loud, somewhat gravelly voice, was above all to preserve, protect, and cherish the collected relics of the Soviet Union's military history. When I suggested that the museum was the central shrine of a war cult, and that, say, the inspirational red divisional banners imbued with so much meaning were analogous to so many icons for centuries carried into battle by believing Russian troops, he did not care for the metaphor, but neither did he dispute it.

The museum's Great Patriotic War exhibits illustrated the entire officially sanctioned war saga, from the surprise of Barbarossa to the triumph of Berlin, with newspaper articles, photographs, weapons, uniforms, posters, drawings, paintings, and a host of other treasured objects. There was a decided focus on singular acts of individual heroism, on the many medals and military orders issued in the post-Stalingrad period, and on banners, of which the most prized was the Victory Banner, the flag hoisted up over the Reichstag building on April 30, 1945.

By 1975, the war cult had so deepened and its accompanying language had become so sentimental that the Victory Banner had gained the epithet "holy of holies," and had been turned into its single most exalted relic, an embodiment of the collective virtue implied in the official remembrance of the victory. In a published letter to members of the Moscow Komsomol in 1975, Leonid Brezhnev revealed that he had "with deep agitation" read a letter from them in which they related their achievements and their "intense yearning" to work like Stakhanovites in this final year of the current five-year plan. "During the war years, right after battle," continued the general secretary, "those soldiers who had demonstrated special courage and valor would be photographed near the unfurled banner of their unit. And today, with the Five Year Plan fulfilled ahead of time . . . you have won the honorific right to be photographed near the legendary banner of our people—The Victory Banner. It is deeply symbolic that today this sacred banner inspires you, the sons, daughters, and grandsons of front-line soldiers, to achieve feats of labor and to execute the decisions of the XXIV congress of the CPSU [Communist Party of the Soviet Union]." And in fact, on January 8, 1975, sixteen "shock workers" of the five-year plan for the Moscow Komsomol were duly photographed in front of the glass case containing that sacred banner in the Victory Hall of the Central Armed Forces Museum. In classic Soviet style, their attractive young faces were set in a requisite vacant, unsmiling gaze.[8]

"Why did our teachers think we would have any desire to look at Soviet banners, when every day we saw them everywhere?" mused the *Moscow News* journalist Dmitrii Radyshevsky as he recalled high school trips to the Central Armed Forces Museum as a teenager in the 1970s. "What we boys liked to look at was the weapons, and as for banners, the only ones we found interesting were the captured German ones!"

After the first hall devoted to the war—"The Perfidious Attack on the Soviet Union by Fascist Germany. Military Activities on the Soviet-German Front in the Summer and Fall of 1941"—all the rest, true to the Brezhnevite standard, comprised displays that ended with military successes. The second hall went up through the Battle of Moscow; the next, Stalingrad; the next, Kursk; and so on. Of the nine halls devoted to the war, six exhibited relics from the more positive, post-Stalingrad period.[9]

THE VISAGE OF HEROES

During the Brezhnev years the apogee of war art was the battle panorama, an expansive, indeed sometimes fully circular representation of battle scenes, aiming to portray absolute realism. In the foreground are three-dimensional models of fighting men, weapons, and other battle paraphernalia, and as the scene recedes toward the horizon, the portrayal flattens out into two dimensions. The first one of these I saw, in a small city in Ukraine, reminded me of the dioramas I used to love to visit in New York's Museum of Natural History when I was a child. Some great black bear with open maw would strech out its fearsome paw behind glass, while small animals would burrow and forage in a remote setting replete with trees, shrubs, and lovely cloud formations painted onto the idyllic background.

For decades battle panoramas were the preserve of the Grekov

Military Art Studio in Moscow. The studio dates from 1938 and was named after the military artist Mitrofan Grekov, who died four years before it was founded. Studio artists concentrated on the theme of warfare ranging over centuries, from dreamy representations of medieval battles against the Tatars all the way to equally mythologized portraits of cosmonauts and soldiers "fulfilling their international duty" in Afghanistan. The overwhelming majority of their work, however, was focused on the Great Patriotic War.

I first visited the studio in the late 1980s and was received by one of its administrators, Marat (*sic!* after the French revolutionary martyr) Samsonov, a well-preserved, middle-aged artist with a kindly, simple, ruddy face, startlingly blue eyes, and gray hair. He had spent many years, together with a team of artists, painting the famed Stalingrad battle panorama that is housed in its own round museum building in Volgograd. I have seen that panorama and remember the oppressive claustrophobia it evoked since it went completely around and there was no getting away from the battle it depicted. Samsonov told me that he and his fellow painters had attempted to recreate battle scenes with such accuracy that wherever possible, studio researchers had tried to determine the actual identity of men occupying individual positions, to locate photographs of those men, and thus to insert into their scenes historically accurate faces and figures.

Until late into the Gorbachev era, artists at the Grekov Studio were expected to concentrate on the showy aspects of their subjects, explained Tania Skorobogatova, head of the studio's propaganda department. She had Kate Smith's body, dyed strawberry blond hair, jangly jewelry, and layers of makeup. "We were supposed to paint a pretend reality consisting of champions and exemplars," added Nikolai Solomin, a charming artist in his early forties whose father had been one of the most famous painters in the studio. Solomin was of medium height with a sweet, round face and shiny brown hair and eyes; he spoke a beautiful, lilting Leningrad Russian with a comfortingly chantlike cadence. His tenor voice resonated with emotion, and was accompanied by extravagant gestures. "Soldiers had to look like perfect heroes. I remember once I painted some soldiers at rest, with their sub-machine guns pointing down. My superiors ordered me to repaint the scene with those guns pointing up."[10] Even while relaxing, the men were to appear ready for battle.

In old Russia, icon worship formed the heart of Christian devotion. An icon was a highly stylized representation of a sacred figure or figures. While the icon was not itself, strictly speaking, an object of worship, it was a vehicle through which believers could communicate with the deity.

In their classic book on the meaning of icons, Leonid Ouspensky and Vladimir Lossky analyze Christian catacomb paintings of the first and second centuries with the following formulation: "the fundamental principle of this art is a pictorial expression of the teaching of the Church, by representing concrete events of sacred History and indicating their inner meaning. This art is intended not to reflect the problems of life but to answer them, and thus, from its very inception, is a vehicle of the Gospel teaching."[11]

This same principle—that art was to answer and not show the problems of life—underlay all the productions of the war cult and socialist realism more generally. The "realism" corresponded to some alternate vision of reality comensurate with the promise of socialism.

Battle panoramas notwithstanding, the graphic arts representing the Great Patriotic War produced during the full-blown war cult tended, by and large, to focus on interaction among a few individuals. Grieving mothers bid their beloved sons farewell; soldiers cradled their wounded comrades; partisan women nursed their babies with one hand while holding rifles with the other. A palpable—usually spectacularly unsuccessful—effort to bring some sort of spiritual component into the paintings was often evident. Decades of enforced socialist realism had given way to clumsy, although undoubtedly frequently sincere, attempts at impressionistic lyricism; large, hollow eyes, thin, elongated figures, heavy use of black and gray dominated gloomy canvases devoted to personally tragic themes such as the painful parting of loved ones.

In some instances, painters delved into Russian iconography for their inspiration. Mikhail Savitskii's *Partisan Madonna* (1967) is a powerful work that features a nursing partisan mother, her serious face caught up in an iconlike hieratic gaze, and her red scarf resembling the garment of a classic *bogomater*. A far less effective example of religiously inspired war art is a 1981 sculpture designed by M. B. Pereaslavets of the Grekov Studio. *The Exploit of Private Iu. Smirnov* shows a stark and stolid bronze crucifixion of a man with the tor-

tured body of Christ and the coarse-featured head of a Russian peasant, gazed upon by a woman companion, while an impassive-looking
comrade stares incomprehendingly at the viewer.

Surely the most striking, indeed, shocking example of art in this
genre is Tatiana Nazarenko's *The Partisans Have Arrived* (1976). The
work is self-consciously painted in the style of an Italian Renaissance
deposition from the cross. A few Russian peasant huts set in the
steppe replace the usual stone towers nestled in Tuscan hillsides, a
gallows looms in the foreground instead of a cross, and one dead victim of Nazi brutality is lying front and center after his comrades have
cut his corpse down from the rafters. But the rest of the painting
shows a pale-skinned Christ brought down from the gallows, with
Mary Magdalene, her hands clasped in adoration, on one side of
Him and the mother of God on the other, being comforted by John
the Evangelist. Even the characters' clothing somehow combines
Soviet World War II dress with the soft flow of Italian fabric. Why
would a painter with a Ukrainian name like Nazarenko, who in
actuality was a restorer of icons and an Orthodox believer, turn for
inspiration to Western religious art? Perhaps because through the
Western artistic idiom she could communicate a generalized sentiment that the victims of Nazi atrocities were true martyrs, deserving
the highest veneration, without at the same time offending the
Orthodox strictures that strictly prescribe the permissible subjects of
icons and the style in which they are to be rendered.

The refinement of a Nazarenko or Savitskii are welcome exceptions in the flood of art on the war theme commissioned in the period between the beginning of Brezhnev's rule and the Gorbachev era.
Herculean soldiers with enormous hands, large noses, high, Slavic
cheekbones, determined eyes, and mouths set with grim determination were the norm. So were flat, affectless faces staring at the viewer, as well as flat, affectless faces in shadow or turned away from the
viewer.[12]

MEMORIALS AND MEMORY

The impulse to commemorate military victory by building some sort
of shrine is as old and as widespread as human civilization itself.
Indeed, it is surely a mark of civilization, and decidedly a secondary,

refined form of activity. More primal is the propensity to celebrate victory by, say, eating the heart of a slain enemy chieftain, or making a drinking chalice out of his skull, as Kuria, chief of the Kuman tribe, did in the tenth century after killing Sviatoslav, the prince of Kiev. Similarly, when Tamerlane celebrated his conquest of Delhi in the fourteenth century by ordering the construction of a mound made up of 30,000 enemy skulls, he was designing a primitive war memorial.

The building of war memorials or shrines is a step removed from such primary activities. For one thing, a shrine is typically not constructed out of the enemy himself—out of his heart or head or the banner he held—although it may incorporate symbolic enemy objects. A shrine or memorial is intended to convey more than the simple message, "We live; they are dead." Even if it is nothing but a pile of stones, it is meant to last, to pass on a history to those who had not been present at the moment of victory. A shrine or memorial is also intended to convey gratitude to a god or gods for their role in the victory, whether such gratitude is genuine or is merely expressed to placate a vengeful deity who might have easily allowed the battle or war to go the other way. Quite possibly, even the most elementary kind of memorial is meant not only to celebrate military victory but simultaneously to mourn the lives of those killed in the effort. Surely for the wives, mothers, daughters, and sisters of the fallen, such shrines are mourning places, even if the men who call for and build them intend for them to be purely triumphal.

A simple cairn will do as a memorial if everyone in the vicinity knows about the battle it is meant to commemorate. The piled stones serve as a reminder, or as a prod to inspire children or newcomers to ask the older generation about the marked event. Such a memorial of stones or sticks depends on living people to tell the story.

The next level of monument is self-contained and independent, one that tells the battle story, usually in the form of paintings or sculptures or bas-reliefs. These appear on many classical monuments, such as Titus's Arch of Triumph in Rome. Such a memorial can stand for centuries, displaying to generations of visitors the saga of trial and triumph.

A further refinement in the evolution of war memorials is a shrine built not only to mark a victory and to tell its story but also to serve as the locus of ritual acts honoring those deemed responsible for the victory, and paying obeisance to the appropriate deity. Such acts can be simple and uniform: at Tokyo's Yasakuni Shrine, a memorial to those Japanese who have died in wars since the late nineteenth century, visitors approach the main shrine, throw a coin into a grate, clap twice, and then bow to summon the spirits of the dead. Or such rituals can be more elaborate: at the Valle de los Caidos (Valley of the Fallen), the memorial to the victims of the Spanish Civil War, visitors must travel to a mountaintop situated at Spain's exact geographical center, and there they enter the largest basilica in the world to hear a complete Catholic Mass.

The organized cult of the Great Patriotic War had its own supershrines, the more than twenty renowned "memorial ensembles," many of which were built during Leonid Brezhnev's rule. Some, like Khatyn' in Belorussia (not to be confused with the Katyn forest, which I discuss in the following chapter), were erected on the actual sites of Nazi atrocities: slender, chimneylike pipes and bells rise up from each of 149 spots where once stood the houses of a village that the Germans destroyed wholesale. Volgograd, with its famed Motherland—that from her bare toes to the tip of her raised sword is reputed to be the tallest statue in the world—boasts the most celebrated of these ensembles. The Volgograd memorial, unveiled in October 1967 for the fiftieth anniversary of the revolution, just a few months after the flame at the Tomb of the Unknown Soldier in Moscow was kindled, served as a kind of objectified merger of the revived cult of the revolution and the newer cult of the Great Patriotic War. In the years before and during the Volgograd memorial's construction, a small group of prominent writers headed by the Stalin Prize–winning novelist Victor Nekrasov, engaged in a heated public debate in an attempt to prevent the monstrosity from going up and destroying the actual historic site of the great battle. They failed.

In 1981 Leonid Brezhnev himself presided at the opening of an enormous monument and museum in Kiev dedicated to the victory. The statue, the work of Evgenii Vuchetich, the designer of the Volgograd memorial, was a particularly ungainly realization of the Heavy Metal Motherland: a gleaming female figure of metal with an impassive, masculine face and a straight, stiff body draped in a classical robe with raised sword and shield. The interior of the pedestal, which looks something like a spaceship, served as a museum of the Great Patriotic War.[13]

For many young adults in the Soviet Union, the local monument to World War II became a significant locus of ritual on their wedding day. In the twenty years following the 1967 opening of the Tomb of the Unkown Soldier in Moscow, it became customary for newlywed couples to make a stop at their nearest significant war memorial immediately after the registry of their marriage but before the wedding reception. In Moscow the traditional stop was the Tomb of the Unknown Soldier. Out of gaily festooned taxis or private cars parked before the intricate wrought iron gate of the Alexander Garden emerged flushed bridegrooms and brides resplendent in gauzy white dresses and kitschy veils. Always accompanied by camera-wielding relatives or friends, they placed flowers near the eternal flame and then drove off to celebrate their weddings. Like the Jewish custom of the bridegroom crushing a glass at the end of his wedding ceremony to commemorate the destruction of the Temple in Jerusalem, the Soviet rite was meant to solemnize youth's happiest moment by taking out time to remember the bitterest chapter of a people's history. It was meant to inspire a sense of obligation to parents and grandparents at precisely the moment when young people were making their statement of independence by getting married.

The Soviet war memorial also served as a locus of military ritual. On my first trip to Leningrad's Piskarevskoe cemetery, I watched a cluster of stalwart army officers stand at attention in front of the eternal flame located near the entrance and then lay flowers at the feet of the stately and feminine motherland statue. With this public act the living warriors honored their dead comrades and other victims of the ordeal.

Another rite that even more dramatically linked past suffering with present resolve was the initiation of soldiers into the Soviet Army. The recruits lined up at a given war memorial and one by one stepped up to the eternal flame and swore an oath of allegiance to the precepts of the army. A striking painting displayed on the penultimate page of the big, glossy volume commemorating the fortieth anniversary of the victory is called *Oath of Allegiance* and portrays a fresh-faced Candide in Soviet Army uniform holding an AK-47 automatic rifle in one hand and a small red book in the other. His boots gleam with the reflection of an eternal flame leaping out of a five-pointed star before which he stands at attention, gazing ahead with a sweetly vacant stare. Three rifle-bearing comrades await their turns to make their pledges.[14]

THE MAKING OF HEROES

The fortress in the city of Brest on the 1941 Polish-Soviet border was ruthlessly besieged by the Germans in the very first days of the war. The Germans bypassed the fortress, encircled the town, and then returned to the fortress. Several thousand soldiers trapped within its walls knew it was the end, that they would eventually be killed. The population of the fortress kept dwindling, and the Germans continued to shell and bomb it for more than a month. When they finally took it on July 24, almost all the inhabitants were dead or seriously wounded. Were they defenders? Were they simply desperate men? At any rate almost all of them died in the process of staving off the capture of the fortress.

The mother of the Harvard historian Vladimir Brovkin worked as a tourist guide in the Soviet Union. As a teenager in the late sixties he accompanied her to Brest, where he saw in the ruins of the fortress a modest exhibition of photographs and newspaper clippings devoted to its wartime fate. In 1971 Brovkin returned to Brest, this time as an Intourist guide leading a group of foreign tourists.

"I couldn't believe my eyes," he recalls. "Rows of granite graves, photographs of the 'heroic defenders' of the fortress, an eternal flame, immense statues, the works! An incident of tragic defeat had been transformed into an exploit of heroic defense. The exhibition in the fortress now emphasized the leading role of the Party during the war. It was incredible."

In fact the "Brest Fortress-Hero Memorial Ensemble," completed in 1971, was not only mendacious and trite, it was—like the ensembles in Volgograd and Kiev—unforgivably ugly. From the entrance a walkway steered visitors under a thick wall pierced with an enormous opening in the shape of a five-pointed star, bringing them to the central esplanade. An erect obelisk soared up from one end of a vast granite plaza, while the center was dominated by the horrid head of an enraged soldier trapped in a hunk of stone; his eyes glowered down at passers-by from under Brezhnev-like thick eyebrows, and the crudely rectangular-shaped monolith was supposed, according to its designers, to symbolize the "inextinguishable will, limitless courage . . . and fearlessness" of the fortress garrison.

Another monument, Thirst, depicted a man stretched out in a cartoonlike caricature of a desert scene, grasping for water with one hand while the other has driven a sword into the ground on which he lies. The complex also contains some ruins from the actual fortress.[15]

REQUIEM

When I first met the sculptor Daniil Mitlianskii in 1987, I thought he looked like Hollywood's version of old man Karamazov—unkempt, matted brown hair streaked with gray, a full gray beard, exhausted, bloodshot eyes, and a slightly loping gait. In 1971 he had sculpted the single most effective monument to World War II I ever saw in the Soviet Union, a modest sculpture of five soldiers that for twenty-one years, until it was heavily damaged by vandals on the eve of Victory Day 1992, stood in the outdoor courtyard of a high school in downtown Moscow.

The monument is titled Requiem, and the vulnerability of those five slim, indeed, wraithlike young boys standing stock-still, poised to march off to their deaths at the front, pulled at my heart every time I saw them. My first visit took place on June 22, 1987, the anniversary of Operation Barbarossa.

My companion was Tamara Ravdina, a Muscovite of around seventy, whom I had met earlier that month in the home of my mentor, the historian Mikhail Gefter. More than a half-century earlier, Ravdina had been a university classmate of Gefter's wife, Lela. Their voices breaking with emotion, both women recalled their wartime years as navy nurses as the most satisfying period of their lives.

"Never again did we feel so absolutely needed," explained Ravdina, a cheerful, athletic-looking woman with close-cropped gray hair and a youthful complexion. "Of course the work was horrible. I spent most of the war in a makeshift hospital along the

Ladoga lifeline that supported Leningrad during the blockade. There was bombing all the time. And I will never forget the incredible stench in the separate tent we had for victims of gangrene. When after the war I had a son, I already knew how to feed him after all those years of feeding paraplegics."

"But those were our finest hours, the most brilliant time of our lives," added Lela Gefter, a small but vigorous woman with a melancholy face. "I know that the regime here has for years exploited the memory of the war to militarize the youth and so on, but nonetheless, for our generation the memory of the war is a holy memory."

Tamara Ravdina's fiancé had been a student at Moscow's 110th School, one of the city's finest high schools, established in 1917 on the site of a *gimnazium* from the imperial period. The boy was in school when the war began, and like so many of his classmates, he went off to the front and never returned. After the war, Ravdina had a son, but never married.

In the late 1960s, when the war cult was moving toward its peak, with obelisks and heavy-headed soldier monuments going up quite literally by the thousands, Daniil Mitlianskii, an alumnus of the 110th School, approached other alumni and teachers with the idea of presenting the school with a monument honoring its ninety-eight students and two teachers who had died in the war. The project was absolutely independent, with no official sponsorship whatsoever. It took the school director, an elderly woman of great integrity, a good deal of persistence to gain the necessary bureaucratic permissions that would enable Mitlianskii to bring the task to completion. His sculptural style was nonconformist, and he was a member of neither the Party nor the Union of Artists. And it did not help matters that he was Jewish.

Finally on June 22, 1971, the thirtieth anniversary of the Barbarossa invasion, the monument was unveiled in the courtyard of the school, which is located in downtown Moscow. One of the finest poets of the frontline generation, David Samoilov, read his poems at the stirring ceremony inaugurating the public life of the memorial.

Requiem was an astonishing sculpture. The five young boys stationed on top of a simple pedestal were shockingly small compared with classic Soviet war memorials. Not quite life-size, thin, with reedy necks, and bayonets and knapsacks strapped to their straight backs, they looked exactly like what they were—children going off to die with hardly a conception of why.

The boys had real identities. They had all just finished out their last, or tenth, grade of high school, except Igor Kuptsov, who had volunteered for the front straight out of ninth grade. He died in Berlin on April 30, the very day that the Victory Banner went flying out over the Reichstag building. The others, Gabor Raab (a Hungarian), Grisha Rodin, who died near Rzhev in 1941, Yura Divilkovskii, and Igor Bogushevskii, were school friends and class-mates of the sculptor. To be precise, four of them had attended the school; the fifth was Mitlianskii's beloved brother-in-law. None of them returned from the front. At the base of the pedestal was a bronze plaque listing the names of all the students and teachers from the 110th School who had died in the war.

June 22 was a date that had typically been noted in the press with articles and editorials about the perfidiousness of the invasion that had occurred in 1941, about the strengths of the Communist Party and Soviet people, and the glory of the eventual victory. While some families and other groups of people may have marked the date with properly lubricated private rituals, no official ceremonies commemo-rated the anniversary of the invasion. The anniversaries that were feted in the press, particularly within the armed forces, were those of the officially touted victorious events of the war: the purportedly tri-umphant finales—no matter what the cost in human lives—of the battles of Moscow, Stalingrad, and the Kursk salient. And, of course, Berlin and the final capitulation. Officially sponsored war memorials were typically opened on Victory Day, *not* on the date of the calami-tous invasion.

June 22 was precisely the right date for the unveiling of Requiem. The young boys sculpted in living, loving contours by hands that undoubtedly trembled with the pain evoked by memory, survivor guilt, and alcohol were archetypal June 1941 recruits, filled with a sense of duty to their country and dangerously false expectations of what was to come. When you are brought up on lies, what do you know about reality?

After the unveiling of the monument a ritual was established at the 110th School. Every year, on the evening of June 22, or *Den Pamiati* (Day of Remembrance), as they liked to call it, alumni and their

Yegor was the ten-year-old grandson of Oleg Lishin, the founder and leader of *Dozor* ("Patrol"), a search organization that I joined on a dig in August 1992. He drowned the following summer in a camping accident. *(Photograph by Nina Tumarkin.)*

"Poor Yorick!" Serega Shpilianskii, young leader of our *Dozor* brigade in the summer of 1992, muses over the skull of a Soviet soldier he has just dug up at the former battle zone outside Rzhev. *(Photograph by Nina Tumarkin.)*

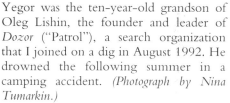

Soldiers from the Great Patriotic War, August 1992. These are some of the remains of the seventy-nine unburied soldiers that *Dozor* volunteers unearthed during nine days of work in the former battlefields around Rzhev. *(Photograph by Nina Tumarkin.)*

Fall 1941. The outbreak of war tore millions of sons and husbands from their mothers and wives. Most Red Army recruits came from simple peasant backgrounds. *(Photograph by Mikhail Trakhman.)*

"Mother," drawing by D. A. Shmarinov, 1942, from a series titled "We will not forget, we will not forgive." Of all the artistic media during World War II, drawings tended to be the most honest in their depictions of the horrors suffered by the civilian population.

Fighting for every floor, Stalingrad, November 1942. The Stalingrad battle, which took hundreds of thousands of Soviet lives, was waged block by block, house by house, floor by floor. *(Photograph by Georgii Zelma.)*

Victory. In the most famed of all Soviet wartime photographs, two Red Army reconnaissance men, M. A. Yegorov and M. V. Kantariia, hoist the "Victory Banner" over the Berlin Reichstag building on the evening of April 30, 1945. The scene was the Soviet analogue to Associated Press photographer Joe Rosenthal's renowned 1945 snapshot of American marines raising Old Glory at Iwo Jima. The Soviet Union suffered more than 300,000 casualties in the Battle of Berlin. *(Photograph by Yevgenii Khaldei.)*

"The Motherland Calls!" Wartime posters—an important medium of wartime propaganda—often depicted determined, angry, or grieving women to inspire the fighting forces. In this famous poster, which was the Soviet equivalent of "Uncle Sam Wants You!" an archetypal mother displays the Red Army oath in her call for recruits. *(Poster by I. Toidze, 1941.)*

"We Shall Make It to Berlin!" Red Army soldiers as portrayed in posters published toward the war's end were wholly mythic figures, exuding health, happiness, and perfect confidence in the impending victory. This young man has just killed a German, whose bullet-pierced helmet lies on the grass. His greatcoat rolled and flung over his shoulder, he grins as he readies himself for the march on Berlin. *(Poster by L. F. Golovanov, 1944.)*

"Glory to the Red Army!" In 1945 L. F. Golovanov incorporated his poster of the previous year into this graphic celebration of the victory. The soldier from the 1944 "We Shall Make It to Berlin" poster stands smiling before a Berlin wall on which that poster is affixed. He is now a proud, bemedaled officer. Nothing about his figure or mien would suggest that he had survived four years of fighting. On the wall his comrades have scribbled the date, May 2, 1945, and triumphant phrases: "We Made It!" and "Glory to the Russian People."

"Letter to the Front." Socialist realism pervaded wartime and postwar painting no less than poster art. In this famed 1947 oil painting by A. I. Laktionov, a wounded and decorated Red Army soldier has brought a letter to his comrade's family and enjoys a smoke while the frontline soldier's son or little brother reads the letter to his beautiful and well-nourished family.

"Soldier-Liberator," a monument to the fighters in the Soviet Army who died in the Battle of Berlin, was erected by the sculptor E. V. Vuchetich in Berlin's Treptower Park in 1949. A symbol of the Soviet Union's domination of East Germany, this statue served for decades as the prime image of the cult of the Great Patriotic War. The highlight of the military parade in Red Square at the forty-fifth anniversary of the victory in May 1990 was a colorful float representing a red-draped live tableau of this monument, with a real uniformed giant of a man holding a real little girl in a white dress.

This motherland that towers over the Volgograd war memorial is reputed to be the world's tallest statue. Together with the Berlin soldier, this monument has been a major symbol of victory since its unveiling in 1967. The sculptor was E. V. Vuchetich. *(Photograph by Nina Tumarkin.)*

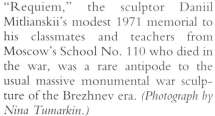

"Requiem," the sculptor Daniil Mitlianskii's modest 1971 memorial to his classmates and teachers from Moscow's School No. 110 who died in the war, was a rare antipode to the usual massive monumental war sculpture of the Brezhnev era. *(Photograph by Nina Tumarkin.)*

In war memorials throughout the Soviet Union, the eternal flame symbolized the immortal power of the war dead. In this 1971 painting by F. P. Usypenko entitled "Oath," a rosy-cheeked young soldier enacts his ritual initiation into the Soviet Army as he declaims his oath of allegiance before an eternal flame at his local war memorial.

Mikhail Savitskii's 1967 painting "Partisan Madonna" gains its power from the religious theme of mother and child transmogrified from Russian iconography to the stark reality of partisan warfare. The nursing mother will have to sacrifice her child as surely as did the Mother of God.

Official Victory Day cards for sale during the fortieth anniversary of the victory celebration in 1985—the climactic year of the war cult—depict classic symbols such as letters sent from the front, which were always triangular for easy recognition, and the fortieth-anniversary medal given out to all surviving veterans of front and labor. *(Card from the collection of Nina Tumarkin.)*

A 1985 poster conveyed the upbeat spirit of the fortieth anniversary of the victory. This bright-eyed, round-faced cherub of a soldier conveyed the false optimism of the war cult's imagery. *(Poster by M. Butkin.)*

"Glory to the Soldier! May 9, 1945." A 1989 poster on sale during the forty-fifth anniversary of the victory showed something closer to the real face of war. By 1990 the official cult of the Great Patriotic War had been undermined by *glasnost* and the propensity toward truth telling that had gripped the Soviet public. *(Poster by E. Tomashevskii.)*

In May 1990, forty-five years after the war's end, a veteran in front of Moscow's Bolshoi Theatre still hoped to find information about his two brothers who had died in the war. One of them was reported missing in action. *(Photograph by Nina Tumarkin.)*

After decades of intrigue and bureaucratic inertia, a plan to construct on Moscow's Hill of Prostrations a central museum and monument to the victory of the Soviet people in the Great Patriotic War resulted in 1984 in a plan for the construction of this monstrosity, entitled "Victory Banner." The banner hoisted over the Berlin Reichstag building in 1945 had become the most sacred relic of the high war cult. This model of the monument was put on display in Moscow in 1986. The public, inspired by Mikhail Gorbachev's new call for *glasnost*, rejected the design.

During the final five years of the Soviet Union's existence, the projected monument on the Hill of Prostrations was a battleground for the symbolic portrayal of the memory of the Soviet experience in World War II. A series of competitions for the monument's design produced hundreds of models and plans, none of which were realized. By Victory Day 1993, the building of the museum of the Great Patriotic War was nearly complete, but no one could agree on what to put into it, since the once cohesive memory of World War II had dissipated. As of that time the monument planned for the plaza in front of the museum was the sculptor Mikhail Anikushin's softly rounded mother and child. *(Photograph by Ella Maximova.)*

families or friends would gather in the little courtyard of the school near the monument to hold a memorial tribute for their classmates who had never made it home from the war.

It was cool and gray at six o'clock on June 22, 1987, when Tamara Ravdina and I met at the Arbat Metro station and made our way through back alleys and courtyards that were smelly and puddly but safe from the noise of traffic. I always can count on losing about three pounds per week in Moscow. What really burns up calories is walking through the city with a Muscovite who invariably has a quick stride, concentrating on listening to all the important things my companion is saying while at the same time avoiding stepping in mud or potholes or getting hit by a car, or bumping into someone, all of this while toting a heavy bag containing camera, dictaphone, a snack, and gifts for whomever I am going to be visiting that day and that evening. Besides, Moscow is vast; when residents tell you that some place is only "two steps away," they usually imply at least a twenty-five-minute hike at a brisk pace.

Tamara and I walked for only about twenty minutes, but despite the cool weather I was in a sweat when we arrived at the school. About forty people, many of them elderly, stood chatting with one another, catching up on news. This was, after all, a reunion of alumni who saw one another only once a year, reunited by real memory and a characteristically Russian indulgence in sad feelings. Everyone carried a small bunch of flowers, except those who had already placed theirs on the monument.

The laying of flowers was the one universal act of paying respects to the dead that was ubiquitous in Soviet culture. No one, for example, would have dreamed of attending a Soviet funeral without bringing flowers, for in an atheistic service, the only ritual act required of all participants was the silent laying of flowers on the coffin of the deceased. It was, and still is, likewise customary for people visiting a grave to place flowers on it. Ravdina and I had flowers too, faded red tulips we had bought at the metro station.

We greeted people briefly and then went in silence to set down our flowers. I suppose I had expected the alumni gathering to be a refreshing shower of wisdom and insight steeped in memory freed from the shackles of propaganda. That is not how things went. The meeting was disappointingly flat and official. The 110th School was a

"Spanish school," meaning that its strongest department was in Spanish language instruction. The first to speak was a Spanish teacher followed by a Komsomol secretary. Next on the program came two alumni. All the speakers came out with stereotyped praise for the boys, gratitude for the victory, and a love of world peace.

Indeed this last theme had become an important component of the war cult in the last years of Brezhnev's rule. With the antinuclear peace movement gaining strength in Europe and then the United States from 1977 onward, the Soviet Union, which had a vested interest in reducing the spiraling costs of arms buildup, had taken to presenting itself as the leader of the peace movement, legitimized by the trauma of having lost twenty million victims in the last world war. "We know what war is, trust us, we will do everything possible to contain American adventurism that might lead to war," was the message.

An alumnus read some genuinely affecting poetry, declaiming it in that rather showy Russian style for which I happen to have a weakness, and then came the most moving part of the meeting: the minute of silence. Some heads were bowed. Some eyes were closed. What were they thinking, those teachers, alumni, Komsomol secretary, and students? I relived the moment of gently placing the little bouquet of tulips at the boot of one of the soldiers. At that very moment my husband was putting our ten-month-old baby son to sleep in our Moscow apartment. He was such a happy, responsive baby. What were Igor or Gabor or any of those five boys like as babies in, say, 1924? What kind of fates had their parents imagined for them?

BE PREPARED!

The alumni and others mostly melted off into small groups. Some of them had been coming to the June 22 reunion for decades. One woman whose boyfriend had attended the school told me she had come to that school courtyard every June 22 since 1942!

I stood chatting with Marina Smaragdova, a seventh-grade teacher in the school and caretaker of its museum, which she offered to show me. Many Soviet schools, especially of the showcase variety, boasted small museums of the Great Patriotic War, but this offbeat, one-room museum filled with documents and old photographs was dedicated to the history of the school itself, with a special emphasis on Mitlianskii's monument.

"Do you mean to say that in the United States, students aren't trained in military preparedness?" Marina Smaragdova asked me, her soft, high-pitched voice resonant with incredulity. I am convinced that there is nothing softer in the world than a certain kind of middle-aged Russian woman, and Marina Smaragdova was a prime example: round, puffy cheeks, sad eyes peering out sweetly over little wrinkled pouches, full figure, plump, freckled hands, fluffy, curly, wispy hair dyed some unnatural color, small feet, and the tiniest, highest-pitched voice of which a healthy adult is physically capable. "Our ninth and tenth graders all spend two hours per week on elementary military preparedness, although as of September 1 of this year, those hours will be reduced."

Charmed by the dissonance between the appealing softness of my interlocutor and the subject about which she was speaking so matter-of-factly, I asked her what kind of military training the children get.

"Oh, they learn all sorts of things," she said, animatedly, "for example, how to take apart and reassemble a grenade." Smaragdova articulated the word *granata* (grenade) with a smile and a lilting chirp, as though she were talking about some Italian musical instrument capable of mellifluous sound.

The need for all citizens to be ready for combat in case of enemy aggression had been articulated by Lenin even before the 1917 revolution, and bellicose imagery figured both in Soviet ritual and rhetoric from the beginning of the Soviet state. Military symbols and gestures were particularly evident in rites connected with the initiation of children into Communist Party organizations such as the Little Octobrists (7–11 years old), Pioneers (9–14 years old), and Komsomol, or Communist League of Youth (14–26 years old). Uniforms, salutes, marching, flags, unison recitations of memorized pledges all figured prominently in rites designed to foster feelings of group solidarity.

But military symbols and rituals devised especially for the young had taken a qualitative leap from 1965 on. The militarization of the youth coincided both with a drastic military buildup—the Soviet Union created a "naval infantry," the counterpart to our marine corps, only beginning in the early sixties—and with the emerging centralized cult of the Great Patriotic War.

Within the armed forces, the glorified history of the war with Germany was the hub connecting the spokes of the Soviet wheel of war. An inviolable narrative of that war provided the basis for an entire military cosmology addressing all the basic questions to assure victory in a future war. In the military, the "immortal exploits of the Red Army in the Great Patriotic War" were held up as models for inspiration and emulation by generations of Soviet officers and soldiers. In military manuals, journals, newspapers, and propaganda brochures—particularly in the issues that appeared around Victory Day and other wartime anniversaries—the idealized story of the war was a beacon whose light illumined the path trod upon by all soldiers and sailors.

The Brezhnev regime suffused rays of that beacon throughout the Soviet polity. In the guise of paying nationwide respect to those who died in the war so that future generations might realize socialism, managers of institutional and public ritual undertook a program of militarizing the youth to an extraordinary degree. In addition to the "elementary military preparedness" training expected of all students in their last two years of high school, war-related activities became a routine part of the regular programs of Pioneers and Komsomols. Projects relating to the Great Patriotic War played a major role in this vast undertaking.

In 1965 the Komsomol and various branches of the army founded the *Krasnye sledopyty* (Red Pathfinders). These were groups that organized hiking expeditions to World War II battle sites for children and youths, who were expected to come away from the experience imbued with awe at the valor of the Red Army's finest and with a determination to serve the motherland with equal courage. Sometimes the expeditions were simply tours, but more often their agenda involved retracing the course of a battle and hunting for relics such as helmets, weapons, and other military paraphernalia. The youngsters also looked for—and frequently found—human remains, which they tried to identify whenever possible.

Beginning in 1965, *Narodnoe obrazovanie* (*Popular Education*), the monthly journal published by the Ministry of Education, was filled with articles discussing the effectiveness of such World War II–related activities in the upbringing of young people. Investigative expeditions to battle sites are a "powerful, vivid, and persuasive means of upbringing," wrote a director of a children's tourist excursion organization for the Orlovsk region. The pioneers on one such expedition found human remains, a gas mask, a pipe, and a razor. On the handle of the razor were engraved the name of its owner, Strochkov, some dates in 1942, and the slogan "not a step backwards!" The youngsters made a coffin for the remains of Comrade Strochkov, buried it with some ceremony, and sought out and found his family.[16]

By the mid-1970s the system of elementary military preparedness involved some thirty million children and adolescents. DOSAAF, the acronym for Voluntary Society for Cooperation with the Army, Air Force, and Navy, was a paramilitary organization that sponsored "evenings of military glory" and children's war games such as the all-union competitions *Zarnitsa* (Summer Lightning) and *Orlenok* (Eaglet), in which twenty-two million children participated.[17]

Tours of battle sites and war museums, investigative work in battlefields, meetings with veterans, the design of school exhibits and museums of the Great Patriotic War, commemorative evenings, war games, the study of modern weapons, practice in wearing gas masks, a plethora of literature about the armed forces, elaborate rituals involving honor guards, oaths, marching, flags, uniforms, salutes, guns—all appeared as jagged pieces of a propaganda kaleidoscope, shifting into new patterns with each successive twist engineered by the management. The emphasis vacillated between past and present, war and peace, depending on the politics of the moment.

In the late 1970s the Soviet Union tried to portray itself as the leader of the European antinuclear peace movement, an undertaking that was incorporated into the military-patriotic plan. The messages sent out to participants and the larger society were not only mixed but also contradictory: the youth must be prepared to serve their motherland with the same unswerving devotion and courage their parents and grandparents demonstrated in the last war; that war had been a struggle between socialism and fascism, which was a form of imperialism, and imperialism is still very much alive; only a strong Soviet armed force will ensure peace, by deterring imperialistic adventurism; having endured the violation of its sacred borders and lost twenty million precious lives, the Soviet Union, fired by the wisdom derived from suffering, stands as an indispensable guardian of world peace; those twenty million did not die in vain, because the socialist system for which they willingly gave their lives is flourishing and will prevail.

At the same time that the authorities moved their war propaganda machine into high gear, from 1968 on, an emerging dissident movement in turn sought to shame the leadership into a recognition of the barbarism of many of its constraints on the freedom of its citizenry. The word "*pozor,*" which means "shame" or "disgrace," figured prominently in antigovernment statements. When, after the untimely death of the wildly popular rebel poet, actor, and singer, Vladimir Vysotsky, in 1980, the police removed his portrait from the window of Moscow's Taganka Theater, where he had worked, an angry crowd of thousands of people shouted "*Pozor, pozor!*"

"Today's successes in the country of Soviets are the result of the victory over fascism, are the realization of the hopes of thousands of fallen soldiers"—this is the underlying thought revealed, frame by frame, in movies about the war, which is the kernel of their effectiveness in teaching the youth, explained the author of a 1975 article in *Popular Education.* "Soviet people of all ages cherish as sacred the events of that terrible time, pay homage to the memory of the heroes who gave their lives for our happiness. . . . The immortal exploit in the name of socialism, which the Soviet people achieved under the leadership of the Communist Party, will always be an inspiring example for new generations of fighters for communism," gushed another author in the ostentatious idiom that characterized the thirtieth anniversary of the victory. Owing to the power of its "emotional effect on participants," the Great Patriotic War plays the most significant role in the system of military-patriotic upbringing, wrote a Moscow schoolteacher in 1975.[18]

Ten years later, at the fortieth anniversary of the victory, school museums of military glory, excursions to battlefields, formal meetings with elderly veterans, honor guard rituals at war memorials abounded along with a flood of books on the subject for children of all ages. In many of these accounts, wartime children figured as heroes (rarely as heroines). Even preschoolers were barraged with war-related propaganda, since "even if a little child does not understand everything right now, the tracks left in his heart will remain, and he will understand the price of the happiness that was won for him." The *"Malysh"* ("Kiddy") press was busy churning out books of stories and poems and even pop-up books about the military and the Great Patriotic War.[19]

SOVIET POLITICAL CULTURE ON TRIAL

In the end—if we consider the end to have come on Christmas Day, 1991, when Mikhail Gorbachev stepped down from the presidency of his country and effectively disbanded the Soviet Union—the dissidents and their spiritual descendants were successful in discrediting the Communist Party and Soviet government in the eyes of the general populace.

But the near quarter-century-long campaign of military-patriotic upbringing, which fizzled out toward the end of the Gorbachev era, together with the system that had engendered it, had been, almost from the beginning, a spectacular failure. And so too had the officially managed cult of the Great Patriotic War. For one thing, it had been run by men with terrible taste; tacky, totalitarian kitsch could not possibly engage the emotions of young people searching for identity and some *modus operandi,* if not *vivendi,* in a kafkaesque world.

The aesthetic dimension of Soviet political culture should not be underestimated in assessing the causes of its inadequacy; the soul, which naturally yearns for beauty, will reject grimacing motherlands and soldier hulks. The war cult, together with the more inclusive umbrella campaign of military-patriotic upbringing, exuded a profound *falseness,* which was perhaps the primary cause of its failure. The withered Lenin cult was no less fraudulent, but it was also incomparably more removed from real and meaningful memory.

There really had been a war in the first half of the 1940s, a traumatic, dramatic ordeal in which tens of millions of men, women, and children had perished. Much of its real history had disappeared, together with those unfortunate victims. And most of the rest of its history had been purposively manipulated, twisted, and tinseled over to serve the political needs of those who ran the country.

It only made matters worse that during much of the Brezhnev period, beginning in about 1970, the authorities inserted into the expanding cult of the Great Patriotic War an official cult of Leonid Brezhnev himself. All high school students had to read *Malaia zemlia* (The Little Land), the general secretary's ghostwritten memoir about his own wartime experience as chief political officer of the Eighteenth Army, which fought—among other places—in the area around Novorossiisk. The slim volume with its overblown self-praise cries out for caricature. "I heard the words, now legendary, 'I want to go into battle a Communist!' before practically every action, and the tougher the fighting was, the more often they were heard."

Although Brezhnev never took part in any fighting, his book contains a passage about how in battle he replaced a dead machine gunner and fended off a fascist attack. "My world shrank down to the dimensions of an observation slit," recalled Brezhnev. On a comprehensive examination in 1984, a classmate of the journalist Dmitrii Radyshevsky wrote and read aloud the following: "For Leonid Ilich, the world shrank to the dimensions of an observation slit. Leonid Ilich fended off an attack." The class laughed; any juggling of the formulaic idiom showed off its absurdity. Indeed, the glorification of the 1943 fighting around Novorossiisk, which was later shown to have been primarily diversionary—and the naming of Novorossiisk as a hero city—were entirely due to Brezhnev's presence in that operation.[20]

There is every reason to believe that as a matter of course youngsters who were chosen to serve as honor guards, who presented veterans with flowers, speeches, and their attention, who traipsed along on group trips to war museums and exhibits did so because they had no way to get out of these activities without jeopardizing their future careers. In his splendid 1986 television movie, *Pictures of Russia,* the Danish correspondent Samuel Rachlin interviewed teenage honor guards at one of Volgograd's many war memorials. When he asked a uniformed boy and girl why they served in that capacity, they came out with stock phrases about hallowing the war dead, but who knows what they said to one another in private, or at home, in the cramped kitchens of their parents' apartments? If they bore any resemblance to the Soviet teenagers I knew, they harbored an inner contempt for the rituals they were forced to enact. In contrast, it is likely that some, or even many, of the boys enjoyed battle site tours and war games, which took them away from their parents, into the country, and usually involved playing with some sort of military hardware.

To the younger generations, the feelings of shame, obligation, respect, awe, and gratitude toward those who had fought in the war against Germany that the Party, armed forces, and government had been so eager to arouse were slow in coming. Indeed, the cult of the Great Patriotic War appeared to have backfired, inspiring a callous derision on the part of many youths who might have shown some interest in the war had the authorities had the intelligence to leave them in peace.

7

GLASNOST AND THE GREAT PATRIOTIC WAR

One spring day in 1986 Andrei Voznesensky was riding in a taxicab along a highway not far from the Crimean city of Simferopol. Ten kilometers from the city, the driver, Vasilii Lesnykh, stopped the cab at a spot where, during two nights in December 1941 the Germans had massacred 12,000 Soviet citizens, most of them Jews. Lesnykh, a native of the area, recalled how, as a child of ten, he had witnessed the atrocity. "An antitank ditch ran from the highway. And at the ditch, people were shot with machine guns. They all screamed horribly—the steppe was overlaid with groans. . . . The soldiers were all drunk. . . . Yes, I also remember a little table at which they took away passports. The whole steppe was sprinkled with passports. They buried many people half-alive. The earth was breathing."

The poet recalled that the driver kept repeating the painful story, and then added a horrible coda to the already gruesome symphony. Some of the victims had brought their most valuable possessions with them to the ditch, but the Germans had shot the people in a hurry, without taking the time to strip them of their valuables or gold teeth. "Recently," said Lesnykh, "people have been digging up this mass grave, looking for gold. They were tried for it last year."

Voznesensky and the driver walked out along the site, which had long since been planted over with grass. Suddenly they saw a portion of earth that had been freshly dug up, along with piles of blackened bones, skulls, and rotted clothing. "Digging again, the bastards!"

muttered Lesnykh. In the black of night, Soviet citizens were driving up to the site of the massacre and by the light of their automobile headlights, extracting gold crowns out of the victims' skulls with pliers. To prevent infection they wore rubber gloves.[1]

Voznesensky had come to Simferopol specifically to visit the site of the crimes committed long ago by the Germans, and more recently by Soviet grave robbers, after having heard about the robbers' trial. The result of his sojourn in the Crimea was a work of poetry and prose entitled "The Ditch: A Spiritual Trial."

At a public performance in the spring of 1987, I watched Voznesensky recite, in his characteristic passionate and measured manner, the narrative about vandals systematically unearthing the bodies of the war's hapless victims and stripping them of valuables. He did not specifically mention that the murdered men, women, and children had been mostly Jews, but the implication was clear to anyone who knew anything about the German occupation. An article in the *New York Times* had indicated that Voznesensky saw "The Ditch" as an attack on Soviet anti-Semitism and most specifically on the official propensity to maintain a lethal silence about the special suffering the Nazi occupiers meted out to Jews.[2]

What, asked Voznesensky, could possibly have so corrupted the souls of those people who would rummage around skulls and skeletons to pull out bits of gold? Moreover, the brazen acts of sacrilege were not even hidden, and passers-by could see their evident traces. The trial took place in 1984. On the first day, wrote Voznesensky, the courtroom was full of people who listened for the location of the ditch. "On the second day it was empty—they had rushed off to utilize the information. . . . Has everyone gone mad? . . . It is souls they are robbing, souls of the dead and buried. Their souls, Your souls."

The prose passages of "The Ditch" are as effective as Voznesensky's characteristically clipped poetry. At one point he simply quotes from "Case No. 1586," the documents cataloguing the crimes the grave robbers had committed in June and July 1984. They made off with jewelry and gold bits worth many thousands of rubles. On July 13 they stole gold crowns and bridges whose total value was 21,925 rubles (about $10,000). The robbers included a physician who had graduated from a Moscow institute affiliated with the prestigious Academy of Sciences. They ranged in age from twenty-eight to fifty. Their nationalities were Russian, Ukrainian, Azerbaijani, and Armenian. "As they answered the judge, their own gold crowns glittered in their mouths."

When one of the robbers was asked how he had felt while digging up the graves, he replied, "And how would you feel yanking out a gold bridge that has been damaged by a bullet? Or pulling out the shoe of a little child together with some remnants of bone?"

It really happened, it really happened.
It really happened, it really happened.
Dust of gold and bone.
A bat removed a bracelet from a skeleton,
While another, behind the wheel, hurried him along . . .

A skull. Night. And a blooming almond tree.
The infernal organizer of a pogrom
Left the spade and calmly pressed on the gas pedal . . .
Emaciated, like a poker,
Hamlet took skulls
And pulled out a row of crowns.
A person is different from a worm.
Worms do not eat gold.

Whither do you lead, ditch?
Not to flowers, nor to orphans.
This is a cemetery of souls—genocide.
A whirlwind of passports moves across the steppe.
And nobody brought any hyacinths.

The authorities had erected no memorial at the site of the massacre. "They could at least put up a post here. One for 12,000. To remember people is a sacred act," wrote Voznesensky. With some satisfaction the poet told me in an interview that as a result of "The Ditch," a modest monument had been hurriedly placed on the site in November 1986.

The 1984 crimes at the Simferopol ditch provided the absolute antipode to the official memorialization of the Great Patriotic War in all its grandeur. What could more graphically appose the reverence for the wartime martyrs than the deliberate desecration of their graves? What psychic process must have taken place to prompt workers, an engineer, a driver, a physician—seemingly ordinary people—to stealthily dig up the remains of Jewish families slain on the orders of Nazi overlords and strip their skeletons of the valuables the Germans had been in too much of a hurry to take themselves? And whence came the callousness of passers-by who knew the acts were being committed but offered no protest? What of the people to whom the gold crowns and pieces of jewelry had been sold? According to Voznesensky, they received stiffer sentences than did the grave robbers, who got off rather lightly. And what do we make of the people who attended the Simferopol trial on the first day to learn the location of the ditch and then themselves rushed off to see what they could plunder? A Soviet journalist wrote that the digging near Simferopol had been not simply a crime but a sin, in the way Tolstoy and Dostoevsky had understood the meaning of the word.[3]

I believe that grave robbing for greed is a truly counterinstinctual activity that breaks the most fundamental kind of taboo. One must have no fear of the dead in order to disturb the eternal rest of innocent genocide victims. Perhaps anti-Semitism had something to do with it; on some subliminal level the criminals might have believed that because the dead were "merely" Jews, they wielded no spiritual power. More likely, the robbers simply saw an opportunity to get money, a scam they saw as no worse than the countless scams that made up the notorious "second economy" in the Soviet Union. Only in this case they were not stealing from the state. They were simply digging for gold.

Voznesensky's poem provoked many hundreds of letters that expressed dismay, disgust, shock, and rage. One reader, who identified herself as "simply a woman," wrote that the poem had filled her with the desire for retribution. A veteran from Kharkov wrote that he had not cried when he was wounded at the front, but that both he and his wife wept while reading "The Ditch." "We are all responsible for this event," wrote a Leningrader. "Apathy always engenders crime."[4]

Was it apathy that prompted six youths hanging out at the Valley of Glory in the area of Murmansk to spend three hours firing rifles at a war memorial one warm summer's night in 1986? Early in this book I described that incident, which occurred in the same month as the publication of "The Ditch." Most of those Murmansk youths were eighteen to twenty-three years old, but one was only fifteen. The owner of the rifle, he was an award-winning high school student. The older boys included Komsomol members and one former border guard, Pavel Guliaev. Apparently when twenty-two-year-old Guliaev had picked up the gun, he had bragged to his pals, "I'll show you how border guards can shoot."

Compared to the Simferopol grave robbings, the Murmansk episode seemed tame: some bored adolescents living in the boondocks got a bit tipsy and found themselves shooting at a piece of funerary architecture. The actual targets might not have been as important as the accuracy of the shooting. But undoubtedly the fact that the Valley of Glory was a place of public ceremony must have heightened the excitement of using it as a shooting gallery. One could take a "boys will be boys" approach. After all, no one had gotten hurt. But the Soviet public was horrified, and not least of all because the boys got off with light sentences—two to five years in the reformatory—and because they were openly supported by their comrades. When the sentences were pronounced in the courtroom a young voice shouted out, "We will avenge you guys!"

The incident prompted a correspondent for the local newspaper, *Poliarnaia pravda* (*Polar Truth*), to write a heartfelt article in which she linked the trial of the "marksmen" with that of the Simferopol gold-diggers. Voznesensky had been correct, she said, in warning that the Simferopol trial had not ended. The young sharpshooters' trial was its continuation. True, the incentives were different, as were the individuals and the articles of the criminal code with which they were charged, but the original offense is identical: "Human soullessness, callousness, underdevelopment, the confusion of all values." The poet had asked, "Whither do you lead, ditch?" Into that ditch in which people turn into hyenas, answered the journalist. And to the Valley of Glory, where for many years people had in fact been stealing the stars off the tombstones and digging up graves and stealing military medals.[5]

The shootings of the Murmansk memorial were publicized among the Moscow intelligentsia by Ivan Stadniuk, an old warhorse and conservative writer of war novels. In the course of a speech to the plenum of the administrative board of the Writers' Union, he expressed the pain he had suffered reading "The Ditch." Unfortunately, he added, the Simferopol crimes were not unique incidents of iconoclasm, and he related to his audience the story of the six Murmansk youths and their shooting spree. From it he drew a moral lesson. We are all at fault, he said. The whole people stands accused for these crimes, because it is up to all of us to inculcate in everyone respect for our history and for our veterans. He then went on to catalog other grave robbings and the vandalism of war memorials in 1978, 1981, and 1984. In the last one, the graves of thirty-one soldiers had been dug up on the seventy-kilometer line of the Pechenga Highway. Military artifacts had been strewn about and the soldiers' skulls had been perched on top of poles stuck into the ground. "It is our sacred duty," concluded Stadniuk, "to remember and think about the young," to teach them about our tragic and heroic past.[6]

Zone of Oblivion is the name of a 1991 television movie by Kazan filmmaker Vladimir Yerkhov, about the work of the search movement devoted to finding and burying the war dead. In the powerful film, which opens with spliced footage of young people digging for battle artifacts in 1990 and documentary film of real wartime scenes, Yerkhov's first narration describes a terrible sight he had witnessed in October 1989 in the environs of Novgorod. He had arrived with a search group at a locus of wartime fighting, only to find that marauders had gotten there first. Forty-seven human skulls and a thick layer of bones had been dug up and strewn about in a search for valuables. Any teeth with metal that looked like gold or silver had been pulled out of the skulls that then had been tossed onto the ground.

Over the years, Daniil Mitlianskii's war memorial, Requiem, which reposed in the courtyard of Moscow's 110th School, had been mutilated many times; time and again he had been called upon to repair its broken bayonets or the limbs of its wraithlike figures. Unprotected by official Party or government sponsorship, that monument had been prey to vandals since its erection in 1971.

Mitlianskii's studio in the north of Moscow was a fabulous place, filled with fanciful sculpture—huge expressive heads, small, graceful soldiers whose slimness conveyed their touching youth and vulnerability. For Mitlianskii war memorials were a passion. He wept as he spoke about the war, and this was before touching a drop of the vodka I had brought.

"Look, have you been to Japan?" the sculptor asked me suddenly, as we perched on little stools, eating bread, fresh dill, and some toxic-looking cheese that he considered a delicacy, all laid out on a small, rickety table in his studio.

"Yes," I replied.

"Well, I haven't, but I hear that in Japan there are temples built out of paper that have lasted hundreds of years. Here in Moscow the bayonets have been broken off my monument twenty times. Twenty times they have had to be replaced! People here destroy whatever they can. The Japanese preserve paper for hundreds of years, and Russians will break metal and even stone if they can. Because no one cares about anything. Listen, what does it say on your country's coat of arms?"

"Coat of arms?" I struggled to come up with the right answer. "It says '*e pluribus unum*,'" I finally responded.

"And what does it mean?" asked the sculptor.

"Out of many, one."

"And on our coat of arms it says 'workers of the world unite' but it should say 'no one gives a damn about anything.'"

In fact, although Mitlianskii's depressing assessment of his people may have been apt for the stagnation era, the Gorbachev regime had begun to foster a respectful attitude toward the past and a renewed pride in old Russia, which was viewed by a steadily growing number of people as a spiritual wellspring and a source of hope, dignity, and meaning. Predictably, the neo-Slavophilism of the late 1980s bore the same xenophobic, exclusive character that had defined the Soviet patriotism of the Brezhnev period.

THE RETURN OF THE REPRESSED

When General Secretary Mikhail Gorbachev called for *glasnost,* or the voicing of ideas and sentiments (the word comes from the Slavic root *glas,* which means "voice"), and an end to the "blank spots" in history—a phrase he used during the commemoration of the seventieth anniversary of the Bolshevik revolution in 1987—he helped unleash a thoroughgoing de-Stalinization that within a year or two called into question the very legitimacy of the government and Party that had produced Stalin's system and continued its legacy. After decades of silence, the Pandora's box containing the demons of the Stalin years was opened, and for more than two years grisly revelations, particularly about the 1930s, dominated newspapers, periodicals, and films, causing great anguish and anxiety to entire generations of people, most of whom had been shielded from the truth. Mass graves were dug up in the courtyards of prisons; both victims and perpetrators of terror and torture, all of them elderly, rushed to go public with secrets they had kept hidden for a half-century.

American reporters lionized the *glasnost* revelations, but for the Soviet people the process of facing and assimilating an ugly past was painfully divisive. It is easy for us Americans with our eighteenth-century sanctification of Truth to assume that the lifting of a veil of secrecy is an unmitigated good. But for many Soviet people the Gorbachev regime's de-Stalinization was genuinely traumatic. "We don't know how to deal with all of these facts," complained a Muscovite historian of architecture in April 1988. She had just finished writing an article on the architectural designs of Moscow prisons in the 1930s. "Everyone is upset, agitated, argumentative."

Mikhail Zaraev, a journalist who in the late 1980s wrote for *Selskaia zhizn'* (*Village Life*), a conservative newpaper geared toward the rural reader, told me in 1988 that in the countryside people were talking about Stalin in household after household. Zaraev had just returned from a collective farm. Almost the first thing the farm's chairman, a weathered and shrewd peasant, had said upon making his acquaintance was, "What do you think of Stalin? Every evening I argue about him with my thirty-year-old son." Zaraev then told me, "I replied to the chairman that without knowing anything else I could assure him that I agreed with his son. I figured that if the son is thirty, the father is fifty-five or sixty, and that if they are arguing, then the son undoubtedly is attacking Stalin and the father is defending him."

Time and again during those days in Moscow I heard the accusation that Soviet people did not know how to accept the fruits of *glasnost* and democratization. My Jewish friend Lena, a computer programmer in her mid-thirties, put it better than anyone else. "Look," she said, "we have just finished celebrating the holiday of Passover. Just think, the Jews had to wander in the desert for forty years after their years of bondage. Well, we had some seventy years of slavery and now it is our turn to wander. . . . "

In his book on the demise of the Soviet Union, *Lenin's Tomb,* David Remnick mused on the accumulated effect of decades of living with a distorted or obliterated past: "It's as if the regime were guilty of two crimes on a massive scale: murder and the unending assault against memory. In making a secret of history, the Kremlin made its subjects just a little more insane, a little more desperate."[7]

Letting the secrets out into the open, I think, made many of them crazier still. Soviet scholars and ordinary citizens alike were gripped by a compulsion to set the record straight about their country's experience in the Stalin years, a compulsion driven by a variety of sentiments, from rage all the way to the yearning for spiritual purification. The Soviet people's devotion to—even obsession with—real memory was at the heart of their spiritual turmoil.

"People once again feel themselves to be descendents," explained historian Mikhail Gefter in the spring of 1988. We were sitting at a table covered with a brown-and-white checkered tablecloth in the "big room" of his small apartment. Gefter was recovering from a major heart attack and showed it; his tiny, wizened frame seemed to have shrunk since my last visit with him the previous summer, and his face was pinched and white. We had just finished a simple supper of buckwheat groats with sour cream and bread and cheese. Gefter's wife, Lela, was coming in with the *zapekanka* she had baked, a rich pudding made of cottage cheese, eggs, cream, sugar, and flour.

"We are all more or less affected by the desire to retrieve our history," she said, as she offered me tea and a plateful of dessert. "You don't know how painful it all has been. Take the town where I was born. Now it is called Zhdanov, but it used to be Mariupol. How many Jews were killed by the occupying Germans I cannot say for sure, but there were many. Near a big ditch into which many of their bodies had been tossed there has been a clumsy little wooden post identifying the site."

Lela explained that the Jews of Zhdanov had collected money to erect a proper memorial to their dead relatives and friends, with a wall on which would be engraved all of their names. She started to weep as she told me how she and her cousin had been struggling to remember the correct names of all their kin who had perished. "For example there was Uncle Ziama. When we were children in the 1930s, we always called him Uncle Ziama. But what was his real first name? If we do not remember it then he cannot be properly honored on the monument."

"Maybe it was Zalmon?" I suggested, "that was a common Russian Jewish name."

"Zalmon," she repeated, her voice breaking with emotion, "that is what we were also thinking."

(Not long after, as part of a national attempt to restore the remnants of a past that had been shattered by Soviet militant postrevolutionary zeal, the city of Zhdanov once again took the name Mariupol.)

On that evening in April 1988 as Mikhail Gefter was telling me how people in the Soviet Union—Russians, Jews, Armenians, and others—were seeking to reforge their links to previous generations, I remembered a conversation from ten years before in which he had described the exact opposite impulse at work during the 1920s. Gefter had grown up in a Jewish family in Simferopol. An active, enthusiastic Pioneer during the years following the close of the Civil War, he had recalled his childhood feelings about the Jews who lived in his neighborhood. "My parents were revolutionaries and non-observant Jews. But I remember seeing the older men in the neighborhood slowly walking down the street in the black suits and broad-brimmed black hats trimmed with fur that they wore even in the summer. To me they represented the dark ages that the revolution had promised to sweep away. They seemed the very opposite of the progress to a bright future promised by the Communist Party. I used to run across the street when I saw them coming."

Like all postrevolutionary regimes, the Bolshevik government in the years following the 1917 seizure of power had consciously sought to rupture all links between old Russia and the bright new political, social, and cultural entity that was purported to have risen from its ashes. Spurred by a similar impulse to control time, the Jacobin heirs to the French Revolution had renamed the months of the year and even rewritten the calendar, with 1789 marking the year 1.

In Soviet Russia, the first generation of Bolshevik leaders was impelled by an urgent need to transform the populace from what they saw as the products of an old and rotting culture into new Soviet men and women with new values, morals, mores, tastes, and exemplars. Beginning in the mid-twenties with the creation of the League of the Militant Godless, this impulse was extended to include active antireligious measures that aimed to replace religious faith with the enthusiastic support of Lenin's legacy. Many churches were destroyed in the effort to purge the land and people of polluting influences, a destructive campaign that was part of a more general attempt to negate the past and turn the present into the beginning of a new and separate epoch.

During World War II came the brief interlude in which both the Orthodox Church and the heroes of Russia's prerevolutionary past were called upon to help mobilize the country and provide sources of national pride and moral sustenance. But when the war ended, the tenor of propaganda and of the postwar reconstruction of cities and towns had once again come to reflect a classic revolutionary antihistorical philosophy, which was continued through the Brezhnev era and beyond.

"Our state," pronounced Mikhail Gefter as we talked in his apartment on a frosty evening in February 1989, "has operated as a monopoly such as no capitalist power has ever dreamed of—a monopoly of the economy, of property, a monopoly of ideas, a monopoly of the arts. That monopoly has now been shown to be the source of our national catastrophe, and it is necessary to abandon the monopoly. But it has proved impossible to alienate one monopoly without cutting into the others. If you touch the monopoly of property, then you affect the monopoly of power; if you touch the monopoly of power, then you affect the monopoly of significant ideas. If you touch the monopoly of these significant ideas," continued Gefter with a soft chuckle, clearly enjoying his monologue as he now looked at me intently through his large glasses, "then you affect the monopoly of tastes, the monopoly of power over people's souls, and so on. This system of interdependent monopolies that made up the skeleton of the Stalinist system—which of course reached a level of absurdity by the end of his life—this system, if disrupted in one place, must necessarily lead to disruption in the others. Now pluralism is something about which you can say, 'well and good,' but pluralism cannot be established by decree or even by a collective will. Pluralism," he said in a whisper (Mikhail Gefter had radio actor Garrison Keillor's habit of shrinking his voice down to an almost inaudible level as he reached the climax of an important train of thought), "pluralism is a culture."

We continued to talk as he walked me to the subway. Although everyone had been complaining about the unusually warm winter weather, on that Monday afternoon it was well below freezing, with a fairly thick snow cover underfoot. Gefter had on the seasonal outerwear uniform for men of his elder generation: ankle-high boots, thick wool coat, plaid scarf, and bushy fur hat. He brandished a ski pole instead of a cane. As we walked down the three flights of stone steps in his little apartment building, his wrinkled skin looked paper white in the dim, harsh light of the stairwell. We started across the courtyard and headed toward the Novye Cheremushkii subway station. Gefter suddenly stopped walking and looked up at me, leaning heavily on his ski pole. "Our people," he said deliberately, "must learn to feel that they are masters of their own fates."

Every reform movement needs to posit in the past some period "before the fall" to whose principles or values it aspires to return. For Martin Luther this was the Christian era before the establishment of the papacy. In the Soviet Union in the late 1980s Mikhail Gorbachev equated the fall with Stalin and marked out 1921–28, the era of the New Economic Policy, as a golden age of humane and sensible socialism that sought gradually to transform the social system without exploiting the long-suffering Russian peasantry or unduly hampering private trade within the country. For most representatives of the Soviet intelligentsia, however, the pre-Stalinist Soviet past was both remote and pallid; a people as intensely emotional as the Russians needed to feed on stronger stuff.

In the 1970s and 1980s—the span of an entire generation—much of what Soviet political mythology had put forward as the source of inspiration, cohesion, and popular loyalty had gone stale. The idealized figure of Lenin, the saga of revolution and civil war, the vision of an industrializing nation united by revolutionary zeal and devotion to Stalin, the tragic splendor of the Great Patriotic War and Stalin's irreplaceable strategic brilliance and inspirational power, the accomplishments of Soviet technology and the socialist economic system, the Communist Party as a bountiful and progressive political and moral force, the success of socialism as a social system steadily gaining global predominance—none of those myths could any longer be summoned before a nation that had watched its economy crumble and its ruling Party deteriorate into corruption and paralysis. The Eastern European empire was breaking away; the Stalin myth was being painfully exploded; in early 1989 the decade-long Afghan war finally ended in a shambles. Only a few diehard communists could sort all this out and retrieve anything much to lean on. Russia's cultural and religious heritage, however, was a rich respository of tradition and rootedness.

HOLY RUSSIA RESURGENT

The mellifluous peal of church bells resounded incongruously through the hockey stadium. Some three thousand people were sitting in their winter coats in the cool vastness of the Soviet Wings Sports Palace located on the outskirts of Moscow. Adjacent to the rear scoreboard, in enormous letters made up of lightbulbs that usually spelled out the names of competing teams, glittered the words TRADITIONS OF THE RUSSIAN LAND. In the front was a big stage on which were seated a line of speakers, and in the middle of the stage, a microphone. On the curtained wall behind the mike was a huge television screen.

It was Friday, February 17, 1989, and the event had been billed as an evening devoted to a Russian national revival. With me was Mikhail Gefter's son Valia. As the bells pealed to signal the beginning of the rally, a group of about a dozen young men and women came into the stadium conspicuously late and unfurled a banner that read The Cathedral of Christ the Savior Shall Be! They also displayed a large red flag depicting, in gold paint, the figure of St. George slaying the dragon. In the early Soviet period Bolshevik iconographers had taken over this famed patron saint of battle, who had in the late 1980s become the symbol of the new Russian nationalism exemplified by the notorious chauvinistic group, *Pamiat* (Memory). This cluster of young people, I later learned, represented a detachment of *Pamiat* called *Khram,* which in Russian means "church" or "shrine."

For a thousand years, since the ruling dynasty of the east Slavic

territories had converted to Christianity, virtually all Russian monuments to victories in battle had taken the form of churches. It was
thus in keeping with ancient tradition when on Christmas Day of
1812, Alexander I issued a manifesto pronouncing his intention to
construct in Moscow a cathedral to Christ the Savior in celebration
of his gratitude to God's Providence for having saved Russia from the
French. The plans soon got bogged down by intrigues and technical
difficulties, and the cathedral, built on the left bank of the Moscow
River, was consecrated only in 1883. The resultant edifice was
immense; it could hold some 10,000 worshippers. As it turned out,
this mammoth cathedral cum war memorial, after seventy-one years
of planning and construction, had a life span of only forty-eight
years. In 1931 the Soviet authorities, inspired by the militant antireligious fervor of the early Stalin years, dynamited the Cathedral of
Christ the Savior. And so the national shrine to the Russian victory
in the Fatherland War was blown to bits. In its place, during the
1950s, the city constructed a correspondingly vast outdoor swim-
ming pool capable of accommodating 20,000 swimmers. Beginning
in the late 1980s Russian nationalists rallied round a cry to rebuild—
preferably on its original site—the Cathedral of Christ the Savior.

A beautiful actress began the "Traditions of the Russian Land"
evening by reciting, in a characteristically Russian emotional
cadence, a poem about a person moving from darkness into the light
of religious faith. Next came a porky looking youngish priest with
red hair and beard, pasty complexion, and a black cassock flowing
down the full length of his rounded torso. He delivered a sermon on
the power of prayer that would have seemed rather ho-hum in a
Sunday morning service, but it packed something of wallop in the
chilly secular vastness of the Soviet Wings Sports Palace, his enormous gold chain and cross glinting on the giant television screen.

Writers, philosophers, philologists followed with more or less
impassioned speeches on the rebirth of Russian culture. "We are *not*
born of October," declared one of the writers, with reference to the
oft-repeated ritual slogan in Soviet propaganda that posited the
Bolshevik revolution as the fountainhead of popular consciousness.
"We are born of a thousand years of Russian history!" he continued,
to a burst of applause. At the end of his talk a mixed choir filed on
stage and filled the stadium with the voluptuous sounds of a capella

Russian church music. There was loud clapping for a suggestion that at least one hour a week of Soviet television be given over to church broadcasts and also for calls for the publication of the complete works of Pushkin and other literary greats. Every mention of the preservation or restoration of churches and monasteries (the original cause embraced by *Pamiat* at its inception) drew noisy salvos of applause.

Some speakers posited the Russian language and literature as the absolute embodiment of the national spirit. Ours was primarily not a stone but a wooden culture, observed a philologist, so few ancient churches and other buildings remain. "What is extant of old Russia is in the domain of *words,* so let us issue collections of Russian folklore, let every neighborhood high school teach the languages from which from which our own is derived, namely classical Greek, Latin, Old Church Slavonic (at this there exploded a hearty round of applause) and—you'll be surprised to hear—Hebrew!" Snickers and murmurs rippled through the stadium. That "you'll be surprised to hear," with its nodding implication that every Russian would naturally assume Hebrew to be utterly alien—this was the level of anti-Semitism evident at the "Traditions of the Russian Land" gathering. It was subtle but palpable. Valia Gefter, whose nose had been broken the previous year by a street thug who had punched him in the face after making a remark about "yids," shot me a knowing look.

The most thunderous applause of the evening was evoked by Vladimir Soloukhin, a gifted writer and poet and master demagogue. A middle-aged man with sandy hair and the face of a bruiser, he rambled on at length in a booming basso that affected a super-Russian accent from his hometown of Vladimir, the mother of Russian cities as early as the twelfth century, when Moscow was little more than a crude cluster of wooden stockades. He got a spirited response when his remarks touched on the restoration of churches and monasteries. "Why do we need to battle on behalf of every monument?" "Why," he continued, his voice rising in a steady crescendo of frustration, "in a civilized, enormous, rich progressive state like ours, why is it necessary to point out that we must save every church, every stone? It ought to be completely obvious!"

The climax occurred a moment later when Soloukhin addressed the jumble of real concerns gnawing at the souls of Russians today. "What are our people currently expecting? Our people are expecting our own Soviet government to say: 'We've had enough! Enough of exporting our raw materials as though we were a colonial power! Enough of spending our gold on bread, we can produce our own bread! Enough of looking at the ruins of tens and hundreds and thousands of ravaged churches! Enough of standing on food lines! Enough of empty shops! Enough of scurrying after Western rags and jackets! Enough of keeping the people in the background! We've had enough!'" At this, most of the three thousand strong audience rushed to their feet, applauding with gusto, and then, in typical Russian fashion, people started clapping rhythmically in unison until the speaker, who had sat down, returned to the microphone.

It was ten or ten-thirty on that cold Friday night as we inched our way out of the stadium. Who were these folks who had finished out their week by traveling straight from work to this rally on the outskirts of the city? Why had they come? My companion and I speculated on these questions as we made our way, arm in arm, along an icy path leading through a little park to the train station. The thicket of people walking with us to the station were mostly fairly young and looked to us to represent neither the intelligentsia nor what Valia called *temnyi narod,* literally "the dark" (in the sense of unenlightened) people. They were somewhere in between, the grandchildren and great- grandchildren of the illiterate, desperately poor *muzhiki,* peasants who in 1918 and 1919 had supported the Reds against the Whites, only to find themselves in every way disenfranchised and stripped of rights, of land, of bread. They were the descendants of men and women who in the 1920s and 1930s finally became literate, only to be given praises of Stalin to read.

They and their ancestors had always been deprived of the fruits of Russian culture, even though their sweat and blood had nurtured the trees that had borne that fruit. In the imperial period, educated society had given rise to a splendid secular culture exclusively of and for the elite, and after the revolution that culture had been jostled around, distorted, and incorporated into something called Soviet culture, which was a pastiche of old and new and excluded entirely the rich religious traditions that had nourished Russian souls for almost a thousand years. And now these Soviet citizens, victims of more than a half-century of cultural starvation, were longing for some mythic incarnation of the culture that had always been denied them.

What Goes Around, Comes Around

In the summer of 1989 in a discussion with members of the USSR Academy of Sciences' Institute of Ethnography, I asked the members to plumb the real meaning of rituals and myths celebrating the Great Patriotic War. Immediately a young man in his late twenties or early thirties stood up. He was tall, pale, and mustachioed, and neatly attired in a light-blue shirt and navy trousers. "The Great Patriotic War was the greatest catastrophe in the history of Soviet foreign policy," he said. "And so to cover up the disgrace, our authorities canonized it and called it a victory. But what kind of victory was it if we lost twenty or thirty million people and the Germans lost two or three million?" After a stunned silence I called on a middle-aged man who, in a bold voice, said that "ours was a victory because even though the costs were enormous, we did save the world from fascism."

"Save the world from fascism?" shouted the young man, jumping up again. "On the contrary, we *brought* fascism to East Europe and enslaved our own people as well. What kind of salvation was that?"

Then a stout elderly woman in a blue-and-white flowered dress slowly stood up. Her thin white hair was pulled back in an old-fashioned knot. She looked directly at the young man and in a quivering but determined voice said, "Russians have always had in their hearts a special place for *victims*. You are right in saying that the war was an incomparable catastrophe. But the victims of that catastrophe—the millions and millions of war dead, the countless orphans and widows—shall always, yes always merit our compassion, and our love."

The old woman was right, of course. No matter who is to blame, the victims' sufferings remain real. Indeed, the pathos of those millions of unfortunates was surely not diminished but, rather, heightened by the fact that so many succumbed to the evils of their own leaders. Self-inflicted wounds can be the most painful to bear.

Much of the struggle that, by the beginning of the 1990s, began to pull the Soviet Union apart was about memory as a source of power. Many of the non-Russian nationalities—Armenians, Azeris, Estonians, Lithuanians, Latvians—were even more quickly swept away than the Russians by the desire to become heirs to their own histories and thereby masters of their own fates.

The Baltic states' struggle for independence—which began the breakup of the Union of Soviet Socialist Republics—was inextricably bound up with the desacralization of the Great Patriotic War myth. The classic Brezhnevite narrative of the war had involved a massive cover-up of the secret protocol of the Nazi-Soviet Pact—signed on August 23, 1939, by Foreign Ministers Joachim von Ribbentrop and Viacheslav Molotov—by which Hitler and Stalin had divided up the Baltics, Poland, and Bessarabia. As recently as New Year's eve 1988, Molotov's grandson, also named Viacheslav, whom a colleague had brought to my Massachusetts home as a dinner guest, assured me (over the incongruent combination of borscht and champagne) that there had been *no* secret protocol to the pact. "Grandfather gave me his word of honor," said the handsome young man earnestly, "and believe me, he would never have lied to me."

Grandfather had indeed lied. Before the end of the decade, Soviet authorities published the clandestine portions of the pact. Publicly a treaty of mutual nonaggression, the settlement had provided for a partition of Poland and other territorial arrangements, including the eventual transfer to the Soviet Union of Romanian Bessarabia and the three Baltic states. A week later Hitler invaded Poland and World War II had begun. After some initial hesitation, Soviet troops moved into eastern Poland. In 1940 they occupied Estonia, Latvia, and Lithuania, only to lose them to Germany after Operation Barbarossa. During the course of 1944 the Red Army replaced the German occupying forces in the Baltic states and incorporated those territories—formerly part of the Russian Empire—into the Union of Soviet Socialist Republics.

On the fiftieth anniversary of the Nazi-Soviet Pact, August 23, 1989, in the wake of the publication of the pact's secret protocol, a human chain of Balts linked hands across the expanse of Estonia, Latvia, and Lithuania four hundred miles long. This powerful protest against the rape of their lands by two evil dictators was an early step in the Baltic states' emancipation from Soviet control, which in turn helped speed the dissolution of the Soviet Union.[8]

Admitting the truth about the prehistory of the Great Patriotic War turned out to be one of the most fateful steps taken by the Gorbachev regime. Predictably, the next momentous admission of truth had to revolve around the bedeviled question of Katyn.

KATYN

On April 13, 1943, Joseph Goebbels, propaganda minister of the Third Reich, announced over German radio the discovery, in the Katyn Forest near Smolensk, of a huge grave containing the remains of thousands of Polish officers who, he said, had been shot by "Jewish commissars" in the spring of 1940, indicating that the victims had been some of the Polish officers and other Polish nationals who had disappeared after having been incarcerated when the Soviet Union had invaded Poland in 1939.

Occupying German forces in the area of the forest had interrogated local inhabitants, who told them that the NKVD had carried out the killings in the spring of 1940. The Polish government in exile (the "London Poles") called for an investigation by the International Red Cross, and the Soviet Union responded to the accusation of responsibility for the crime by charging the Germans with having perpetrated the murders in 1941, and by breaking off diplomatic relations with Poland.

Early in 1944 an official Soviet investigative commission, headed by an N. Burdenko, concluded that Germans had done the killings, which had taken place in the fall of 1941. In June 1946 the subject of Katyn came up in the Nuremberg trials but was dismissed for lack of sufficient evidence. Soviet authorities continued to insist on German responsibility for the villainy done to the Polish officers and, with a subordinate government in place in Warsaw, turned Katyn into an utterly taboo subject.

The massacres had in fact taken place in the spring of 1940 at Katyn, Kalinin, Starobelsk, and other secret locations. The killers, who were typically each rewarded with several glasses of vodka after each night's work, shot their prey methodically, night after night, over a period of weeks. The thousands of victims represented the cream of the Polish officer corps and the potential germ of a vigorous postwar administration. Stalin had his own designs on postwar Poland that did not include anything like independent governance. There is every reason to believe that the slayings had been a prophylactic genocide. From the very first, elaborate precautions had been taken to cover up the NKVD executioners' work.

In April 1993, exactly fifty years after the discovery of the atrocity was made public, Dr. Mark Kramer, a colleague at Harvard's Russian

Research Center, handed me a sheaf of photocopied documents he had just brought back from Moscow, where he had been working in the presidential archive's "special archive," in which, among other things, the secret protocol to the Nazi-Soviet Pact had been kept. Scholars have long known about the discovery of the mass graves in 1943, and the bitter counteraccusations in the conflicting explanations of the massacre proferred by Germans, Poles, and Russians, which over the course of decades was the single thorniest issue in the otherwise already prickly Soviet-Polish relationship. But that clutch of papers I took home with me that spring day in 1993, stamped TOP SECRET, contained new evidence documenting the massacre, its cover-up, and the tortuous path to the Soviet admission of guilt for the killings of the Polish officers.

The original idea for the arrest and execution of the Poles had come from the notorious comissar of internal affairs, Lavrentii Beria, who on March 5, 1940, informed Stalin that NKVD prisoner-of-war camps and prisons in western Ukraine and Belorussia were holding a "relatively large number" of former officers in the Polish Army, members of the Polish police force, spies, members of Polish nationalist parties, and others who "all appear to be sworn enemies of Soviet power." Beria broke down by rank and occupation 14,736 (almost all Polish) suspects in the camps and 18,632 (10,685 of them Poles) suspects in the prisons of western Ukraine and Belorussia, and suggested that the NKVD examine the files of most of the above and "apply the most severe punishment—execution." Stalin read this letter and scrawled his signature on the first page.

Almost twenty years later, in March 1959, Aleksandr Shelepin, head of the KGB (successor to the NKVD) sent his boss, Nikita Khrushchev, a handwritten letter detailing the exact numbers of Polish officers, policemen, nobles, "and others" shot in 1940 in accordance with the findings of an NKVD "troika" (three-person commission). "21,857 persons were shot: in the Katyn forest 4,421 people; in the Starobelsk camp near Kharkov 3,820 people; in the Ostashkovsk camp in the Kalinin region 6,311 people; and 7,305 people were shot in other camps and prisons of western Ukraine and western Belorussia."

The figure I had always heard quoted in reference to those killings was approximately 15,000. Now, sitting at my desk at home, I sud-

denly learned from Shelepin's neat, even handwriting that that estimate had omitted 6,857 men. At a loss for what to do with those
victims whose murder fifty-three years earlier was an entirely new
revelation, I telephoned Mark Kramer and asked whether he had
noted those thousands of additional dead men; he replied that he
had. He sounded calm, implying that those of us who study Russia
have to assimilate those kinds of news as a matter of course. And to
be sure, what are 6,857 people compared to the Soviet losses in the
war, which can only be *estimated* at the nearest several million? The
answer to that question, which I have pondered over the years in
many guises, is that when God said, "Thou shalt not kill," He meant
it. Every murder victim deserves to be mourned.

I paced around my study. My hands pulled a prayer book off a
bookshelf, and I walked over to the window. Stumbling over the
English transliteration, I slowly recited the *Kaddish,* the Jewish prayer
for the dead. Fully aware of the irony that some, indeed, many of
those slain Poles had doubtless been the basest kind of anti-Semites, I
nonetheless chanted the words of the ancient prayer as I meditated
on the newly discovered 6,857 victims of the NKVD.

"Since the moment the above-named operation was carried out,"
wrote Shelepin to Khrushchev, "no information about these dossiers
has been given out to anyone; all 21,857 of them remain in the
above-named place [KGB]. For Soviet organs all these files contain
neither operational interest nor historic value. They could hardly be
of genuine interest to our Polish friends (*sic!*)." Warning that "unde-
sirable consequences for our government" could ensue should there
be any publicity about the operation, Shelepin requested permission
to destroy all the dossiers, retaining only the minutes of the meetings
of the three NKVD officials who had sentenced the accused to
death. As it turned out, the files were not destroyed.

In April 1971 the BBC in London had shown a television film
on the Katyn affair at the same time that a book about the Katyn
tragedy had been published in Britain. Foreign Minister Andrei
Gromyko transmitted to the Soviet ambassador in London a draft
of an official response to the British foreign minister. "It cannot
fail to evoke astonishment and dismay that certain circles in
England are once again unearthing insinuations of a Goebbels-like
propaganda in order to cast slurs upon the Soviet Union, whose

people saved Europe from fascist enslavement by spilling their own blood."

Press the pause button. Right here is the cult of the Great Patriotic War at its very worst, conjuring up the blood of those millions of Soviet citizens who actually had died at the hands of the Germans to drown out warranted accusations that even before Hitler had gotten around to such mass slaying, Soviet authorities had committed international atrocities to match those that would be perpetrated by the Nazis.

On March 30, 1976, a shrill memo by three high-level leaders, including Yuri Andropov, who would later succeed Brezhnev as general secretary, expressed indignation at continuing efforts in Poland "to construct 'memorials to the victims of Katyn' with anti-Soviet inscriptions." The memo continued with a warning that the upcoming thirty-fifth anniversary of the "crimes of the German fascists in the Katyn forest"—which Soviet authorities set at the fall of 1976 to correspond with their contention that the enemy had committed those crimes in fall 1941—might intensify such "anti-Soviet provocations." Five years later, in 1981, members of the Solidarity movement in Poland constructed a memorial to the Katyn victims and dated the massacre in 1940. The Polish government confiscated the memorial.

A few years later, Colonel Jaruzelski's regime put up its own monument in the exact spot where the Solidarity memorial had been. The inscription read: "To the Polish soldiers—victims of Hitlerite fascism—reposing in the soil of Katyn."

In May 1987, in the first flush of the Gorbachev phenomenon, a joint Soviet-Polish commission of historians was established to clarify "blank spots" in the history of the relations between the two countries. The following year, a document signed by Eduard Shevardnadze, Aleksandr Yakovlev, Viktor Chebrikov, and Vadim Medvedev, all highly prominent officials in the Gorbachev administration, requested that in the vicinity of the memorial to the slain Polish officers an *additional* monument be erected, to some five hundred Soviet prisoners of war who had later been killed by the "Hitlerites" and buried in the same territory.

Ah, the politics of victimization! In order not to completely lose face when the truth about the murderers came out, the executioners had to remind the world that their countrymen also had suffered at the very same site.

In early March 1989 Valentin Falin, head of the International Section of the Central Committee of the Communist Party of the Soviet Union, addressed a letter to the Central Committee pointing out that the upcoming fiftieth anniversary of the beginning of the war in Poland had brought up some serious concerns in Poland, with Katyn at the top of the list. "Most Poles are convinced that the Polish officers died at the hands of Stalin and Beria, and that the crime itself occurred in the spring of 1940. According to our official version of the events made public in 1944, those officers were shot by the Hitlerites in 1941." The Polish leadership was maneuvering "to somehow satisfy its own public and at the same time avoid Soviet reproaches of disloyalty."

Two weeks later, on March 22, another letter to the Central Committee, titled "About the Question of Katyn," signed by Falin, Foreign Minister Eduard Shevardnadze, and KGB head Vladimir Kriuchkov, presented a calculated and forthright argument for making public the whole truth about the fate of Polish officers and others executed by the NKVD a half-century earlier: the longer the matter drags on, the more of a stumbling block the Katyn question will be in the relations between Poland and the USSR; a brochure put out by the Catholic Church in 1988 had called Katyn one of the most brutal crimes in the history of humankind; other publications suggest that until the Katyn tragedy is brought to light, there cannot be normal relations between Poland and the USSR; the Katyn question is now obscuring Polish interest in the German invasion and outbreak of war in a campaign whose "subtext gives Poles the idea that the Soviet Union is in no way better—and perhaps even worse—than Nazi Germany, and that the Soviet Union is no less responsible for the outbreak of war and even for the military rout of the government of Poland [that had been in power at that time]." Moreover, the longer the Katyn question remains unanswered, the more insistently will the issue of the fates of other Polish officers whose traces were lost in Kharkov and other areas interest the Polish public.

Apparently we cannot avoid an explanation to the government of the PRP [People's Republic of Poland] and Polish society about the tragic affairs of the past. In this instance time is not on our side. Perhaps it would be advisable to say how it really was and who is concretely to blame for what occurred, and with that to close the question. In the final accounting, the costs of such an action will be smaller than the losses we are accumulating from our current inactivity.

April 13, 1990, exactly forty-seven years after Goebbels's radio announcement of the discovery of mass graves in the Katyn Forest, Soviet President Mikhail Gorbachev officially laid the blame for the Katyn massacre on the NKVD and delivered to Wojciech Jaruzelski a collection of pertinent documents. Meanwhile in the Katyn Forest at the site of the executions, a large wooden cross had been set up and a mass was held in memory of all the victims. That is, for all fifteen thousand of them. Mr. Gorbachev's statement had apparently made no mention of the additional 6,857 men who had filled out the statistics in the president's special archive.[9]

TRUTH OR CONSEQUENCES

So truth had come out after all, or rather had been squeezed out like toothpaste from the old-fashioned kind of tube my mother used to buy in the 1950s, a serious-looking brand called Squibb. It was strong-tasting pink stuff that came in a stiff metallic yellow tube that retained the traces of each depression my little fingers made in it. The more the toothpaste came out, the more distorted and wrecked the tube became. In contrast to today's tubes, which neatly smooth themselves out, the tube of Squibb was honest. As the toothpaste squished out, the tube was altered; the more the toothpaste was pushed out, the more the tube's shape changed again until the end, when we threw away a wrinkled metal mess. After being contained, truths emerge in squiggles and blobs, and the pressure of those who force them out puts its stamp both on what comes out and on that which had restrained it.

I say "truth" or "truths," and not "the truth," because perceptions of reality vary. No wife or husband can insist on there being one truthful version of anything and stay married for more than a day. Neither should one expect that truths emerge cleanly or clearly. Real events of the Soviet Union in wartime could no more leap out

undistorted and painlessly than could confessions of adultery in marriage. They come out together with a bloody placenta of shame,
guilt, and recriminations.

"Bury memory like a stone in water—only a bubble or two will
show," reads a Russian proverb. Even during Brezhnev's time bubbles
of truth had kept floating up to the surface along with the flotsam
and jetsam of the Great Patriotic War cult. The Belorussian writer
Ales Adamovich's book, *Out of the Fire,* published in 1977, is a compilation of interviews with survivors of the German occupation of
his homeland, complete with riveting photographs of the interviewees, most of them common folk with tragic histories mapped out
on their lined faces. In his preface, the author articulated his hope
that oral history, "the people's memory, if we record and write it
down in the entire fullness of truth [and] honesty," would have a
salutary effect on literature as whole, because within that popular
memory lives "a genuine measure of pain and truth, beauty and
strength, a moral measure." Two years later Adamovich put out
another book together with the Leningrad writer Daniil Granin,
called *Book of the Blockade.* Another collection of recorded interviews
and reminiscences, this one focused on the great siege of
Leningrad.[10]

Many of those recorded interviews, larded with emotive com-
ments by the authors, were indeed nuggets of truth that mingled
with the posturing, self-congratulatory hyperbole that characterized
the mainstream literature about the war.

Of the books in the oral history genre, my favorite is *The Face of
War Is Not Womanly,* published by a young Belorussian writer,
Svetlana Aleksievich, in 1985. Her interviewees, all women who had
participated in the war effort, pour out their stories with a heartfelt
simplicity that bring the war to life. Maria Timofeevna Savitskaia-
Radyukovich had worked for the underground in the town of Slutsk
and given birth to a baby in 1943, while all around her villages,
together with their inhabitants, were burning up in fires set by the
occupying German forces.

> I had a three-month-old baby and would take it along on mis-
> sions. . . . I brought medicines, bandages and serum from the town,
> putting them between the baby's arms and legs in swaddles. Wounded

soldiers were dying in the forest and I had to go. Nobody else managed to pass the German and police sentries—I alone could do it.

I find it hard even to speak about it now. . . . To make the baby run
temperature and cry, I rubbed it with salt. It would turn red then,
develop a rash and wiggle in its swaddles. I would approach the sentries with the words: 'Typhus, herr, typhus . . . ' They would shout to
chase me away: 'Weg! . . . Weg . . . '

As soon as we passed the sentries, I would enter a forest and cry my
heart out there, groaning with pity for my baby. But in a day or two I
would again have to go through the ordeal . . . [11]

The women Aleksievich interviewed had, of course, all volunteered to serve as nurses, doctors, field surgeons, snipers, sappers,
paratroopers, antiaircraft gunners, fighter pilots, tank drivers, partisan
fighters. Their stories are snippets that frequently follow the same
pattern: inspired by the tales of a Zoya Kosmodemianskaia, or by a
selfless need to serve, or by the fervor of patriotism, a young woman
would throw herself into the war; confronted with the brutal reality
of the front, she would struggle with her own sense of horror and
grief, often weeping incessantly; after a while the tears dried up in
the routine of grisly work. "We lost two crews during the early days
of training," recalled Capt. Klavdiia Terekhova, who had been an airplane pilot. "All the three regiments, all of us sobbing, stood in front
of the four coffins. . . . Afterwards, at the front, we did not cry when
we buried our dead."

Maria Smirnova was a medical orderly from Kazakhstan: "When I
crawled under shellfire for the first time to help a wounded soldier, I
cried and it seemed to me that my crying was louder than the roar of
the battle. Then I got accustomed to it. . . . In about ten days I was
wounded, I myself extracted the fragment and dressed the wound."

One of the most poignant recorded conversations in Aleksievich's
volume was a dialogue with a male veteran she had met on a train.
He talked about how unfairly he and others had treated those
women volunteers after the war was over:

"There were many good-looking girls among those at the
front. . . . But we did not look upon them as women, although, in my
opinion, they were wonderful girls. We looked on them as friends."

"Didn't you like them?"

"What do you mean? They were our friends, who carried us from the battlefield. I was thus carried on two occasions when I was wounded. How could I not like them? But you don't marry your own sister, do you? They were our sisters."

"And after the war?"

"Once the war was over, they turned out to be frightfully defenseless. . . . Take, for instance, my wife. She is a wonderful woman and I've lived heart to heart with her for thirty-five years now. And she, too, is of a very low opinion of the girls who had gone to the front. She thinks that they went there to look for husbands and that all of them had affairs there. Though in real fact—and I'm telling it to you quite sincerely—they were modest girls. But after the war every one of us went his own way." Nikolai Borisovich grew pensive. "You won't be able to understand it. We longed for something beautiful after all the filth, lice and deaths. We wanted beautiful women. . . . I had a friend who was loved at the front by, as I see it now, a wonderful girl, a nurse. But he did not marry her after demobilisation but found another, perhaps prettier, girl. He is very unhappy with his wife . . . and is now recalling the other one, who would have been his friend. And yet he had no desire to marry her after they had been at the front together. For four years in a row he had seen her in the down-at-heels boots and a man's quilted jacket. . . . And he wanted to forget about the war as soon as possible. We tried to forget everything. And we also forgot our wartime girlfriends. . . . "[12]

Other bubbles of truth that rose to the surface during the pre-perestroika period had taken the form of song. The two beloved, indeed, wildly popular singers of the Brezhnev era, the crooner Bulat Okudzhava and the raspy, Bob Dylanesque Vladimir Vysotsky—who in 1980 drank himself to death at age forty-two—had both composed and performed wonderfully rich songs about the war in all its facets. Until the mid-eighties or later, most of them had not been accepted into the official mainstream culture. But by Gorbachev's time, the words of Okudzhava songs graced the front pages of the central press on Victory Day, and in 1990 one of his melodies was even played in the celebratory military parade in Red Square.

Bulat Okudzhava had fought in the war as a sergeant, and his many poems and songs about those years betray a deep but gentle realism. "Boys—try to return! Don't hide yourselves, stand tall, don't spare either bullets or shells, and don't spare yourselves, but still try to return!"[13]

Vysotsky was only seven years old in 1945. Nonetheless, he composed many of his numerous songs about the war in the first person. "I write about the war not because I remember it," he once said. "We have all been brought up on the war; I come from a military family and lost many relatives in the war, as we all did in this country. But I write about those times simply because it is challenging to write about people who are in the most extreme circumstances, at a moment of risk; in the next second they might be staring death in the face. I readily find such people in such situations in those times. That is why I write so much about the war."[14]

The *glasnost* revelations were slow to make their way to the bottom of the ravine at Babi Yar. In 1987 the first and only film on the Babi Yar massacre produced in the Soviet Union was shown on Soviet television. It was aired only once, recalled the journalist Vitaly Korotich, who had been instrumental in making that film in 1981. In June 1993 I bought a videotaped copy of it in the gift shop of the newly opened United States Holocaust Memorial Museum in Washington, D.C.

"This film may be considered a work of Soviet Propaganda," warns the text on the sleeve of the video. In fact, the movie is a head-spinning mixture of truth and artifice. Korotich, a Kievan by birth who had spent the war in that city as a child, narrates the story, which is a tapestry of documentary footage, interviews with some of the few remaining survivors of the atrocities, and classic Soviet overdone cinematography, heavy with colored filters and bodies rolling down the ravine in slow motion to the sound of swelling choral music. The text that Korotich reads as a voice-over is an indictment of German fascism but also of "fascism" the world over. Equating Nazism and the Babi Yar massacre to American racism and Israeli Zionism, the film brings in footage of Ku Klux Klanners burning crosses, American and German neo-Nazis, and United States bombers dropping napalm on Vietnamese children, who writhe on the ground in an agony of flames.

The massacre of Jews in Babi Yar is specifically mentioned, and the film even shows and reads out the order published in the fall 1941 newspapers, commanding "all Yids" to come to a specific site in Kiev, with their valuables and belongings. "We all thought we were going to be sent on a journey," recalled a survivor. In fact, even though the huge stream of people moved in the direction of the railroad station, it was herded on to Babi Yar, where the people's belongings were taken from them before they were ordered to strip. Then they were shot.

The text says that Jews were slaughtered at the dread ravine for the first five days, but for the remaining hundreds of days of the German occupation, Soviet citizens of all nationalities were massacred there—Russians, Ukrainians, Jews, Kazakhs—for the crime of being Soviet.

The implication: the Soviet people suffered more than anyone else during the war; and they were united in death as in life. In the film Korotich stated that the remains of approximately two hundred thousand Soviet citizens reposed under the grassy knoll at Babi Yar, including the ashes of those many thousands who were incinerated after having been killed in mobile gas chambers.

"We put all kinds of things into the film to get it past the censor," explained Korotich in 1993. "But we failed anyway; the film was not allowed to be shown, and only in 1987, when I had become prominent as editor of *Ogonek* [an illustrated weekly magazine that enjoyed vast popularity during the *glasnost* period] did I succeed, through an enormous effort, to get the film shown on television—once. But then, while the film would have made a profound impact in 1981, which was a terrible period of cold war and official anti-Semitism, it was not quite right for 1987."

"Tell me something," asked Korotich hopefully, "does the film evoke only negative feelings? Watching it can you feel the film makers' deep respect for the subject? Remember, this was the first and only film made about Babi Yar, and the first forum to recognize publicly that huge number of Jews had been slaughtered there."

After speaking with Korotich, I watched the film again. "They were trying to kill memory," pronounced Korotich, speaking of the Germans, while the screen showed bulldozers turning over soil mingled with human remains. And what had Korotich and his fellow filmmakers been trying to do?

They had been trying to squeeze some truth out of a vessel they could not touch—they had not been given access to relevant archives. And they had felt constrained to weave that truth into a tapestry that would adequately serve the functions of the cult of the Great Patriotic War. What happened at Babi Yar had to emphasize the unique nature of the wrong done to the *Soviet* people, and by implication confirm that people's sole right to judge itself and the rest of the world.

The fiftieth anniversary of the Babi Yar massacre was commemorated in October 1991, an act of official recognition by the government of Ukraine that one hundred thousand people, most of them Jews, had been slain by the Germans at what had then been a gaping ravine. Israeli guests had been invited to the ceremony, and streamers that read NEVER AGAIN in Ukrainian and Hebrew had been put up in the streets of Kiev. A few days before the event a large menorah of bronze was erected at the site where the Germans had killed thirty-three thousand Jews in thirty-six hours beginning on September 29, 1941. "People don't have the right to forget," said Aleksandr Shlayen, a filmmaker who had made two documentary films on Babi Yar. "They simply don't have that right."[15]

DESACRALIZATION

"Right now," said Mikhail Gefter as we sat on little wooden chairs in the lush, fragrant, and Russianly overgrown garden of the dacha he was renting in the summer of 1989, "especially since the historic Congress of People's Deputies that met in May and June and irrevocably changed the face of Soviet politics, we are witnessing a massive *desacralization* of the Soviet leadership and Soviet state, a process that has touched even Gorbachev himself as well as formerly sacrosanct institutions such as the KGB and the army." This process had also begun to erode the fundamental symbols and myths that had for so many decades shaped the higher reality in whose name the Communist Party and Soviet government had operated. By 1990 the generalized desacralization had reached the two great legitimizing myths that had long sustained the Communist Party's mandate to rule. The first was the cult of Lenin as the dynamo of revolutionary change, brilliant architect of the Soviet government, and immortal author of precepts that could forever be a lodestar for keeping the ship of state on course through the dangerous waters of the ongoing conlict with the capitalist world. The other ravaged myth was that of the Great Patriotic War.

Almost fifty years after the invasion, the winds of *glasnost* and *perestroika* had demolished that sonorous combination of self-pity and self-congratulation that for so long had characterized the official memorialization of the war. The bronzed saga of the Great Patriotic War was being replaced with raw human memory. "Our understanding of the war," observed Mikhail Gefter, "is being transformed from a heroic farce to the tragedy that it really was." And the loss of this shared memory had left many Soviet people in the throes of a spiritual crisis to match the political and economic shocks that had sent their country spinning toward chaos, a crisis that had been brewing for many years.

In June 1989, Nikolai Volkov, an official at the Soviet Committee of War Veterans, his silver-studded teeth glinting in the shafts of spring sun that had found their way into his little Moscow office, leaned forward in his chair and with great animation assured me that the forty-fifth anniversary of the victory in 1990 would be commemorated with great fanfare. "At the fortieth anniversary our country had seven and one-half million veterans. There are now about five million left and our numbers are rapidly diminishing. For most of us the forty-fifth will be our last. It must be memorable."

But by May 1990 hard times had arrived. Really hard times. The Union of Soviet Socialist Republics had melted down into an unhappy collection of warring nationalities. As in earlier upheavals in the seventeenth and eighteenth centuries, social protest and brigandage, often indistinguishable from each other, had permeated the polity with a lurking sense of danger and the nearness of chaos. Violent crime had increased dramatically. The Soviet Army was rife with revolt: senior officers denounced Gorbachev's "sellout" to the West; junior officers were calling for the army's liberation from the tutelage of the Party; soldiers—and their anguished mothers—demanded an end to the grisly hazing of new recruits that in recent years had killed thousands of youths. Non-Russian soldiers, especially representatives of rebellious nationalities, such as Lithuanians, were prey to vicious beatings by other soldiers and frustrated officers. The Communist Party of the Soviet Union, which for decades had claimed most of the credit for the victory in the war, was in utter disarray. The socialist economic system, also previously touted as largely responsible for the victory, had collapsed, as evidenced by the infamous "empty shelves" syndrome in the shops. With dizzying speed Eastern Europe had overthrown Soviet-imposed communist regimes, and the Germanies were busy uniting.

The *glasnost*-inspired national mania for new and ever more gruesome details about the terror of the thirties that had long oversaturated the media had abated somewhat. The de-Stalinization compulsion now extended to war-related themes, as the desacralization process that inexorably followed the early stages of the Gorbachev reforms irretrievably eroded the cult of the Great Patriotic War, along with the last vestiges of authority represented by the Communist Party.

The roseate version of the war experience had been a carefully orchestrated symphony in a major key, promoting an image of national harmony and unity. But now that symphony was drowned out by a cacophonous clamor of voices, memories, and passions. The war had become a prism that refracted an entire spectrum of emotions unleashed by five years of *perestroika* and the most fundamental social disintegration.

The mass of Soviet people who not so long ago had genuinely believed the official hype about how well they all lived, or at any rate, how wonderfully well they would be living soon, now saw themselves as pitifully poor. "We live like beggars. There is nothing in our stores, nothing. And our former enemies are living like kings. So for what kind of victory did we sacrifice tens of millions of Soviet lives?" an old veteran asked me as we strolled down Gorky Street shortly after my arrival in Moscow a few days before the May 1990 commemoration of the forty-fifth anniversary of the victory of the Soviet people in the Great Patriotic War.

In eastern and central Europe, symbol bashing, both figuratively and literally, became something of a national sport in the 1989 revolutions, as angry crowds toppled statues of Soviet sacred cows. Within the Soviet Union, especially in the breakaway Baltic states and non-Russian republics, the previously untouchable image of Vladimir Ilich Lenin was now up for grabs quite literally, as statues of the Founder of Bolshevism were dismantled and carted away. For the Moldavian and Baltic republics, de-Stalinization meant an end to the

domination that was the product of an illegitimate, clandestine agreement between Hitler and Stalin. In some of those regions newly
constructed monuments to the local militiamen who had fought on
the side of the Nazis stood in dramatic apposition to the Brezhnevite
myth about the unity and gratitude of all peoples saved from fascist
slavery by the self-sacrificial effort of the Red Army. The implicit
statement: even German fascist rule would have been better than the
hated heel of Moscow.

Secession from the Soviet Union had become a logical—indeed,
the only logical—consequence of de-Stalinization. And it underscored Stalin's silent but mighty presence in the legends about the
Great Patriotic War that had continued to inform the popular consciousness of the Russian people until well into the 1980s.

In early May 1990 I returned to Moscow to witness the celebration
of the forty-fifth anniversary of the victory. The city felt solemn and
hard-edged, with none of the ready-for-a-party feel I had found at
the 1985 commemoration of the fortieth. The conspicuous absence
from Moscow buildings and streets of the usual megaholiday slogans,
gargantuan posters, and omnipresent red bunting was perhaps
indicative of the management's nerves following a May Day coun-
terdemonstration in Red Square at which people jeered Gorbachev,
shouting, among other things, "Hands off Lithuania!"

The fortieth had marked the climax of the Great Patriotic War
cult; at the forty-fifth, the cult was manifestly finished as an institution. In 1985, of the dozens of commemorative posters for sale in
Dom knigi (House of Books), Moscow's largest bookstore, I remember one with special vividness. Entitled *"Pobeda"* (victory), it depicted the face and upper torso of a young soldier who, in a visual short-
hand, represented the old view of the victory. The boy was clean,
handsome, and stocky, with adorable, regular features and a smiling,
dimpled, pudgy face vaguely reminiscent of Yuri Gagarin, the first
man to go into space. He was supposed to be an Everyman version
of the Boys who Brought us Victory, but he looked so clear-eyed,
innocent, proud, and stupid that you couldn't imagine his ever having seen combat. In May 1990 *Dom knigi* was selling only a handful
of posters honoring the victory. I bought them all. The one that best
symbolized the new approach to the war also showed a soldier close

up. Although he was clumsily drawn, you could see that this man had gone through four years of war. He was middle-aged, with a bandaged head, lined face, and sad, weary eyes.

A RUSSIAN WAR

Situated in the broad expanse between the Kremlin and what was in 1990 still called the Lenin Library, Moscow's Central Exhibition Hall, the Manezh, is a fine example of early-nineteenth-century Muscovite architecture, with thick walls the color of beaten eggs stretching out over an entire city block and an elegant, neoclassical facade punctuated with fat white columns. When I had visited Moscow five years earlier for the 1985 jubilee, the Manezh had predictably displayed the traditional all-Union exhibition of commemorative art. Filled with resolute soldiers and grieving mothers, it was a collection of the worst kind of romantic, military kitsch and featured an enormous mosaic of Marshals Zhukov and Rokossovskii on white and black horses, respectively.

Now, in 1990, the same building held a quite different exhibition, indeed, the first of its kind. Entitled "Defenders of the Fatherland," it was an all-*Russian* collection of art devoted to the victory. Its organizer was Col. Nikolai Solomin, the smallish, brown-haired gentleman in early middle age whom I had met previously at the Grekov studio of military art. He took me firmly by the elbow and steered me through the vast hall, percolating with great enthusiasm in fast-paced, melodious prose.

The Manezh exhibit underscored new forces at work in the army. It was a Russian affair, reflecting the nationalism that had become the army's main claim to legitimacy in the previous year or so. Far from restricting itself to the usual 1941–45 period, "Defenders of the Fatherland," as my voluble host proudly pointed out to me, opened with icons of Alexander Nevsky, the grand prince who defeated the Teutonic Knights in the thirteenth century and moved through the later wars against Tatars, Poles, Lithuanians, and Swedes. There was a magnificent display of nineteenth-century art commemorating the Patriotic War against the French. And at the end ranged a motley collection of works paying homage to the Great Patriotic War. Gone were the familiar battle scenes. Most of the more recent paintings had no visible relationship to the war at all. They showed mainly lovely, peaceful landscapes of villages and churches in the style of romantic nationalism so popular today. As a token to *glasnost,* the far corner of the exhibition hall included a small display of dissident posters protesting Stalinism and the war's tens of millions of needless losses.

When I asked Solomin why the exhibition was all-Russian and not representative of the whole Soviet Union, even though every republic had sent fighters to the front, he answered that the artist unions of some of the republics had declined to participate in the exhibition. But Mikhail Gefter, to whom I later recounted my experience in the Manezh, assured me that Solomin had not been forthcoming. "Take a look at the outrageous things that have happened to the *Voenno-istoricheskii zhurnal* [*Journal of Military History*] in the past year or so. It has become ultra-nationalistic and openly anti-Semitic in an effort to gain support for the army among the nation's most reactionary forces. The cause of Russian nationalism is what the all-Russian exhibition was about!"[16]

The next day, May 8, 1990, I saw the army's strident nationalism at work again at a meeting to honor those employees of Moscow's Museum of the Armed Forces who had fought in the war. After a number of flowery speeches, the veterans each came up to the stage to receive gifts featuring a glossy book of Russian and Soviet military medals. (As a foreign guest, I too received a copy of the book and made an appropriately flowery speech of my own.)

After decades of disassociating themselves from early and imperial Russian heroes, Soviet wartime propagandists in 1941 had appealed to the memories of ancient warriors and tsarist generals to mobilize the spirits of the Soviet people at a time of utmost crisis. By 1990, with republic after republic protecting its boys from the draft, liberal officers demanding true *perestroika,* and senior officers deploring the collapse of discipline in the army and the country at large, the Soviet Army was confronted with a crisis of authority greater than any it had encountered since the war. And its leaders had responded much as Stalin did fifty years ago, by sidestepping the bankrupt communist ideals in favor of the atavistic pull of the vast Russian land and its bloody history.[17]

RAVAGED RITUALS

The hollowness of Party propaganda and the flabby remnants of the war cult were nowhere better evident than in Moscow's 110th School, in whose muddy courtyard stood Daniil Mitlianskii's Requiem, the modest and graceful monument dedicated to his school chums who died at the front. In addition to a yearly commemoration on June 22 by teachers, students, and alumni, on May 8, the day before Victory Day, students would go, class by class, to lay flowers on the monument's pedestal. And on Victory Day itself, it was traditional for them to meet with veterans, especially those who were alumni of their school, and present them with small bouquets of flowers.

On the forty-fifth, the children were not buying into any part of those rituals. During the flower laying in the courtyard not even the older ones could muster up a few moments of respectful silence following the teacher's canned little speech about "that generation to whom we owe so much." When one boy made believe he was going to eat his flower instead of placing it at the foot of the monument, the teacher slapped him across the face.

After witnessing this most unsatisfying scene, I persuaded Marina Smaragdova, the plump teacher and curator of the school's little museum, to let me spend an hour in charge of her class of seventh-graders. At the beginning of the hour another teacher came into the classroom and reminded the children to show up the next day at the designated meeting with veterans. "I don't want to see a repeat of last year's sorry performance, when not a single one of you turned out!" she warned in a nasty tone of voice. After she left, the children told me they would not spend their holiday putting on school uniforms and going out to greet the veterans. "We feel silly doing it and besides, why should our parents have to pay for the flowers?" said one intelligent-looking boy with big glasses.

In May 1990 even the gaggles of bemedaled veterans that five years earlier, at the fortieth, had dominated the downtown streets of the capital were hardly in evidence. Many had died or become too ill to travel to Moscow or to go out at all. Others had left their medals and *znachki* (small, commemorative metal badges) at home. No one was wearing *znachki* anymore, although kiosks and souvenir shops still carried them. They smacked of the old order, when you were supposed to wear your loyalty on your sleeve, or rather, on your chest, as little Pioneers did in sporting *znachki* depicting the cherubic face of three-year-old Volodia Ulianov (Lenin) embedded in a red plastic five-pointed star. As for the military medals that so many veterans had worn with pride in years past, in many quarters they were no longer socially acceptable.

I had already noted by the end of the 1980s that veterans were choosing not to wear their medals, or even their battle stripes, in public to avoid ridicule or criticism. As early as the spring of 1988, my colleague Yuri Volchok, an architectural historian, told me that his father, a decorated Muscovite veteran, had pinned his medals onto his suit jacket on the morning of an afternoon veterans' meeting and had then gone about his business. He had returned that evening with the medals in his pocket, and quietly announced that he would never again take them out of their box. "Someone on the street had made a derisive comment to my father about flaunting his medals," Yuri explained. "He was devastated."

"OLD AGE IS NO JOY" (RUSSIAN PROVERB)

In 1980 the Brezhnev regime had for the first time granted special privileges to Soviet veterans of World War II. Veterans of front (who had fought) and labor (who had worked in the rear) were issued cards that entitled them to go to the head of food lines and other queues, and to ride on public transportation free of charge. Later in the decade, veterans got the right to buy special foodstuffs not available to the general public.

From the first, those privileges irritated members of the general public, all the more so because those little benefits were accompanied by an organized homage—sometimes specious, sometimes genuine— to those who fought in the war. Veterans, for example, were now routinely brought to the nation's schools and, after introductions of purple prose, were invited to recount their battle sagas before young audiences who had a hard time suppressing their yawns.

"My mother was never at the front, and she didn't work in war industry," a taxi driver explained to me en route to a Moscow veterans' hospital where my great-uncle Saadia was convalescing. "But," he continued, "she ran herself ragged trying to feed her children in our Urals region evacuation, where there was far less food than at the front. She worked and suffered as much as any veteran. Why shouldn't she be entitled to privileges too?"

As a woman—and a mother—I wholeheartedly agreed with the driver, who was about my age. Most veterans are men, although, as everywhere, the majority of elderly citizens are women struggling to survive on meager pensions. The advantages given to veterans continue the favoritism of men over women that always characterized Soviet society.

Moreover, the veterans' access to coveted goods and conveniences had exacerbated an already troublesome tension between the generations that, like so much else, gained freer expression when, by the end of the decade, *glasnost*—and a growing disdain for the military—combined with almost unprecedented shortages of consumer goods to make tempers short. Again and again I read in the Soviet press letters from indignant veterans, complaining of shabby treatment by their compatriots.

In April 1990, some three weeks before Victory Day, the weekly newspaper, *Soviet Culture* (*Sovetskaia kultura*) published a typical protest. "I walked, limping (my wounded leg was hurting) and hesitantly placed myself at the head of a taxi queue at the Kievskii Railroad Station," began the author, Grigorii Pozhenian. "'Look at the *vova*,' curtly remarked a woman with a string bag."

The derisive term *vova* came from the acronym for the words *Velikaia Otechestvennaia Voina* (Great Patriotic War). "Where do you think you're coming from?" snapped one of the people on line to whom the author showed his veteran's card.

"As a rule, I almost never avail myself of my insignificant privileges," wrote Mr. Pozhenian, "since they elicit only humiliation and insults." He went on to say that he prided himself on his service in the navy, on his father's heroic participation in the Civil War, and on the military exploits of his comrades.

"I yearn to hear military bands in our parks, to have the military uniform—which we never betrayed—no longer be an object of shame. '*Vovy*' indeed! Like mammoths we are disappearing from the face of the earth. We limp, get sick, forget things, repeat ourselves. We cling to our battle stripes, our wounds and medals, only because they dare to demean us with pitiful privileges, pitiful pensions, vacant glances."[18]

As the spring of 1990 progressed and the social fabric increasingly unraveled, intergenerational strains intensified. On the evening of Victory Day, Liuba Dikov, a twenty-two-year-old Muscovite acquaintance with a terrific eye for relationship dynamics, recounted a scene she had witnessed in a dry-cleaning establishment. She was waiting to be served along with about a dozen other people, while the staff, an assortment of wrinkled, stubbly-face men in dirty suits and tired, round-faced old women in faded, flowered dresses, sat around with their hands folded over their large bellies and made no move to help the customers.

Suddenly an irate man of about thirty holding a bag of clothes in need of cleaning shook his fist at the old people and shouted, "Why doesn't someone take these clothes? You're all too lazy even to get up! You, old folks, it was *you* who stuck us with this terrible life, you who ruined everything for us!"

"What did we ruin?" countered one of the men. "We suffered, we fought for you and our country."

"And what kind of life did you fight for?" retorted the young man angrily. "Fascism couldn't have been any worse!"

In part because of such scenes and the intense passion with which public debate had been flaring up at the slightest instigation, some of my Muscovite friends predicted that the forty-fifth victory anniversary might present an occasion for more social turbulence.

From the Thrill of Victory to the Agony of Defeat

On the eve of the holiday, President Mikhail Gorbachev delivered his keynote address before an assembly of dignitaries and honorees. Departing from the traditional title for this speech, "The Immortal Exploit of the Soviet People," he had titled this one "The Lessons of the War and Victory."

The tone of this speech differed radically from that of previous anniversaries. From the very start Gorbachev emphasized the tragic aspect of the war. "Tomorrow," he began, "is one of the very brightest and most tragic of our holidays." He toned down talk about socialism, focusing rather on the laudable patriotic sentiments of the war generation. The Communist Party hardly figured in the speech. Instead the president singled out categories of ordinary Soviet citizens who had helped bring the country to victory, including teachers, writers, actors, composers, and filmmakers. The leader's previous pecking order of thanks to the fighting forces was reversed, with the Western allies mentioned first. And he dwelled at length on the "colossal loss" his country had suffered, on the staggering cost of the victory in human lives.

Mr. Gorbachev acknowledged that the truth about the cost of the victory had become terribly difficult to even utter. But it was also impossible to keep silent about it. He asked those gathered to rise in memory of the fallen and said that the war had carried off nearly twenty-seven million Soviet people, not counting the wounded, frostbitten, and shell-shocked. "On this forty-fifth," added Gorbachev, "let us remember those about whom there was silence for long decades, who had been illegally stripped of their honorable names and their citizenship rights, and locked up in camps." Labor camp inmates, continued Gorbachev, "had also contributed to the war effort through their work in the mines and forests of Siberia." He also remembered the engineers and technicians who had been forced to work behind barbed wire in special institutes. "We repeat," intoned Gorbachev, "no one is forgotten and nothing is forgotten. This is not a call for vengeance. It is spoken as a remembrance from the heart, which is what makes a human being human . . . "

After inviting the audience to sit down, Gorbachev talked about the necessity of understanding the lessons of the war. How was it that the Soviet Union, which was the first country to articulate the extent of fascism as a threat, was itself so unprepared for the aggression when it came? (This was the strongest admission by a Soviet leader of his country's lack of preparedness for the war). What explains the number and degree of our defeats? Why was the road to victory so difficult and why did we sacrifice so much?

The explanations proffered by Mr. Gorbachev included observations that had never before fallen from the lips of a Soviet leader in a public speech. Chances for a prewar alliance with the West had partly been subverted by the Western countries' aversion to the "repressions" (purge and Great Terror) of the thirties. The Soviet-German nonaggression pact had been a mistake in many respects, and the consequent delay in the invasion by Germany had not been properly utilized. The Red Army had been ill-equipped and its officer corps decimated by Stalin's repressions. Stalin had not heeded the warnings of imminent attack by Germany, and when the invasion did come, he refused to believe the news and take appropriate actions.

Gorbachev did add, however, that for all of Stalin's mistakes, it would be wrong to underestimate the dictator's commendable performance as commander in chief and head of the State Defense Council, "which did play its own role."

In describing the course of the war itself, Mr. Gorbachev reversed the previously enshrined official pattern of depicting the entire post-Stalingrad phase as a positive movement toward victory, and admitted that there had been defeats and setbacks as late as 1945. He also acknowledged that in plotting the course of the war, the general staff had not always tried to minimize the sacrifice in human lives. The president toned down the impact of such remarks by weaving in plenty of phrases from the war cult: "We broke the backbone of the aggressor at the Kursk salient."

What then was the source of the victory? It was not the enormous size of the country, nor bad roads, nor severe frosts. It was not because we were prepared to spill any amount of blood necessary to achieve victory. The main source of victory was the Soviet people, who united to face the enemy together. This was a people's war. There had been a true fraternity of nations. All nations in the union contributed to the victory, and Stalin had been wrong in considering some nations to be traitorous.

Only toward the end of this list did Gorbachev mention the Communist Party, and he emphasized not its leadership but the rank-and-file members.

Moving to the postwar period and into the present, Mr. Gorbachev focused on the nearly six million surviving veterans of the front, many of whom were invalids, and on the estimated twenty-three million veterans of the rear, who had contributed their labor to the war effort. "We have put up many monuments in honor of the Victory. We are still putting them up today." But more important is the well-being of veterans and their families. Almost two years ago, continued the president, veterans of front and labor received various material privileges. Now, in accordance with a decision made by the first Congress of People's Deputies, the minimum pension has been raised for veterans and for families of those who died at the front. In all, the government has spent nearly one billion rubles on veterans' benefits.

The conclusion of the speech came full circle to its title. The lessons of the war and victory were as follows: "a people who was victorious in this war is capable of overcoming any difficulties and resolving any problems; a people who endured such a war cannot but wish for peace with all its soul; in today's affairs and cares, let us remember the lessons of the war and victory."

No less than his predecessors, Mikhail Sergeevich Gorbachev sought in his own version of the World War II myth salvation from a troubled reality, or at the very least, something of a model with which to cure the diseased body politic. Forty-five years after the victory, the people of the Soviet Union were living through a time of troubles as terrifying as any they had confronted since the war. The breakdown of the economy, the utter despoliation of the environment, the fear of civil war, the loss of their status as a global superpower, the collapse of every legitimizing myth that had bound them together had led to menacing societal atomization.

A DAY OF GRACE

On Victory Day 1990 brilliant sunshine added dazzle to the military parade in Red Square, which was doubtless held to placate the army leadership. Veterans marching in Red Square were followed by military units parading in synchronized blocks to the sound of sprightly band music interspersed with haunting wartime marches. Then came the antique tanks, roaring and spewing foul-smelling smoke; the first one to rumble into Red Square bore the words "1941, Motherland." As always, the minister of defense rode around the square in a convertible, exchanging ritualized greetings with massed blocks of troops, and then delivered a brief, entirely predictable speech from atop the Lenin Mausoleum. The parade's highlight was a magnificent float, a live tableau of the famed monument to Soviet soldiers in Berlin, of the Russian soldier saving a little German girl. On the float was a real giant of a man in a soldier's uniform, clasping a real little girl dressed in white.

The parade was short and, by the standards of totalitarian kitsch, decidedly modest, quite unlike the extravaganza at the fortieth, five years earlier. (The presence in the parade stands of the comedian Bob Hope, resplendent in white shoes and a baseball cap, added a surreal twist to the proceedings; he and his wife happened to be the guests of United States Ambassador, the Hon. Jack F. Matlock, Jr.)

As I tried to get the best view of the proceedings, teetering on a stone ledge to the left of the mausoleum and only a few feet from a line of elegantly uniformed KGB guards, I sensed that I was witnessing the swan song of the cult of the Great Patriotic War. The swagger, the self-congratulation, the hyperbole about the USSR having defeated the enemy single-handedly were already missing. And the old hype about the victory proving the superiority of socialism would have been laughable, in view of its recent and painful collapse.

The informal meetings of veterans in front of the Bolshoi Theater and in Gorky Park were subdued and only partly focused on the Great Patriotic War. For the first time in anyone's memory, uniformed *afgantsy,* young veterans of the decade-long embroilment in Afghanistan, some of them in wheelchairs, made their appearance at a Victory Day celebration. According to tradition, old folks sang war songs on the steps of the Bolshoi; only fifty yards away, young adults danced in graceful pairs, while others belted out Russian folk songs that had become so popular in the revived nationalism of the day.

Some people still bore placards pleading for information about their missing fathers, brothers, grandfathers, front buddies. I saw a man, no longer young, with a face utterly void of emotion, standing stock-still in the Bolshoi Theater park and holding a sign asking for information about his father, whose wartime photograph showed a handsome young soldier with the same vacant face. A passer-by told me in a whisper that every year, for as long as he could remember, that soldier's widow had held up that same photograph in exactly the same spot in the park; now the son had taken over, so the old woman was presumably infirm, or dead.

In Gorky Park I threw a ten-ruble note into an enormous plastic bowl half-filled with money being collected for a planned *kniga pamiati* (book of memory) listing the names of every single victim of the Great Patriotic War. No mention here of the victory. Just an effort to pay respects to the war dead.

That night I dined at the home of the writer Elena Rzhevskaia, who was an interpreter during the war and had helped locate Hitler's bunker. "Victory Day is the only holiday we have left. No one is going to take it away from us," she said. At 6:50 we clicked on the television set, expecting to see the familiar flickering flame of the Tomb of the Unknown Soldier and hear the unctuous voice of the high priest of the war cult extolling the glory of the victory and its bitter costs in the annual Victory Day television service. What we saw instead was an unspeakably moving collage of scenes depicting wartime horrors. The narrator reminded his viewers of the current turbulence in the country and called upon them to find in the memory of the war a source of healing and reconciliation. "Let us free our hearts of anger and spite," we heard. "Before their common grave, let us forgive one another." Waves of choral singing filled the cozy kitchen.

Astonishingly, the text included references to the Jewish contribution to the war effort and refrained from singling out the Communist Party as the most valued segment of wartime society. "Everyone is equal in war, in death—man and woman, general and soldier, communist and non-communist, Russian, Lithuanian, Uzbek, Jew . . . " We looked at each other. What a dramatic end to the pervasive Soviet silence about the Jewish contribution to the war effort!

At ten o'clock, I was back in Red Square to watch the fireworks. *"Ura!"* the crowd shouted with each explosion. "Hooray!" There were forty-five salvos, one for each year of peace. Everyone I spoke to agreed that Victory Day 1990 had been a day of healing and of genuine commemoration. For the first time in months, the street crowds in Moscow were not shouting and scuffling in anger. They had been reveling in the beautiful spring weather, in a day off from work, and, perhaps, in the memory of a time, decades ago, when their country was united, striving toward a common goal.

"I just shopped around in my neighborhood stores today," Rzhevskaia's son-in-law had said at dinner. "But I could sense the magnitude of the holiday. It was bigger than Victory Day. It was for all of us a respite from our daily struggles and gloom. It was a day of grace."

8

RUSSIA REMEMBERS THE WAR

By 1990, as the Soviet period of Russian history was drawing to a close, the cult of the Great Patriotic War had been replaced by a rich amalgam of passion, regret, nostalgia, rage, and remembrance. A few days before Victory Day 1990, a newspaper article entitled "Stolen Victory" brought into high relief some of the most sensitive questions tugging at the war myth. It began with a conversation that had recently taken place between two elderly veterans: "We've given away Germany, we've given away Europe—for what then did we lay down so many lives during the war?"

"What's there to discuss?" responded the other veteran, "they've stolen our Victory, and that's the whole story."

Did Soviet people really believe that their country had fought fascism in order to take over half of Europe? Gennadii Bordiugov, a scholarly commentator interviewed in the article, was not surprised at this reaction to the recent liberation of Europe: "Our sea of spilled blood was too vast, our wounds too deep to expect our people, especially those who fought, to respond to the events in East Europe without pain." But he went on to assert that in fact the victory *had* been stolen from the people—by Stalin and his system—on the very day of the victory, May 9, 1945. For Stalin, the imperative to rein in the anti-Stalinist and anti-Party sentiments in the country at large had been at least as important a goal as defeating fascism. In the end, "Who was victorious and who was conquered, who won the war against whom, if the vanquished are now sending food to the victors?"[1]

A united Germany supplying an impoverished Soviet Union with food! Who could have predicted it five or even three years earlier? Who was victorious indeed? More than once in 1990 I had heard young people (including Jews) assert that it would have been better had Hitler won the war, contending that a fascist regime would have been no worse, and probably better, than the Soviet system that had brought them nothing but frustration and grief. Such inanities were not common, but many members of the intelligentsia had, in fact, come to equate communism and fascism, Stalin and Hitler.

Soviet publications and films about the war had become relentless in their drive to reveal the ugliest aspects of the war and, in particular, Stalin's brutality toward his own populace. Early in 1990 *Shtrafniki,* a documentary film by Lev Danilov, created a major stir. It graphically detailed the wartime fates of some of the notorious punishment battalions (*shtrafnye bataliony* for officers, *shtrafnye roty* for soldiers) of former political prisoners and other "undesirables," who were sent on the most dangerous, often suicidal missions, followed by commissars pointing guns at their backs to make sure they followed orders. The film also underscored the work of those dread so-called *zagraditelnye otriady* (defensive detachments) of former border or NKVD guards, established after the summer 1942 "Not a Step Back" order, to prevent acts of "cowardice"—like surrendering to the enemy when surrounded. The writer Viacheslav Kondratiev wrote a sympathetic review of *Shtrafniki* that he titled "Pariahs of the War." "How many were killed on reconnaissance by the Germans, and how many by the bullets of our own defensive detachments, we will probably never know. . . . Poor, unfortunate Russia, the poor, unfortunate Russian people that has had to live through all this . . . "[2]

Kondratiev, a tall, lean figure whose expressive mouth is a patchwork of nicotine-stained yellow-and-brown teeth marked by gaps, returned after twenty years to the environs of Rzhev, where he had served as a soldier during the war. As he told me in an interview some thirty years later, when I myself was about to go to Rzhev to search for unburied war dead, "When in 1961 I was on my way to visit the Rzhev front area for the first time since the war, I felt like I was going to a lovers' tryst—I knew I would be overwhelmed by powerful emotions, as indeed I was." But the experience he got was unexpected. The writer was shocked to find the former battle zone littered with the remains of his dead comrades and after a number of years wrote the famed novella *Sashka,* about a teenager who finds the remains of war dead in the Rzhev area, a book that served as a powerful inspiration to the people in *Dozor* and in many other search groups.

In the Victory Day 1990 edition of the then still-respected weekly newspaper published by the USSR Writers' Union, *Literaturnaia gazeta* (*Literary Newspaper*), Kondratiev was one of three writers to publish a lengthy retrospective article on the Great Patriotic War. His piece was a scathing indictment of the way the war had been fought. "What depressed us in the front lines was that our commanding officers did not pity us. They threw us into ill-considered attacks that they knew were doomed. Now you wonder how many men we lost for no purpose, but from incompetence, from ambition, because they took towns just to help celebrate Soviet holidays. And always, always—*at any price!* How many lives could have been saved if we had fought just a little more intelligently, a little more prudently, with a bit more compassion for people." The author then extended his charge further back into the Soviet past: "No, they did not pity their own people, just as they did not pity them in 1917, in 1921, in 1929, and in 1937 [the enumerated years refer, respectively, to the Bolshevik revolution, the brutal suppression of worker, peasant, and sailors' rebellions at the end of the Civil War, the forced collectivization drive, and the great terror]. During the war, God himself said not to pity, victory was more important. In our country results of some kind are always more important than anything else, more than people. Russia has plenty of people, she has enough of them to waste."[3]

Kondratiev had titled his article "Paradox of Nostalgia for the Front," and after sketching out such a terrible wartime scenario, he posed the puzzling question of why such a war would generate feelings of nostalgia in so many people. His answer recalls the de-Stalinization wrought by the war and the temporary freedom it had bestowed on the populace. "There was one strange thing about the war—we felt freer than we had during peacetime." This freedom, wrote Kondratiev, came from the sense that one was truly *responsible* for one's country. This sensation was not present in all circumstances: "if you are driven to attack and are running across a field under a shower of bullets and shells, then you are 'cannon fodder' and nothing much depends on you. But if you are lucky and get yourself to a line of enemy trenches . . . there no one commands you and much, if not all, is in your own hands." The author quotes a passage from a story he had once written in which one war veteran points out to another that at work he could be replaced by someone else, "but during the war I was necessary as necessary could be. If another soldier had been in my place, he might have let the Germans get through . . . " Right there is the source of nostalgia for the war, concluded Kondratiev, "in that genuine feeling of *citizenship,* of responsibility for one's Fatherland." Such sentiments were painfully absent in the Soviet Union of the Gorbachev years.

The bitterness of the remembrance of war in those confused times was nowhere more evident than in a photo-essay that ran in the same issue of the *Literaturnaia gazeta* as Kondratiev's article. A dramatic, full-front photograph of an old and shabbily dressed veteran with a raised hand and clumsy prosthesis instead of a right leg was accompanied by a long caption that included the following thoughts:

Is Everything Forgiven?

Victory—and much is forgiven.

Victory—and the victims are justified: the millions including those (whom we especially remember today) hundreds of thousands of lives lost on the eve of the Day we are now commemorating, lost by one military commander only in order to seize Berlin, which already had one foot in the grave, before another military commander.

And the lies, the brutality of a regime that drowned the humane in human beings, that sowed enmity everywhere; this too is justified.

I feel shame before those who stole the Victory—who gave out commemorative parades instead of apartments, token gifts instead of food, honorary badges instead of normal lives, lives that people deserve. . . .

He raised his hand to stop me taking his photograph. His only medal from the war was a wooden leg. "Don't take my photo!" he said harshly. "We won the war, but we did not liberate ourselves or you . . . "

I took his photo anyhow.[4]

NUMBERS MADNESS: A PERORATION

In his 1990 Victory Day speech Mikhail Gorbachev had upped the estimate of Soviet wartime deaths from the legendary twenty million to twenty-seven million. The assessment of wartime losses had turned into a politicized numbers game in which the more radical, anti-Stalinist, anti-Soviet critics estimated ever-higher losses and pointed to them as a reflection both of the system's incompetence at waging war and of Stalin's direct and indirect role in those millions of deaths. The historian Boris Sokolov's controversial book *The Price of Victory*, published in Moscow in 1991, an obsessively determined effort to pin down both Soviet and German wartime losses, put Soviet real and potential (that is, people who would have been born had it not been for the war) dead at forty-six million. Other estimates ran as high as almost fifty million wartime losses.[5]

How many of the tens of millions of Soviet lives lost in the war must be blamed on the Soviet people and their Supreme Leader? The Soviet Union's enormous wartime losses, which so deeply impressed themselves on its allies, and President Roosevelt in particular, had been decisive at the war's end in enabling Stalin to capitalize on those losses and build for himself a vast empire in Eastern Europe.

Some might argue that the numbers are unimportant, that "war is war," and that any belligerent power inevitably destroys many of its finest sons needlessly through error or the chaotic circumstances of war. But such an assertion willy-nilly leads to the troubling question of numbers. What if it turned out that in fact the Soviet Union had been directly or indirectly responsible for the deaths of two million of its own men, or four million, or fifteen million? Should one say that two million self-inflicted losses properly can fall under the rubric of "war is war," but fifteen cannot? And if it could indeed be determined that Stalin and his compatriots must be blamed for fifteen million, or one-half of all wartime losses, do we accord the Soviet Union 50 percent less respect and sympathy than if the Germans had in fact killed the entire thirty million?

That way lies madness. It spills over into the whole bedeviled question of the quantification of suffering. Did the Soviet people suffer five times as much as the Jews because they lost more than five times the number of people? The answer to that question is clearly no. Victims of terrible ordeals, such as enslaved African-Americans, the Jews in the Holocaust, the Soviet people in World War II, become aggregates of national suffering on behalf of which future generations make compensatory claims. Few would dispute the legitimacy of such claims in principle. However, fewer still would be prepared to rationalize numerically the intensity of a nation's ordeal and the assessment of its demand for recompense.

And yet on some level numbers do matter. It does in fact matter whether a significant portion of the Soviet war deaths cannot be blamed on the Germans, not because we need to know just how much to temper our sympathy for the Soviet side but because in that case the decades-long Soviet mourning for their twenty million martyrs was in part a cover-up for the past sins of Stalin, his system, his policies, and his legacy.

SPEAK, MEMORY

In the summer of 1990 Ales Adamovich, the Belorussian writer, political activist, and deputy to the Soviet parliament, published an article about Stalinism and the war that he called "the war with Hitler." The term "Great Patriotic War" had become so loaded that its very usage identified the user as a conservative, a traditionalist, or an old fogy. In the article, published in *Literaturnaia gazeta,* Adamovich reiterated an argument that had come to represent the revisionist interpretation of the 1945 victory: "In paying an immense price for the victory over Hitler, the people facilitated the complete victory of Stalin's absolutist tyranny."

Of course, it was necessary to defeat Hitler, Adamovich wrote. The big challenge during the war had been to remain human while being squeezed by two inhumane tyrannies. Hitler and Stalin were each other's doubles. Hitler had his Khatyn, and Stalin his Kuropaty. Kuropaty is a wooded area in Belorussia containing mass graves from 1937–38 that had recently been discovered. Khatyn was a Belorussian village. In 1943, the Germans rounded up all the residents of the village—including the children—into a wooden barn and burned them to death. "How to distinguish between those Hitler killed and those Stalin killed, if they killed our people the same way—one entering the country from the outside, the other—from within?" During a visit to Belarus (Belorussia's post-Soviet name) in January 1994, U.S. president Bill Clinton found himself caught on the horns of the Stalin-Hitler dilemma when his original plans to visit Kuropaty, which bears a wooden cross encircled in barbed wire, *before* paying his respects at the main World War II memorial in downtown Minsk, angered some officials. In the end, Mr. Clinton honored the victims of fascism before going to Kuropaty to remember the victims of Stalinism.

Stalin and Hitler did each other's work, wrote Adamovich. Stalin served Hitler's cause when he shot those tens of thousands of experienced Soviet military commanders in the purge of the army and navy. And Hitler did Stalin's work, killing off the bespectacled members of the intelligentsia, only he wasn't thorough enough about the Jews to satisfy the Georgian leader.

Adamovich, himself a former partisan, exploded the war cult's "Glory to our partisans!" myth. He recalled that in 1944, in the Vitebsk region, the high command of the army had managed to pull together most of Belorussia's partisans, tens of thousands of them, to await reinforcements from the regular army—but those never came, and thousands of partisans were mowed down by German tanks. Adamovich suggested that this all happened according to plan, that Stalin had feared partisans as potential postwar terrorists and had arranged to have them taken care of before the war's end. "'Glory to our partisans!' but it is better, easier, safer, if they have first died a heroic death!"

Adamovich also took apart the legend about the wartime unity of the Soviet people. He characterized the war as in many ways a continuation of the 1918–21 Civil War—virulently divisive, conflicted, strife-filled. Gentiles against Jews, collaborators against noncollaborators, Stalinists versus anti-Stalinists—these were just some of the wars being waged on Soviet territory in 1941–45 during the war with Germany.[6]

Not all memories of the war were so negative. Other survivors—particularly women—recalled the war years as a positive experience in which the national divisiveness that had lacerated the USSR in recent years was nowhere in evidence. "I was a participant in the war and from 1941 until 1954 I helped the wounded," wrote a woman with a Ukrainian name in a letter published in *Izvestiia*. "They were all dear to me. I was with the 223rd Azerbaijani division defending the Caucasus. And it never came into my head to think about which of my friends were Azerbaijani, and which ones were Armenian or Georgian. . . . Let the memory of the war, the friendship of peoples tempered in its fires, be an example for our conscience today."[7]

CLIO ON THE MOVE

Professional historians in the Soviet Union, most of whom had been a conservative lot, scrambled to keep up with the imperatives and opportunities offered by *glasnost* and the call to fill in the "blank spots" in Russian and Soviet history. Characteristically, the dominant figures in the Academy of Sciences' Institute of History were rather slow to join the de-Stalinization bandwagon. First they waited a while to check how the wind was blowing, and then to check again. Meanwhile, a small group of radical historians was active in founding *Memorial,* a movement dedicated to investigating and preserving evidence about the Stalin years in an archive, research center, museum, and monument dedicated to the memory of Stalinism's millions of victims.

By and large, in their reexaminations of the past, historians began by focusing on the Great Terror of 1937–39. From there they moved back in time to the breakneck industrialization and the forced collectivization of the peasants beginning in the late twenties, and then were pushed even further back into the early Soviet period in order to explore the roots of Stalinism and its relationship to Leninism.

Only toward the end of the 1980s, after the country had long been convulsed by the tumult of truths about the reality of high Stalinism, did the previously sacrosanct topics of Lenin and the Great Patriotic War come under scrutiny. Historians moved up to the war gradually and chronologically. In 1989 the Institute of History took on the Molotov-Ribbentrop Pact and the Finnish War of 1939–40, and only later did it move on to Operation Barbarossa and after.

Among the thousands, indeed, tens of thousands of books about the war published after Stalin's death, the classic compendiums of officially sanctioned truths about the war took the form of massive multi-volume histories of the Great Patriotic War. In 1960–65 the Institute of Military History (under the tutelage of the Soviet Armed

Forces) published a six-volume *History of the Great Patriotic War of the Soviet Union, 1941–1945*. This was followed in the Brezhnev period by a twelve-volume work that appeared in the mid-seventies. All these volumes had enshrined politically correct sagas of the war in all its facets. Historians of the war who challenged their tenets often found themselves in big trouble.

At the end of the 1980s the Institute of Military History undertook the research, writing, and publication of a ten-volume work titled *History of the Great Patriotic War of the Soviet People*, underlining the populist twist to the war generated by *glasnost* and *perestroika*. The project included many scholars of varying skills and political views. The editorial board boasted some excellent military historians who themselves were high-level officers in the army—Col. V. M. Kulish, Col. V. I. Dashychev, and Col. General Dmitrii Volkogonov, who supervised the work on the first volume.

I met Volkogonov in May 1992, when he held the post of special advisor to President Yeltsin on military affairs. He was also the Russian official in charge of a joint United States and Russian commission to investigate the fate of American citizens who had been missing on Soviet/Russian territory since 1917. In addition, Volkogonov headed a committee to create a new Russian army. In sum, he was what Russians call a *bol'shaia ptitsa*, or bigwig (literally "big bird").

His office in the unmarked building in downtown Moscow that used to house the Central Committee, was large and airy, and sixty-three year old Volkogonov looked decidedly unimposing, with tired eyes looking out at me over big bluish pouches, an unhealthy, splotchy complexion and unrefined features. But his voice was wonderful, with a fluent, bell-like tintinnabulation.

He had long before attained the rank of a three-star general and had been for years in charge of the Soviet Army's Department of Psychological Warfare. In 1986 he suggested that the entire political organ of the army be done away with and turned into a simple information-gathering agency. "Within *hours* of making this proposal I was demoted several ranks and sent away to head the Institute of Military History," he recalled with a wry smile. It was then that he began to work on the ten-volume history of the war.

Early in 1991 he presented the first volume, on the Soviet Union on the eve of the war, to the Ministry of Defense, and on March 7, 1991 he and the volume were the focus of a heated discussion, excerpts of which were published the next week by the editors of the enterprising newspaper, *Nezavisimaia gazeta* (*Independent Newspaper*). Minister of Defense Yazov and others vilified Volkogonov for having "blackened" Soviet history by describing the country and the army on the eve of the war as thoroughly disorganized and crippled by Stalin's policies.

"We need to understand that those crimes," Volkonov said to me leaning forward and raising his smooth tenor voice ever so slightly, "the military unpreparedness, the stupid pre-war diplomacy, the ill-advised pact with Hitler—were not just Stalin's crimes, but crimes of the entire system." Two examples followed.

"By December 1941, 8 per cent of the army that had met the German advance remained alive and in service. Those millions who fought in the rest of the war were entirely new officers and soldiers, peasants who had no idea how to fight, who could only serve as cannon fodder."

"In 1942, when the army needed every last man, Beria wrote Stalin, requesting men to guard the NKVD labor camps. In the war years, between three and four hundred thousand men served as guards in the Gulag, the equivalent of a whole army."

Dmitrii Volkogonov, who had recently published biographies of Stalin and Trotsky, was hard at work to get out a new book on Lenin. He seemed like a man in an enormous rush to get the truth out and have his say. When I pointed this out he told me the reason: he was dying of liver cancer.

Volkogonov resigned from the directorship of the Institute of Military History, and the ten-volume history of the war was abandoned. But only a few months would pass before his accusers would participate in an unsuccessful coup d'etat that would land some of them in jail and bring Volkogonov to within a telephone call from the president.

The most provocative of all the revisionist books on the Soviet Union in the Second World War was without a doubt Viktor Suvorov's *Icebreaker: Who Started the Second World War?* which appeared in translation in France in 1988, in Germany in 1989, and in England in 1990. It was not published in his native country until

1992, when the Soviet Union had already ceased to exist. This daring, possibly reckless, volume posited the thesis that Stalin was in the fullest sense responsible for having started the war: determined to bring about the socialist revolution in Europe that Lenin had dreamed of in 1918, Stalin had supported the Nazis almost from the beginning, envisioning Hitler and his party as the "icebreaker" that would forge the path to revolution in Europe by exhausting that continent with a debilitating war. According to Sokolov, Stalin was planning all along an offensive war in Europe, and was ready to give up everything—including millions of Soviet lives—for the goal of world revolution.[8]

Almost as unorthodox as Sokolov's book was the new line on General Vlasov. Although some Western scholars had argued that he had been an anti-Stalinist patriot, General Andrei Vlasov, the Red Army's highest-ranking collaborator, for decades had been villified in the Soviet Union as an arch-traitor to his country. Even worse, he had been transmogrified into a nonperson; the official multivolume histories of the Great Patriotic War that came out in the 1960s and 1970s entirely omitted mention of his participation in the defense of Moscow in 1941 and in the liberation of Prague at the war's end. None of the documents circulated by Vlasov spelling out his anti-Bolshevik program had been published. Furthermore, the entire Second Shock Army, from which Vlasov had defected and which had played an important role in the defense of Leningrad, had been denied military decorations because of its Vlasov connection. During the Gorbachev years the Second Shock Army was rehabilitated and a movement was set up to find and bury the remains of its soldiers in the swamps around Leningrad. In 1989 and 1990, articles began to appear that vindicated General Vlasov and blamed not him but Stalin for the defections of Soviet soldiers to the Vlasov army.[9]

DAY OF REMEMBRANCE

June 22, 1991, marked the fiftieth anniversary of Operation Barbarossa. In the old days of the war cult June 22 had been passed over with little more than some contemplative articles in the press that somehow pointed the way to the victory. But on this occasion the half-century of the invasion was widely recognized as *Den pamiati*

(Day of Remembrance). This recognition was less a tribute to the weight of a fifty-year mark and more a demonstration of the general reassessment of the war with a greater emphasis on its tragic aspects.

Conferences abounded—in the Academy of Sciences' Institute of History, at the Union of Writers, in the Soviet Army. Those weeks before the attempted coup of August 19, 1991, were filled with tension and foreboding, with the conservative forces very much in evidence. "Our choice was either a pact with Germany or an attack by a coalition of capitalist countries," declared the novelist Ivan Stadniuk in the House of Writers' big, ornate auditorium, which was only about one-fifth occupied. The conference, held on June 19, was called "Memory of the Year 1941" and was televised, no doubt because the featured speaker was Dmitrii Yazov, minister of defense.

Yazov, a stocky, ruddy man with something of the bulldog, or maybe bullfrog, in his face, focused his remarks on Volkogonov's shocking first volume of the planned ten-volume history. "The authors of that book wanted to show nothing but the losses we had suffered in every operation! We must remember the bright deeds of our Soviet soldiers! That volume contained not one single positive statement about the Red Army!"

In his speech Vladimir Karpov, the head of the Writers' Union and a representative of the old line, reached for similarities between 1941 and 1991. We have now experienced a surprise invasion by enemies (from within, meaning liberals), he said. "In 1941 we did not surrender Moscow; today we have given up not only Moscow but Leningrad as well." The last remark was doubtless a reference to Leningrad's decision to rename itself St. Petersburg.

The fiftieth anniversary conference at the central meeting house of the Soviet Army was held simultaneously with the one at the Writers' Union. Rushing over from the writers' conference, I came in late to a session chaired by Prof. Georgii Kumanev, an established member of the Academy of Sciences' Institute of History who had served as my official adviser on one of my visits to Moscow as an exchange scholar. "We were wrong to underestimate Lendlease when we used to say that it represented only four per cent of the totality of our war matériel," he was saying as I walked in. "In fact, if it hadn't been for Lendlease the war would have dragged on for another year and a half," Kumanev added authoritatively, giving me (the *amerikan-*

ka) an unprofessional wink as I quietly took a seat. Acknowledging a significant Allied role in the war effort had become totally acceptable—even chic—among the old guard.

Dmitrii Yazov too had come over from the Writers' Union and had taken center stage at the plenary session of the army conference. The defense minister repeated the speech I had already heard, but for this audience, which was mostly in uniform, the tone was more strident. While we are commemorating the fiftieth anniversary of the invasion, he said, we are getting ready for a series of fiftieth anniversaries of the war's victories—those of the battles of Moscow, Stalingrad, Kursk, and finally Berlin and the Victory in 1995. Yazov also echoed Karpov's eerie remarks about the analogy between 1941 and 1991, and the invasion by enemies from within and by foreign capitalists who are all destroying the Soviet Union.

On the night of June 22, on the notoriously reactionary Leningrad television talk show, "600 Seconds," the KGB head Vladimir Kriuchkov also came out with the analogy between the attack on Stalin and the Soviet Union in 1941 and enemies stalking the Soviet system in 1991. The difference, he warned, was that Stalin had been set upon by a surprise attack, whereas we—the embodiments of Soviet power—are prepared to repel the enemy.

After hearing all this in June I was not at all surprised by the attempted coup that took place two months later. Indeed, I was shocked that President Bush had been so astonished by the coup; perhaps he ought to have sent someone to those June 22 conferences.

HILL OF PROSTRATIONS

In the western part of Moscow, along the old Smolensk Road, there once stood a hill called *Poklonnaia Gora* (Hill of Prostrations). From its grassy height travelers and pilgrims approaching Moscow from the west first caught sight of the magnificent panorama of the "city of churches." Seeing the hundreds of gleaming golden domes, they would prostrate themselves in reverence.

Most Russians know of the Hill of Prostrations from Tolstoy's *War and Peace.* First we see General Kutuzov, commander of the Russian forces, approach the hill, dismount, and convene a council of war during which he lets his officers babble on to one another about possible strategies for battle, while he himself ponders deeply and concludes that the city will have to be abandoned to the French. Then, five days later, on September 2, 1812, fresh from his Pyrrhic victory at Borodino, Napoleon appears with his troops on the same hill. "A town occupied by the enemy is like a maid who has lost her honor," he thinks to himself as he gazes greedily upon the city whose countless cupolas are "twinkling like stars" in the early autumn sunlight.

He sends his adjutants galloping off to Moscow to fetch "*les boyars*" who will enact the formal surrender of the city. While awaiting the deputation, he strolls back and forth along the hill, composing in his mind the dignified and magnanimous speech he will make to the vanquished boyars. But none are found by the French officers. The emperor, impatient and irritated, rides off toward the city only to find it empty and in flames. This marks the beginning of his defeat.[10]

As of 1957, the Hill of Prostrations was the designated site of a central, all-Union memorial complex dedicated to the victory of the Soviet people in the Great Patriotic War. For the better part of the four following decades, the proposed monument on the site was the focus, first, of infighting among the denizens of the Moscow cultural elite, and, during the Gorbachev era, of major public debate. The Hill of Prostrations had played no significant role in World War II, and the area had clearly been chosen for its association with the victory of the Russian nation in 1812.

In 1957 the Hill of Prostrations had been leveled, but not because of the proposed monument. As Margarita Astafieva-Dlugach, a sophisticated and well-connnected researcher in an institute of architectural history, explained, the hill had been razed for security reasons. When Kutuzovskii Prospekt was broadened and big apartment buildings went up to house Party dignitaries, "it was deemed unacceptable to retain any height from which someone could shoot down at their limousines," she said. "A tunnel was equally risky. So the hill was removed, or rather moved, since the excavated earth was piled up into a large mound. Added to it was a front portion of the hill that was taken down to make way for the construction of a large apartment building. People came gradually to call that mound Poklonnaia Hill."

A closed competition in 1979 eventually yielded plans for a grandiose memorial ensemble with an elaborately contrived symbolic structure. Visitors were to ascend a vast set of stairs arranged in five groups—one for each year of the war—with bas-reliefs recounting the main events. On either side there were to be fountains with precisely 1,418 jets of water—one for each day of the war.

At the rear of the complex, a museum was planned, and its most dramatic room was to be the circular Hall of Glory, a locus for the ritualized exaltation of the victory. Along the walls of that hall, white marble posts topped with bronze wreaths symbolizing glory were to display the engraved names of all twelve thousand four hundred Heroes of the Soviet Union. A glass case in the center of the room was to display the original Victory Banner—the "holy of holies."

This Victory Banner provided the theme of the central monument to the victory planned for the Hill of Prostrations. The design was a creation of Nikolai Tomskii, the president of the Academy of Arts. A seventy-meter-high wavy banner of red granite with a huge bas-relief of Lenin's familiar three-quarter profile would be held aloft by a group of diminutive Soviet people crowded onto a tall pedestal. The design was graceless, stolid, and ugly, and its small figures dwarfed by the Lenin banner hardly seemed to commemorate the victory of the Soviet *people.*

By the spring of 1984, one year before the fortieth anniversary of the victory, the construction of the ensemble finally got underway, more than a quarter-century after the initial Politburo resolution. The mound people called the Hill of Prostrations was removed and a lovely woods destroyed to make way for the foundation. Vast sums of money had been collected to fund the project, most of it from *subbotniki* "voluntary" labor days.[11]

But before the Victory Banner monument could be constructed, intrigue within the powerful community of Soviet architects and sculptors (major monuments were a *big* business in the old Soviet Union) combined with a growing *glasnost*-inspired sentiment that the people should have the right to control public culture, did away with the Victory Banner plan. Instead, a series of open competitions allowed a broad spectrum of designers to make a bid for the authorship of what was billed as the Soviet Union's central monument to the victory of the Soviet people in the Great Patriotic War.

In April 1988 I traveled to Moscow to see the exhibit of 470 designs for the monument on the Hill of Prostrations, all displayed in the cavernous Manezh central exhibition hall. I found myself strongly drawn to precisely those designs that any proper jury would immediately eliminate from serious consideration. They included a grouping of primitively crafted people and centaurs made of colored clay and grouped on and around an elaborate clay pedestal; a gaily painted hemisphere bearing Lenin's stern profile and into whose north polar region was stuck a matrix of metal wires studded with star-shaped twinky lights (visitors were invited to press a button to turn the lights on); a truly adorable, enormous tableau populated by charming clay figures, some of which held up globes while others supported a map of the USSR displaying the mythic number 20,000,000; a large, funky collage that included cut-out photographs of a variety of Soviet people plus a red toy tank at the foot of a mock obelisk; two enormously long, skinny, modernistic brass arms extended upward to support a wire globe (one of several handheld globes featured in the exhibit) with a brass soldier posing awkwardly between the two arms. These and several others appealed to me because they were bold, fanciful, and even playful, and very unlike the tens of thousands of actual ponderous and stolid monuments evident in Soviet cities and towns. I also took note of the many homely, even dreadful designs that often represented clumsy attempts to realize forms that had long since become traditional: red stars, rifle-bearing soldiers, mothers (with or without children, wings, branches, or orbs); Lenin (and sometimes Marx), eternal flames; columns, obelisks, Kremlin towers and other phallic objects; eagles, doves, flowers, rainbows; globes, banners, and arches. How small the repertoire of meaningful images seemed to be!

Some of the most publicized designs expressed the neo-Slavophilism of the Gorbachev years. Churchlike structures replete with onion domes and eight-pointed crosses embodied the mood of the times, as did several models that envisioned as a victory monument a reconstructed Cathedral of Christ the Savior. "The Russian past is a source of redemption," said Viacheslav Klykov, the designer of the most popular of the churchlike models at the exhibition as we strolled through his Moscow studio. "The past is a source of morals, of traditions," continued Klykov, who was rumored to be linked with the ultranationalist organization, *Pamiat*. "Not only I and my circle of friends feel this way. I think it is a nationwide phenomenon. Our heritage is our main support in life."

"Is the renewed passion for the Russian church a religious phenomenon, does it come, say, from a desire to praise God, or is it rather the expression of some other kind of impulse, something more social or political?" I asked, knowing it was an impossible question to answer.

"Religious and political imperatives are united in the human spirit," answered the sculptor eloquently. "And in Russia's past the church has often acted as a unifying force. When the nation was attacked and even defeated, the church held the country and culture together and acted as the most effective source of inspiration."

Of all the designs I encountered in visits to two competitions in 1988 and 1989, the most moving was one endorsed by Viktor Agashkov, secretary of the jury that the Ministry of Culture had appointed to be in charge of a design selection. The idea was to rebuild the Hill of Prostrations in the form of a handmade burial mound, with volunteers from all over the country bringing fistfuls of earth. The *kurgan* (burial mound) was an ancient Slavic form of funerary edifice. This symbolic *kurgan* would be made out of earth brought from every part of the Soviet Union where the soldiers who fought in World War II had lived, earth that in Russia has always been an archetypal sacral object, and the process of creating the mound was itself to be a unifying ritual. When I asked Victor Aleksandrovich to tell me more about the scenario he envisioned, he explained, "on some appointed day, say, May 9, people in a village would gather in some central park, and after some ceremony a representative would transfer a small amount of earth into a designated vessel, which would then be conveyed to Moscow by messenger precisely along the road on which soldiers from that village had gone off to the front. The road that once led them to their deaths now will convey the sacred capsule."

"The road to death becomes the road to immortality?" I asked.

"You can put it that way," answered Agashkov.

In the end, none of the competitions yielded any winning designs that the jury would endorse, and while democrats were saying that no monument should be built, but rather the money should go to aid elderly veterans, the army and its supporters insisted on a monument.

As the years went by and the Soviet Union imploded, the plans for a central victory monument fizzled, but the building to house the museum of the Great Patriotic War was in fact constructed.

I was last on the Hill of Prostrations on the afternoon of June 22, 1991, the fiftieth anniversary of the German invasion of the Soviet Union. Accompanied by a bushy-haired philologist with the Gogolian name of Flavius, who worked on the staff of the not-yet-completed Central Museum of the Great Patriotic War, I ascended a grassy mound not far from the museum construction site and joined a crowd of some two hundred people assembled near a large, rough-hewn wooden cross. Like most everyone else, Flavius and I each bought a tan candle from a kerchiefed woman who was selling them out of a worn tote bag.

To the tolling of bells suspended from a wooden frame, a Russian Orthodox priest and church choir appeared, followed by parishioners bearing icons. When he reached the cross the priest, an enormous man in golden robes, performed a requiem mass in memory of the victims of the Great Patriotic War.

The priest chanted out the names of the war dead given to him by the crowd and also invited the congregation to pronounce out loud the names of their loved ones who had died in the war. Women and men called out those names simultaneously in a cacophonous cry of mourning followed by a stream of *Alleluia*s that wafted out into the warm gray summer air. For me, the event was only slightly soured by the fact that it was evidently inspired by the Russian nationalism of the early nineties—at once prideful and xenophobic. Prominently displayed in front of the cross was a large icon of St. George the Dragon-Slayer.

The sounds of the requiem mass, a timeless combination of calculated grandeur and humble piety, resonated through the still air as an ephemeral, but fitting, memorial to the Soviet people who fought and died in the war with Germany a half-century earlier.

By 1993, no monument had yet been erected on the Hill of Prostrations, although a large stone statue of a mother and child, done up in realist (or post-socialist realist) style and submitted by the famed sculptor M. K. Anikushin, who is perhaps best known for his work on the victory monument erected in Leningrad in 1975, had been chosen by the Russian Ministry of Culture. Some people had put forward another plan for the Hill of Prostrations monument: to transport to the designated Moscow site the monument erected by the Soviet sculptor Evgenii Vuchetich in Berlin's Treptower Park in 1949 as a memorial to the Soviet soldiers who died in the storm of Berlin. The statue, which shows a resolute representative of the Red Army's finest holding in his powerful arms a little German girl, had long been a prime symbol of the mature war cult. Even more to the point, some canny individuals doubtless had figured out that it would be better to remove the ponderous reminder of the Soviet domination of East Germany than to wait for an angry German populace to tear it down. And, as an article on the monument published in *Komsomolskaia pravda* put it, "The army is going away from there— why leave that one Soldier standing?"[11]

By Victory Day 1993, the building that would house the new museum of the Great Patriotic War—nicknamed "the Reichstag" because of its large cupola—was nearly complete. On that day, May 9, President Yeltsin greeted veterans from its front steps. There had been rumors of impending antigovernment demonstrations in downtown Moscow, and the authorities had cleverly arranged for buses to take veterans and their irate supporters out of the center of town to the hill.

It was a gorgeous, sunny day. That morning Yeltsin had placed a wreath on the Tomb of the Unknown Soldier. The Russian Army had brought World War II tanks and other military hardware up to the Hill of Prostrations. The museum was complete but displayed only one exhibit, a temporary exhibition of writings and drawings produced during and after the war by people who had fought in it. At ten o'clock in the morning on May 9, the Central Museum of the Great Patriotic War opened to the public.

The scene on the Hill of Prostrations was peaceful, benign. The celebration took place near the museum at Victory Park. Children were clambering all over the tanks. Veterans strolled in the sunshine, clutching flowers that they had been given. The atmosphere was festive. The armed forces had arranged an air show of planes that dropped parachutists into the crowd, to the delight of the many children among the spectators. Stands were selling buckwheat kasha and—unusual for an official public celebration—small containers of vodka. Cooperative ventures were also selling expensive champagne and Marlboro cigarettes.

At noon President Yeltsin made a short speech of welcome to the crowd, after which many people followed him into the museum. The wooden cross that had been brought to the hill area in June 1991 had now been moved to a spot not far from the museum's entrance, and had become the locus for the laying of flowers. Its base was piled high with bouquets. In the museum, staff members near the temporary exhibit informed the visitors that the full museum would open two years hence, for the fiftieth anniversary of the victory in May 1995. At the museum's entrance stood a bust of Marshal Zhukov; some people crossed themselves in front of the bust, and others touched it with their lips. Documentary film clips from the war were being shown at one end of the picture gallery. A computer-generated "Book of Remembrance" that would give visitors information on their loved ones who fought in the war was planned for 1995, but on this 1993 Victory Day, information was available only on war veterans from Moscow and the Moscow region, and people queued up to put in their queries.

My Muscovite friend Ania Narinskaia, a brilliant journalist in her late twenties, spent the day of May 9 on the Hill of Prostrations and then wrote me about the experience. She had spoken with a number of veterans gathered at the museum, and all of them were pleased with the holiday celebration the authorities had arranged, although one veteran complained, "We went to fight for the Motherland, for Stalin. But now—our Motherland is gone!"

"Most of the people who had come to Victory Park did not seem to experience any feelings about the war," observed Ania. "They simply came to stroll, to look, to drink (alcoholic beverages were available at every step), in general to enjoy themselves. Even when a singer sang one of those most moving of wartime songs, I didn't see anyone wiping away a tear.

"Probably in order that people who did not live through the war should experience profound emotions about it, we need a war myth which, however, has already been almost completely destroyed."

9

PARTING THOUGHTS

On June 12, 1993, someone smashed the windows of Moscow's main synagogue. Later that day, angry demonstrators were reported to have swarmed through the streets of the city carrying antigovernment slogans, including one that read, STALIN AWAKEN! THE FASCISTS HAVE INVADED AGAIN!

In Russia the term "fascist" had long since become a synonym for "enemy." Democracts called commmunists "fascists," while the latter made the same accusation of the former. Everything had turned inside out and upside down. Communists had become nationalists. Russians were putting up war memorials to the memory of Germans who had died in the war. During the war a young Hamburger had died in the area of Pskov. Fifty years later, his wealthy family loaded the community in which he had died with large quantities of foodstuffs and other provisions, and in gratitude the inhabitants constructed a monument to the slain German soldier. His family came to Russia for the unveiling.

On a basic biological level, there is nothing more fundamentally important for human beings to know than who their enemies are, and whom it is they can trust. If Moscow's Jews or liberal democrats could become 1993's incarnation of Nazi invaders from whom Russia needed immediate salvation, then something much worse than the distortion or even the killing of memory had gone on in the

Russian polity during the many decades of Soviet rule. At worst, a portion of society had lost the innate capacity to distinguish friend from foe, support from threat, good from evil, and was passing this affliction on to its descendants.

At best, years of lying and manipulation by the Party and government, and to the Party and government, and by and to each other—following a legacy of terror toward a populace that had not been able to figure out how to protect itself from abuse by the authorities—had so confused some people's understanding of reality that their capacity to locate sensible objects of blame and fear was in serious need of repair.

It all comes down to the question of trust and betrayal that in our country is perhaps most vividly laid out in the United States Holocaust Memorial Museum in Washington, D.C. As you see the photomontage of naked women lined up on a ridge at Babi Yar, as you walk through the cattle car, past the detailed model of a gas chamber, through a room that contains nothing but thousands of shoes that had belonged to Holocaust victims, shoes that still carry a musty, human smell, it is hard to avoid the conclusion that if people can order tens of thousands of other people to gather up their belongings as though to indicate that a long journey was in the offing, and then can rob, strip, and shoot all of them, making no distinctions between them on the basis of age or sex or anything else, then it is impossible for anyone to ever put their trust in anyone else. If millions of ordinary people could be herded into huge chambers, told they were going to shower, and then be gassed, one would think that humankind could simply not recover the equanimity to live in anything resembling normal society.

The good news is that somehow, miraculously, life went on after the war, after those atrocities. Some survivors, perhaps even many, did go mad, and spawned mad, abused children. But others—like so many starfish regenerating amputated limbs—many others, continued to love, honor, and respect other human beings. This was the case in the Soviet Union no less than in any other belligerent country. But in the Soviet Union, the process of growing new limbs was complicated by a quarter-century of Stalinism, which had specialized in recognizing—and meting out terrible punishments to—unseen enemies. Whom can you trust if your colleague or neighbor or spouse might denounce you to the authorities? How can an NKVD interrogator prevent his own interrogation and arrest further down the road if accusations, and death sentences, are based on nothing but some crazed logic?

"Ambivalence, I think, is the chief characteristic of my nation," wrote the poet Joseph Brodsky in 1976. "There isn't a Russian executioner who isn't scared of turning victim one day, nor is there the sorriest victim who would not acknowledge (if only to himself) a mental ability to become an executioner. Our immediate history has provided well for both."[1]

It is fair to suggest that for decades the populace of the Soviet Union was both individually and collectively suffering from post-traumatic stress syndrome. It is also possible that the postwar decades of official lies about the Stalin years, about the war, indeed, about the world in general delayed what might have been for many a more expeditious process of healing. Truth telling, however painful it may be, is sometimes the only mechanism that can heal a troubled spirit. On the other hand, the too frequent or too intense retelling of the source of post-traumatic stress may exacerbate the condition. So the problem is very complicated indeed. The changes that take place in people who undergo traumas are physiological. The chemistry of the body becomes too finely attuned to danger and, in a quite physical sense, cannot forget it. Therefore, therapies are usually not nearly as helpful in alleviating the condition as is medication.

Entire cultures that live through the kinds of traumas that visited the people of the Soviet Union in the 1930s and 1940s become transformed by the experience. It is often the case that when life is going on in some predictable groove, the syndrome seems to fade. But when the going becomes hard, scary, filled with uncertainty, as it did in the post-Soviet Union beginning in the late 1980s, the syndrome comes back, and people smash in the windows of synagogues in order to fight fascism.

In a powerful article titled "The Politics of Memory," about the remembrance of the Holocaust in Israel, Amos Elon quoted a conversation he had witnessed in 1972 between a British Labour politician and a retired Israeli diplomat. "We're a traumatized people. Please understand," pleaded the diplomat as he tried to defend Prime

Minister Golda Meir's intransigence on the issue of Palestinian rights. "You certainly are a traumatized people!" countered the British politician. "But you are a traumatized people with an atom bomb! Such people belong behind bars!"

The point of Elon's article was that an obsessive recounting of the Holocaust and an inability to let any of it go had helped create a genuinely bleak philosophy of life in Israel, and had opened the way to the exploitation of the Holocaust for political purposes. Students had been steeped in Holocaust studies and encouraged to travel to Poland on organized tours of extermination camps, trips that were fraught with high ritual. The author went on to laud his country's more recent willingness to allow itself some healing forgetfulness: "where there is so much traumatic memory, so much pain, so much memory innocently or deliberately mobilized for political purposes, a little forgetfulness might finally be in order. This should not be seen as a banal plea to 'forgive and forget.' Forgiveness has nothing to do with it."[2]

Perhaps Russia could use a little forgetfulness as well. As another traumatized country with nuclear weapons, the retelling of past evils of which it was both victim and perpetrator might best be delayed until some more stable identity takes shape on the Russian land.

The deterioration of the cult of the Great Patriotic War made room for the emergence of memory and truth—a good thing insofar as authenticity itself is a value. On Sunday, June 22, 1993, the Day of Remembrance, the Russian poet Anatolii Naiman attended church as usual. The liturgy for the day had included prayers for the "tranquility of all the leaders and soldiers who [had] laid down their lives on the field [of battle] for their faith, country, and church." In his sermon, the priest maintained that despite its horror, the war had been the best period of his people's lives, because everything during the war had been genuine, because people had been open with their feelings, including their basest ones. Authenticity, even of baseness, is a treasure, said the priest.

At the same time, the loss of the war cult was another loss of something familiar, and to many citizens, comforting. Once the imposed, standard story of the war had been exploded, the public memory of World War II—once envisioned by its managers as a unifying, cohesive force—now reflected, and indeed exacerbated, the fragmentation of the troubled society at large. St. Petersburg marked the tragedy of its siege; Belarus, the decimation of its population; Ukraine, its own wartime catastrophe. Soviet power, which, it was now understood, had contributed to the carnage, could no longer serve as a focus of venerational remembrance—except on the part of communists and their supporters. For many others, the current politics of victimization dictated new truths: the regions had suffered, and continued to suffer, primarily as victims not of German fascism, but of Soviet communism.

By spring 1994, as Britain and France revealed elaborate plans to commemorate the fiftieth anniversary of D-Day, some entrepreneurs in Russia—which had been left out of those plans—competed among themselves for control of Volvograd's shabby but elegant old Intourist Hotel in the hopes that European and American tourists would wish to spend large sums of money there while touring the site of the great Stalingrad battle and the Volvograd memorial. The Volvograd entrepreneurs hoped that the victory, almost a half-century old, would now take on new life as a marketable consumer product.[3]

FROM COLLECTIVE BACK TO PERSONAL GRIEF

Masha was home in her New York apartment after a protracted stay in the hospital. She was unimaginably weak, barely able to move from room to room. It was a crisp winter day. In her beautiful living room with its warm pink walls and soft lighting (she kept little holiday lights in her big potted plants all year round, for effect), we were stretched out on the white sofa facing each other, our feet resting on each other's thighs.

Masha closed her eyes, and I read aloud those portions of the beginning of this book that speak about our family and about her cancer, leaving out the physical descriptions of her illness. We got to talking about death. I asked her how it felt to be dying.

"It's not that bad," she replied. "If only I didn't feel so sick." That struck her as funny, and we both laughed.

After enduring years of childhood operations necessitated by the radiation damage she had suffered (that is likely to have brought on her adult leukemia), Masha grew up with a high tolerance for pain. She was the only mother I have ever heard say that childbirth "wasn't that bad."

I tried to communicate my impression, formed during my dig with *Dozor,* that in the long run death looks peaceful, clean, restful. No matter now much pain and despair those men had suffered while they were alive and while they were dying, no matter how muddy and war-torn and stench-filled the battlefield and trenches in which they died, fifty years later their brown remains are quietly nestled in a beautiful forest.

As an historian and as a woman who lost her father in childhood, I am always trying to touch the dead in some way or another. There was something sweet and comforting in doing it directly. Just thinking about the dead, remembering them, talking about them does not do the trick. You need something tactile.

I love to look at a decorated bowl I made for my father when I was a little girl. First I smeared glue on the outside of a clear glass bowl I had bought at Woolworth's; the glue came in a bottle with an opening that looked like a pig's snout. Onto the layer of glue went something ropelike called raffia, colored dark green and silver, which wound around the bowl, covering it completely. As a final touch I had taken a bit more raffia and glued on the word "POP." He kept his pipes in it.

Now I wear Masha's clothes, but it feels unsettling. Early in her illness I had bought her a beautiful white cotton nightgown. After she died, time and time again I tried to bleach out the bloodstains, but they would not quite come out. The blood on my sister's nightgown should have been a sign of life, coming from menstrual flow, and not the effluvia of punctures in her lung that enabled her to breathe.

"Life is freedom, and dying is a gradual denying of freedom," wrote Vasilii Grossman in *Life and Fate.* He was right. Maybe death really is the liberation that some say it is, but if so, it is a liberation not from a painful life but from the ever-tightening shackles of the dying process. The sicker Masha got, the smaller the range of choices left open to her. Jello or tapioca pudding? Attempt to shower now or wait until she could summon up a little more strength?

Masha and I had always shared a room till I was a high school senior, when she went away to college. And we shared a room on her last night, March 12, 1993. Earlier that day she had slipped into a coma. By the time I arrived at her room in St. Vincent's Hospital at the north edge of Greenwich Village, her eyes were closed and her mouth open as she noisily gulped in oxygen through a mask over her face. She did not respond to anything that was said to her by her children and other loving relatives.

Shortly after ten o'clock in the evening everyone went home and left me alone with Masha. I changed into a hospital gown so we could be dressed alike, just as we sometimes were as children. When we were little and even into our high school years, I would sing myself to sleep, sitting up with my legs crossed and rocking from side to side; Masha teased me about it a bit but never questioned my right to take over our joint space with my voice.

Now she was dying—the doctor had said that she probably would not make it through the night. I turned out the light, sat down on the cot next to her bed, and, assuming my old cross-legged position, began to sing *Katiusha,* a Russian song that had been enormously popular during World War II.

> Apple trees and pear trees were blooming,
> Fog was gliding along the river.
> To the river bank came our Katiusha
> To its bank, to its high steep bank.

When we were young, Masha and I used to sing that song without any harmony for the grown-ups. We sounded like one strong voice. But now I sang *Katiusha* alone.

Then I dozed off and was touched awake by a nurse. "Did she die?" I asked immediately. "Yes," she nodded. Despite everything I could not believe it. Maybe it was a mistake. Maybe if I did not tell anyone what had happened, the death would go away. The nurse had turned the light on and the contours of Masha's face were becoming pointy and skull-like, but still I stayed away from the telephone.

I had stopped time. I held her hand, now bluish and cold. We stayed together in a place between the living and the dead. It was a half-hour before I picked up the phone to call my mother, Masha's children, their father, and her husband.

NOTES

CHAPTER 1: INTRODUCTORY THOUGHTS

1. I. I. Illiustrov, *Zhizn' russkago naroda v ego poslovitsakh i pogovorkakh. Sbornik russkikh poslovits i pogovorok,* 3d ed. (Moscow, 1915), pp. 456–57.

2. Jamaica Kincaid, "A Fire by Ice," *New Yorker,* Feb. 22, 1993, p. 64.

CHAPTER 2: VALLY OF DEATH

1. O. V. Lishin and A. K. Lishina, *Eto nuzhno zhivym* (Moscow, 1990), p. 32.

2. "Nikto ne zabyt?" *Ogonek,* No. 31, July 1989, p. 32.

3. Timothy W. Ryback, "Stalingrad: Letters from the Dead," *New Yorker,* Feb. 1, 1993, pp. 58–71.

4. Alexander Werth, *Russia at War* (New York, 1964), p. 630.

5. Leonid Gurevich, "Ostanovite pulio," *Iunost',* No. 7, July 1987, p. 11.

6. *Komsomol'skaia pravda,* Dec. 4, 1985.

CHAPTER 3: THE LAST HURRAH

1. The speech was published in *Pravda,* May 9, 1985, and in English translation in *FBIS Daily Report,* May 9, 1985.

2. The letters were finally published ten years later. See Mikhail Gefter, ed., *Golos iz mira kotorago uzhe net: Vypuskniki istoricheskogo fakulteta MGU 1941 goda v pish'makh i vospominaniiakh* (Moscow, 1995).

CHAPTER 4: "NO SEA WITHOUT WATER, NO WAR WITHOUT BLOOD"

1. Vladimir Nabokov, trans., *The Song of Igor's Campaign* (New York, 1960), p. 46.

2. J. V. Stalin, "The Tasks of Business Executives," *Works,* vol. 13, July 1930–January 1934 (Moscow, 1955), pp. 40–41.

3. The classic, and heartbreaking, book on the spirit of youth in 1914 and after is Paul Fussell, *The Great War and Modern Memory* (New York, 1975).

4. John Erickson, *The Road to Stalingrad* (New York, 1975), p. 98.

5. Seweryn Bialer, *Stalin and His Generals* (New York, 1969), p. 188.

6. Bialer, *Stalin and His Generals,* p. 196.

7. Dmitri Volkogonov, *Stalin: Triumph and Tragedy,* Harold Shukman, ed. and trans. (New York, 1988), p. 402.

8. Konstantin Simonov, *The Living and the Dead* (New York, 1962), pp. 75–76.

9. Professor Georgii Kumanev, Institute of History, USSR Academy of Sciences, interview, June 1991; Lazar Lazarev, "Kak by ni byla gor'ka . . . ," *Kommunist,* No. 8, May 1991, p. 30.

10. Iurii Belash, *Okopnye stikhi* (Moscow, 1990), p. 222.

11. John Barber, "Popular Reactions in Moscow to the German Invasion of June 22, 1941," *Soviet Union/Union Sovietique,* vol. 18, nos. 1–3 (1991).

12. I. V. Stalin, *Sochineniia,* vol. 2 [xv], 1941–45 (Stanford, Calif., 1967), p. 35.

13. On the retention of Stalin and socialism as the prime foci of wartime propaganda, see Jeffrey Brooks, "*Pravda* Goes to War," in *The Heart of War: Culture and Entertainment in Wartime Russia, 1941–1945,* ed. Richard Stites (Bloomington, Ind., 1995). For the wartime propaganda about Stalin, see John Barber, "The Image of Stalin in Soviet Propaganda and Public Opinion During World War 2," in John Garrard and Carol Garrard, eds., *World War 2 and the Soviet People* (London, 1993), pp. 38–49.

14. *Izvestiia,* Dec. 22, 1943.

15. Ol'ga Berggolts, *Sobranie sochinenii v trekh tomakh,* vol. 2 (Leningrad, 1989), p. 38. See also Deming Brown, "World War II in Soviet Literature," Susan J. Linz, ed., *The Impact of World War II on the Soviet Union* (Totowa, N.J., 1985), p. 245.

16. Lazarev, "Kak by ni byla gor'ka . . . ," p. 27.

17. Julia Neiman, "1941," *Literaturnaia Moskva,* no. 2, Nov. 1956. Translated by Walter N. Vickery in Patricia Blake and Max Hayward, eds., *Dissonant Voices in Soviet Literature* (New York, 1964), pp. 156–57.

18. A. Anatoli (Kuznetsov), *Babi Yar: A Document in the Form of a Novel* (New York, 1970), pp. 93, 96.

19. Ales Adamovich, *Ia iz ognennoi derevni* (Moscow, 1991).

20. Dmitri V. Pavlov, *Leningrad 1941: The Blockade,* John Clinton Adams, trans., Foreword by Harrison Salisbury (Chicago and London, 1965), p. xiv. The figure of nine hundred days and nights to measure the blockade is approximate and legendary. The siege was lifted on January 27, 1944, and historians vary in their dating of its inception. The duration was probably somewhere between 872–82 days (Harrison Salisbury, *The 900 Days* [New York, 1969, 1985], p. 567n.).

21. I am indebted to Professor Edward Keenan of Harvard University for this story.

22. *Soviet Life,* May 1985, p. 14. This child's diary was displayed in the museum attached to the Piskarevskoe cemetery.

23. In *Russia at War,* Alexander Werth claimed that the general nationwide shock and dismay at the fall of Rostov had in part been orchestrated by the leadership in order to prepare the country for the post-Rostov reforms that tightened discipline in the front and rear (chap. 5).

24. John Barber and Mark Harrison, eds., *The Soviet Home Front 1941–1945* (London and New York, 1991), p. 31.

25. Maksim Gor'kii, *O russkom krest'iantve* (Berlin, 1922), p. 5.

26. Ilya Ehrenburg, *The War: 1941–1945* (Cleveland and New York, 1964), p. 30.

27. Aleksei Surkov, *Sobranie sochinenii,* vol. 1 (Moscow, 1978), p. 288. When it was published in *Krasnaia zvezda* in August 1942, the poem was entitled

"I Hate." It was subsequently renamed "Fields of Battle," the title under which it appears in Surkov's collected works.

28. Quoted in Alexander Werth, *Russia at War* (New York, 1964), p. 417.

29. Konstantin Simonov, *Sobranie sochinenii,* vol. 1 (Moscow, 1979), pp. 105–7. The poem is untitled.

30. Kukriniksy,"Besposhchadno razgromim i unichtozhim vraga!" poster, 1941; V. B. Koretskii, "Voin krasnoi armii, spasi!" poster, 1941; D. A. Shmarinov, "Otomsti!" poster, 1942.

31. I. Toidze, "Rodina-mat' zovet," poster, 1941.

32. *Izvestiia,* Jan. 22, 1942.

33. Gastello's feat was first mentioned in a Soviet Information Bureau (Sovinform) report of July 5, 1941. All twenty-eight "Panfilovtsy" are named in *Izvestiia,* Jan. 22, 1942.

34. Under Khrushchev, Shelepin was a member of the Party's ruling Presidium. I learned the story of the real Zoya from Lazar Lazarev, who knew Lev Arnshtam. For a splendid discussion of the cult of Zoya, see Rosalinde Sartorti, "On the Making of Heroes, Heroines, and Saints," in *The Heart of War.*

35. Ehrenburg, *The War,* p. 78.

36. John Erickson, "Soviet Women at War," John Garrard and Carol Garrard, eds., *World War 2 and the Soviet People* (London, 1993), p. 50.

37. Mikhail Gefter, ed., *Ikh prizvaniem byla istoriia* (Moscow, 1995), pp. 26–27, 31.

38. Alexander Tvardovsky, *Vassili Tyorkin: A Book About a Soldier,* Alex Miller, trans. (Moscow, 1975), pp. 19–21.

39. Ilya Ehrenburg and Konstantin Simonov, *In One Newspaper: A Chronicle of Unforgettable Years* (New York, 1985), p. 203.

40. Ehrenburg, *The War,* p. 107.

41. T. G. Malinina, "Proektirovanie pamiatnikov i memorialov v gody voiny," *Arkhitektura 40 let velikoi pobedy* (Moscow, 1965), pp. 14–15.

42. A. K. Zaitsev, *Memorial'nye ansambli v gorodakh-geroiakh* (Moscow, 1985), p. 13; *Arkhitektura 40 let pobedy,* p. 58.

43. Zaitsev, *Memorial'nye ansambli v gorodakh-geroiakh,* pp. 27, 43. Both designs were made in 1943, and the artists were, respectively, I. Sobolev and L. Rudnev.

44. I. Rzhekhina, P. N. Blashkevich, and P. G. Burova, *A. K. Burov* (Moscow, 1984), pp. 94–97.

45. Michael Cherniavsky, "Corporal Hitler, General Winter and the Russian Peasant," *Yale Review* (Summer 1962): 547–58.

46. Leo Tolstoy, *War and Peace,* Rosemary Edmonds, trans. (Harmondsworth, England, 1975), p. 717.

47. For a brilliant and brief exposition of this argument, see H. R. Trevor-Roper, "The 'Blitz' That Failed," *New York Times Magazine,* June 18, 1961, pp. 8–9, 33–38.

48. Catherine Andreyev, *Vlasov and the Russian Liberation Movement* (Cambridge, England, 1987), pp. 2–3.

49. Quoted in Donald Treadgold, *Twentieth Century Russia* (Boulder, San Francisco, and London, 1990), p. 361.

50. Vera Tolz, "New Information About the Deportation of Ethnic Groups in the USSR During World War 2," in Garrard and Garrard, *World War 2 and the Soviet People,* p. 164. See also Aleksandr Nekrich, *The Punished Peoples* (New York, 1978).

51. "Prazdnik pobedy," *Pravda,* May 9, 1945.

52. Ehrenburg, *The War,* p. 188.

53. George Kennan, *Memoirs: 1925–1950* (Boston, 1967), pp. 240–41.

54. Ehrenburg, *The War,* p. 188.

55. For the text of the speech, see "Obrashchenie Tov. I. V. Stalina k narodu," *Krasnaia zvezda,* May 10, 1945.

56. J. V. Stalin, *The Great Patriotic War of the Soviet Union* (Moscow, 1950), p. 352.

57. *Pravda,* June 25, 1945.

CHAPTER 5: AFTER THE WAR WAS OVER

1. See Sheila Fitzpatrick's excellent article, "Postwar Soviet Society," in Susan J. Linz, ed., *The Impact of World War II on the Soviet Union* (Totowa, New Jersey, 1985), especially pp. 150–51. The 1939 figure of 190.7 million population of the Soviet Union includes the territories annexed during the war in western Ukraine and Belorussia, Moldavia, and the Baltic states. *Narodnoe khoziaistvo SSSR v 1960 g. Statisticheskii ezhegodnik* (Moscow, 1961), p. 7, cited in Fitzpatrick, "Postwar Soviet Society," p. 131.

2. Alec Nove, *An Economic History of the U.S.S.R.* (London, 1972), p. 298, cited in Fitzpatrick, "Postwar Soviet Society, " p. 146.

3. Joseph Brodsky, *Less Than One: Selected Essays* (New York, 1986), p. 18.

4. Fitzpatrick, "Postwar Soviet Society, " p. 136.

5. The author also notes with sadness that in fifty years production of prostheses has not improved considerably, judging by the fact that veterans of the Afghan war try to get theirs from abroad. Lazarev, "Kak by ni byla gor'ka . . . ," p. 31.

6. Vera Dunham, *In Stalin's Time: Middleclass Values in Soviet Fiction* (Cambridge, England, 1976).

7. Dunham, *In Stalin's Time,* p. 43.

8. *Vechernaia Moskva,* May 10, 1946, and I. Azizyan and I. Ivanova, *Honour Eternal: Second World War Memorials* (Moscow, 1982); the sculptor of the Berlin monument was Evgenii Vuchetich; *Literaturnaia gazeta,* Feb. 2, 1952.

9. *Literatura i iskusstvo,* May 1, 1946.

10. Lazar Lazarev, "Russian Literature on the War," Garrard and Garrard, eds., *World War 2 and the Soviet People* (London, 1993), pp. 30–31.

11. Ibid., p. 31.

12. *Pravda,* May 9, 1949; *Krasnaia zvezda,* May 9, 1949; *Izvestiia,* May 8, 1949; *Vechernaia Moskva,* May 8, 1950; *Pravda,* May 9, 1949; *Pravda,* May 9, 1950.

13. Ilya Ehrenburg, *Post-War Years: 1945–54,* Tatiana Shebunina, trans. (Cleveland and New York, 1967), p. 301.

14. Yevgenii Yevtushenko, *A Precocious Autobiography* (New York, 1964), p. 85.

15. *Crimes of the Stalin Era: Special Report to the 20th Congress of the Communist Party of the Soviet Union*, Boris Nicolaevsky, annot. (New York, 1962), pp. S36–S45.

16. Lazarev, "Kak by ni byla gor'ka . . . , " p. 33.

17. Lazarev, "Russian Literature on the War," John Garrard and Carol Garrard, eds., *World War 2 and the Soviet People*, pp. 32–33.

18. *Zhivye i mertvye* was published in 1958. *The Living and the Dead* is actually the title of the first novel in a trilogy with the same name. The second volume, *Soldatami ne rozhdaiutsia* (*Soldiers Are Not Born*), appeared in 1964, and the third, *Poslednee leto* (*Last Summer*), in 1970. Of the three, only the first, the title volume, is available in English translation.

19. This fact was pointed out by Robert Chandler in the introduction to his English translation, Vasilii Grossman, *Life and Fate: A Novel* (New York, 1987), p. 9.; John Garrard, "Stepsons in the Motherland: The Architectonics of Vasilii Grossman's *Zhizn' i sud'ba*," *Slavic Review* 50, no. 2 (Summer 1991): 337n. For Grossman's report of his meeting with Suslov, see D. Fel'dman, "Do i posle aresta," *Literaturnaia gazeta*, Nov. 11, 1988.

20. Grossman, *Life and Fate*, pp. 213, 216.

21. "Treblinskii ad," *Znamia*, no. 10 (1944), cited in Garrard, "Stepsons in the Motherland," p. 338; *The Black Book*, sponsored in part by United States Jewish organizations, was never published in the Soviet Union, although a Russian edition appeared in Jerusalem in 1980. An insignificant portion of the manuscript was published in the United States in 1946, and in 1981 a fuller (although still incomplete) version was published in New York. *The Black Book*, John S. Glad and James S. Levine, trans. (New York, 1981).

22. Grossman, *Life and Fate*, pp. 484–487ff., p. 555. The critic John Garrard apposes the notion of death as slavery to the "Christian view that for the faithful 'death is the gateway to eternal life,'" and suggests a primal Jewish source of Grossman's view ("Stepsons in the Motherland," p. 344).

23. Grossman, *Life and Fate*, p. 93.

24. *Life and Fate*, pp. 207, 553–54.

25. *Nabat pamiati: sovetskie memorial'nye ansambli, posveshchennye zhertvam fashizma* (Leningrad, 1975); E. A. Levinson and A. V. Vasil'ev, "Pamiatnik na piskarevskom kladbishche," *Arkhitektura i stroitel'stvo*, no. 4 (1957): 51. Levinson and Vasil'ev were the architects. The Motherland figure was sculpted by V. V. Isaeva and R. K. Taurit.

26. Yevgeny Yevtushenko, *Selected Poems*, trans. Robin Miller-Gulland and Peter Levi, S.J. (Baltimore, 1962), pp. 82–84.

27. For my discussion of Babi Yar I have drawn heavily on Richard Sheldon's excellent article, "The Transformations of Babi Yar," Terry Thompson and Richard Sheldon, eds., *Soviet Society and Culture* (Boulder and London, 1988).

28. Anatoly Kuznetsov, "My Diary in the Other World, " *New York Times*, August 10, 1969, cited in Sheldon, "Transformations of Babi Yar," p. 144.

29. A. Anatoli (Kuznetsov), *Babi Yar: A Document in the Form of a Novel*, David Floyd, trans. (New York, 1970).

CHAPTER 6: "NO ONE IS FORGOTTEN, NOTHING IS FORGOTTEN"

1. *Leningradskaia pravda,* May 10, 1960.

2. David Riesman, Nathan Glazer, and Reuel Denney, *The Lonely Crowd* (New Haven and London, 1971), p. 65.

3. Robert C. Tucker, *The Soviet Political Mind: Stalinism and Post-Stalin Change* (New York, 1971), pp. 188–89.

4. For a discussion of shame and guilt quite different from my own, see Donald Capps, *The Depleted Self: Sin in a Narcissistic Age* (Minneapolis, 1993), pp. 71–100. See also Helen Merrell Lynd, *On Shame and Search for Identity* (New York, 1958).

5. Lazarev, "Russian Literature on the War," John Garrard and Carol Garrard, eds., *World War 2 and the Soviet People* (London, 1993), pp. 34–35.

6. Aleksandr Nekrich detailed the "Nekrich Affair" in his autobiography, *Forsake Fear: Memoirs of an Historian* (Boston, 1991).

7. Aleksandr Nekrich, *Forsake Fear,* p. 103.

8. V. Shelekasov, *Vstan' pod znamia geroev!* (Moscow, 1975), pp. 1, 58–59.

9. *Pamiat' o podvige* (Moscow, 1985) is a detailed official guidebook of the Central Museum of the Armed Forces of the USSR.

10. On the Grekov studio, see *Studiia voennykh khudozhnikov imeni M.B. Grekova* (Moscow, 1989).

11. Leonid Ouspensky and Vladimir Lossky, *The Meaning of Icons* (Olten, Switzerland, and Boston, 1952), pp. 28–29.

12. See, for example, M. V. Kornetskii, "Soldiers of '41" (1967); P. A. Batarshin, "Women of the '40s" (1975); S. S. Safarian, "Triangular Letters" (1982); and A. L. Khudiakov, "Wait for Me" (1982), all reproduced in *Podvigu 40 let* (Moscow, 1985).

13. For a brilliant analysis of that memorial—and the spaceship simile—see Michael Ignatieff, "Soviet War Memorials," *History Workshop* (Spring 1984).

14. F. P. Usypenko, "Prisiaga" (1971), reproduced in *Podvigu 40 let.*

15. V. Anikin, *Brestskaia krepost'-geroi* (Moscow, 1981), p. 111; A. K. Zaitsev, *Memorialnye ansambli v gorodakh-geroiakh* (Moscow, 1985), pp. 98–107ff.

16. Z. Bonks, "Dorogami slavnykh pobed," *Narodnoe obrazovanie,* no. 6 (1965): 74–76.

17. V. G. Sinitsyn, ed., *Nashi prazdniki* (Moscow, 1977), pp. 114–16.

18. A. Bernshtein, "Fil'my o Velikoi Otechestvennoi voine," *Narodnoe obrazovanie,* no. 5 (1975): 68; "Velikaia pobeda sovetskogo naroda," *Narodnoe obrazovanie,* No. 5 (1975): 5–6; I. Ozerskii, "Vechno zhivye stranitsy . . . ," *Narodnoe obrazovanie,* no. 5 (1975): 57.

19. L. Ostrovskaia, "Rastim grazhdanina," *Doshkol'noe vospitanie,* no. 10 (1985): 57. Notable were the books of doggerel by Sergei Mikhalkov. See, for example, his *Pobeda: Stikhi* (Moscow, 1985).

20. L. I. Brezhnev, "The War," *How It Was: The War and Post-War Reconstruction in the Soviet Union* (Oxford and New York, 1979), p. 12.

CHAPTER 7: *GLASNOST* AND THE GREAT PATRIOTIC WAR

1. Andrei Voznesenskii, "Rov, dukhovnyi protsess," *Iunost'*, no. 7, 1986, p. 6.

2. *New York Times*, Oct. 20, 1986.

3. "Sovest', bol' i nadezhda," *Sovetskaia kul'tura*, Oct. 9, 1986.

4. Ibid.

5. Adel' Kalinichenko, "Predavshie pamiat'," *Poliarnaia pravda*, Nov. 30, 1986.

6. *Literaturnaia gazeta*, May 6, 1987.

7. David Remnick, *Lenin's Tomb: The Last Days of the Soviet Empire* (New York, 1993), p. 101.

8. *New York Times*, Aug. 19 and 23, 1993.

9. Vladimir Abarinov, *Katynskii labirint* (Moscow, 1991), pp. 7–8. For the write-up of an interview with one of the executioners, see David Remnick, *Lenin's Tomb: The Last Days of the Soviet Empire* (New York, 1993), pp. 3–9, *passim*. See also "Katyn Tragedy, New Light on the Deaths of 15,000 Polish Officers in 1940," *Moscow News*, no. 12, 1990.

10. Ales Adamovich, Ianka Bryl, and Vladimir Kolesnik, *Ia iz ognennoi derevni* (Minsk, 1977); Ales Adamovich and Daniil Granin, *Blokadnaia kniga* (Leningrad, 1979). Both books are available in English translation.

11. Svetlana Aleksievich, *War's Unwomanly Face* (Moscow, 1988), pp. 40–41. Originally published as *U voiny ne zhenskoe litso* (Moscow, 1985).

12. Ibid, pp. 50, 55, 65.

13. Vladimir Frumkin, ed., *Bulat Okudzhava: 65 Songs* (Ann Arbor, Mich., 1980), p. 43.

14. Vladimir Vysotsky, "Vladimir Vysotsky Speaks of his Songs," *Sons Are Leaving for Battle* (Melodiia, 1986), side 1.

15. *New York Times*, Oct. 5, 1991.

16. For more on the chauvinist turn of *Voenno-istoricheskii zhurnal*, see *New York Times*, Jan. 10, 1991.

17. Interview with the historian V. M. Kulish, May 5, 1990.

18. *Sovetskaia kultura*, April 14, 1990.

CHAPTER 8: RUSSIA REMEMBERS THE WAR

1. *Komsomolskaia pravda*, May 5, 1990.

2. Viacheslav Kondratiev, "Parii voiny," *Literaturnaia gazeta*, Jan. 31, 1990; for a letter to the editor by a group of veterans protesting Kondratiev's sympathetic review of the film, see *Literaturnaia gazeta*, Mar. 7, 1990.

3. Cited in George Gibian, "World War 2 in Russian National Consciousness: Pristavkin (1981–7) and Kondratyev (1990)," John Garrard and Carol Garrard, eds., *World War 2 and the Soviet People* (London, 1993), p. 153.

4. Viacheslav Kondratiev, "Paradoks frontovoi nostalgii," Iu. Rost, "Proshcheno?" *Literaturnaia gazeta*, May 9, 1990.

5. Boris Sokolov, *Tsena pobedy* (Moscow, 1991). See also Iurii Geller, "Nevernoe ekho bylogo," *Druzhba narodov*, no. 9, 1989, pp. 229–44.

6. "Kuropaty, Khatyn, Chernobyl," *Literaturnaia gazeta,* Aug. 15, 1990.

7. *Izvestiia,* Apr. 28, 1990.

8. Viktor Suvorov, *Icebreaker: Who Started the Second World War?* (London, 1990).

9. Vera Tolz, "Discussion of General Vlasov in the Soviet Press," *Radio Liberty Report on the USSR* 2, no. 52 (1990): 1–3.

10. Leo Tolstoy, *War and Peace,* trans. Louise Maude and Aylmer Maude (London, 1965), bk. xi, chap. 19, pp. 70–73.

11. In all, by 1986 some 190 million rubles were collected.

12. I. Virabov, "Manevry na Poklonnoi gore," *Komsomolskaia pravda,* Sept. 12, 1991. The novelist Vladimir Karpov figured among those who favored moving Vuchetich's monument from Berlin to the Hill of Prostrations. See his article in *Literaturnaia gazeta,* May 9, 1990.

CHAPTER 9: PARTING THOUGHTS

1. Brodsky, *Less Than One: Selected Essays* (New York, 1986), p. 10.

2. Amos Elon, "The Politics of Memory," *New York Review of Books,* Oct. 7, 1993, pp. 3, 5.

3. Louis Uchitelle, "In the New Russia, an Era of Takeovers," *New York Times,* Apr. 17, 1994, sec. 3, pp. 1, 8.

INDEX

Adamovich, Ales, 68–69, 207–8
Aleshin, Sasha, 26–27
Anti-Semitism, 102, 114–15, 159,
    161; and Babi Yar, 67–69, 119–24,
    185–87; politics of, 49–51. *See also*
    Holocaust
Armed Forces of the Committee for
    the Liberation of the Peoples of
    Russia, 86–87
Art: cult, 138–41, 191–92; postwar,
    100–101, 112–13; wartime, 75–81.
    See also Music; Poetry
Association of United Search Organi-
    zations, 14–15, 17. *See also* Dozor
Astafieva-Dlugach, Margarita, 215

Babi Yar, 67–69; and *glasnost*,
    185–87; memorial, 124; postwar,
    119–24
"Babi Yar" (Yevtushenko), 119–24
Belash, Iurii, 59–60
Berggolts, Olga, 32, 64
Beria, Lavrentii, 177
"Big Deal" (Dunham), 99–100
Black Book, The (Grossman), 115,
    233n20
"Black summer," 70–76
Blockade Diary (Kochina), 118
Bolshoi Theater, 37, 39
"Brest Fortress–Hero Memorial
    Ensemble," 145–46
Brezhnev, Leonid, 127; cult of,
    155–56; and stagnation era, 28,
    129–33
Brodsky, Joseph, 97, 224

Censorship, 104, 113, 119–24,
    134–35, 186
Central Armed Forces Museum,
    136–38
Chernenko, Konstantin, 29
Cherniavsky, Michael, 85
Churchill, Winston, 87, 95
Clinton, Bill, 207–8
Cold war, 95, 104–5
Communism, 6–7, 132; vs. fascism,
    114–15, 189–90, 202–3, 222
Communist Youth Organization. *See*
    Komsomol
Cranes are Flying, The (Kalatozov),
    112

Danilov, Lev, 203
Day of Remembrance, 212–14
Death: medallion, 18; and war casual-
    ties, 56, 82, 85, 96, 135, 206–7
Demidov, Volodia, 17, 21, 23
Den Pobedy. See Victory Day
De-Stalinization: and freedom,
    64–66, 86–87; and *glasnost*,
    164–70, 181–85, 187–91; and
    historians, 209–12; and war cult,
    129–33. *See also* Stalin, Joseph;
    Stalinism
"Ditch: A Spiritual Trial, The"
    (Voznesensky), 159–63
"Dizzy with Success" (Stalin), 58
Dozor (Patrol), 11–27; and German
    soldiers, 15, 23; and Rzhev,
    11–12, 18, 20–21, 203–4; theme
    song, 21–22

Dubcek, Alexander, 132
Dunham, Vera, 99

Ehrenburg, Ilya, 82, 121; and fascism, 73, 115; and Stalin's death, 105–6; and Victory Day, 89–90; and war heroes, 78–79
Eisenstein, Sergei, 62–63
Elon, Amos, 224–25
Exploit of Private Iu. Smirnov, The (Pereaslavets), 140–41

Falin, Valentin, 180
Fascism, 72–73, 185–86; vs. Communism, 114–15, 189–90, 202–3, 222
"February Diary" (Berggolts), 64
Fetisov, Georgii, 48–49
Field of Mars memorial, 126–29
For His Native Land (Krasnov), 112–13
From Stalingrad to Vienna (Vasilevskii), 104

Gastello, Nikolai, 76
Gefter, Lela, 87, 146–47, 166–67
Gefter, Mikhail, 166–69, 192; and desacralization, 187–88; and de-Stalinization, 64–65; and Rzhev, 21; and Victory Day, 34–37
Gefter, Valia, 44–45
Ginzburg, Musia, 35–36
Glasnost: and Babi Yar, 185–87; and de-Stalinization, 164–70, 181–85, 187–91; and Katyn, 176–81; and Nazi-Soviet Pact, 175; and propaganda, 185–86, 192–94; and Russian culture, 170–73, 191–92; and Simferopol grave robbings, 158–63; and veterans, 194–96, 198–99; and Victory Day, 199–201

Gorbachev, Mikhail, 14, 91, 155; "Lessons of the War and Victory, The," 196–99; and Victory Day, 34–35, 39, 41. *See also Glasnost*
Gorky, Maxim, 72
Great Patriotic War: and anti-Semitism, 49–51, 102, 114–15, 119–24, 159, 161, 185–87; "black summer," 70–76; casualties, 56, 82, 85, 96, 135, 206–7; Day of Remembrance, 212–14; and de-Stalinization, 64–66, 86–87, 129–33, 164–70, 181–85, 187–91, 209–12; development, 52–55; German occupation, 67–69; and Hill of Prostrations, 214–21; Leningrad blockade, 56, 69–70, 230n20; military diplomacy of, 55–60, 85, 197–98, 211–12; Nazi-Soviet pact, 50, 175, 211; Operation Barbarossa, 55–57; Russian remembrance of, 202–5, 207–9, 209–12; sacralization of, 61–64, 76–81; and Soviet victory, 84–92; and Stalingrad, 81–82; and Stalinism, 53–55, 56, 86–87, 90–92, 99–100, 106–9; Victory Day, 28–29, 88–90, 92–94; and women, 40, 182–84, 208–9. *See also Dozor; Glasnost*; Great Patriotic War cult; Postwar period
Great Patriotic War cult: art, 138–41, 191–92; and Central Armed Forces Museum, 136–38; deterioration, 222–26; development, 8–10, 110, 133–36; memorials, 141–46; and militarization, 150–55; and political culture, 155–57; and Requiem monument, 146–50, 163–64, 193; saints/martyrs of, 76–81; and stagnation era, 28, 129–33; symbolic flame, 125–29; theme, 14, 32, 51, 124, 197; and Victory Day, 41, 44–45, 135–36. *See also Dozor; Glasnost*

"Great Patriotic War of the Soviet People, The" (*Pravda*), 61
Great Terror, 56, 59, 134
Grekov Military Art Studio, 138–39
Gromyko, Andrei, 178–79
Grossman, Vasilii, 113–17, 227

"Hell of Treblinka, The" (Grossman), 115
Hill of Prostrations memorial, 214–21
History of the Great Patriotic War of the Soviet People (Institute of Military History), 210
History of the Great Patriotic War of the Soviet Union, 1941–1945 (Institute of Military History), 209–10
Hitler, Adolf: and German occupation, 67–69; and Leningrad blockade, 69–70; military diplomacy of, 85; and Operation Barbarossa, 55–57; vs. Stalin, 189–90, 202–3, 207–8
Holocaust, 114–15, 224–25; denial of, 49–51; Memorial Museum, 50, 223. *See also* Anti-Semitism

Icebreaker: Who Started the Second World War? (Suvorov), 211–12
Iconoclasm, 24–25, 158–64
Idi i smotri (*Come and See*) (Adamovich), 68–69
"I Hate" (Surkov), 73–74, 230n26
Ikonnikov, Iulii, 15
In Stalin's Time: Middleclass Values in Soviet Fiction (Dunham), 99
Institute of Military History, 209–10
"Is No One Forgotten?" (*Ogonek*), 14
Iunost (*Youth*), 24, 122–23
Ivan's Childhood (Tarkovskii), 112
Izvestiia, 76, 127, 208–9

Jews. *See* Anti-Semitism

Kalatozov, Mikhail, 112
Karpov, Vladimir, 213–14

Katiusha, 228
Katyn, 50, 176–81
Kennan, George, 89
Kerbel, Lev, 1–2
Khatyn, 207–8
Khrushchev, Nikita, 106–10, 131–32
"Kill Him!" (Simonov), 74–75
Kincaid, Jamaica, 10
Kochina, Elena, 118
Komsomol (Communist Youth Organization), 14, 17. *See also Dozor*
Kondratiev, Viacheslav, 203–5
Korotich, Vitaly, 185–87
Kosmodemianskaia, Zoya, 76–78
Kosygin, Alexei, 129, 132
Krasnaia Zvezda. See Red Star
Krasnov, A. P., 112–13
Kumanev, Georgii, 213–14
Kuropaty, 207–8
Kursk, 82
Kuznetsov, Anatoli, 67–68, 119–20, 122–23

Lazarev, Lazar, 99, 133–34; and de-Stalinization, 65–66; and wartime memoirs, 104, 110, 111
Lend-lease agreement, 50, 87, 213–14
Lenin cult, 53–54, 187–88
Leningrad: Affair, 102, 118; blockade, 56, 69–70, 230n20; and Victory Day, 29–32
Lenin's Tomb (Remnick), 166
"Lessons of the War and Victory, The" (Gorbachev), 196–99
Letter from the Front (1947), 100–101
Life and Fate (Grossman), 113–17, 227
Lifelong Cause, A (Vasilevskii), 104
Lishin, Ada, 13, 16, 20
Lishin, Oleg, 12–13, 16, 26
Lishin, Tania, 16, 26–27
Living and the Dead, The (Simonov), 58, 111
Lonely Crowd, The (Riesman), 131
Lossky, Vladimir, 140

Matrosov, Aleksandr, 45, 78
Medvedev, Roy, 60–61, 84
Memorial movement, 209
Memorials, war, 1–2, 82–84, 141–46;
    Babi Yar, 124; "Brest Fortress-
    Hero Memorial Ensemble,
    145–46; Central Armed Forces
    Museum, 136–38; Field of Mars,
    126–29; Hill of Prostrations,
    214–21; "Motherland," 32, 143;
    Piskarevskoe Cemetery, 31-32,
    118–19, 126–29; *Requiem,* 146–50,
    163–64, 193; "Soldier-
    Liberator," 17; Soldier's Field,
    46–48; Thirst, 146; Tomb of the
    Unknown Soldier, 41–42, 127–29,
    143–44; "Valley of Glory," 24–25,
    161–63; Volgograd, 47–48, 51,
    143
"Minute of Silence," 41–43
Mishin, Avgust, 12
Mitlianskii, Daniil, 146–47, 163–64,
    193
Morozov, Pavlik, 45, 54
Moscow, 20; and Victory Day, 33-38
"Motherland" memorial, 32, 143
Music: "Sacred War," 62; "Valley of
    Death" (Yerkhov), 22

Nabokov, Vladimir, 52–53
Nagibin, Yuri, 98–99
Nazarenko, Tatiana, 141
Nazi-Soviet Pact, 50, 175, 211
Neiman, Julia, 66
Nekrich, Aleksandr, 135
Nevsky, Alexander (Eisenstein), 62–63
NKVD, 59, 203, 211; and Katyn,
    176–81
"Not a Step Back" order, 71, 102–3,
    203
Nove, Alec, 96

Ogonek, 14, 102

Operation Barbarossa, 55–57
Ouspensky, Leonid, 140

"Panfilovtsy," 76
"Paradox of Nostalgia for the Front"
    (Kondratiev), 204–5
"Pariahs of the War" (Kondratiev),
    203
Partisan Madonna (Savitskii), 140
Partisans Have Arrived, The
    (Nazarenko), 141
"Patience" (Nagibin), 98–99
Patrol. *See Dozor*
Pereaslavets, M. B., 140–41
Petrakov, Dmitrii, 46–47
Petrova, Lena, 20
Piskarevskoe Cemetery Memorial,
    31–32, 118–19, 126–29
Poetry of: Belash, Iurii, 59–60;
    Berggolts, Olga, 32, 64; Neiman,
    Julia, 66; Simonov, Konstantin,
    74–75; Surkov, Aleksei, 73–74;
    Tvardovsky, Aleksandr, 80–81;
    Voznesensky, Andrei, 160;
    Yevtushenko, Yevgenii, 119–21
"Politics of Memory, The" (Elon),
    224–25
Postwar period: art, 100–101,
    112–13; and Babi Yar, 119–24;
    and Khrushchev, 106–10, 131–32;
    and *Life and Fate* (Grossman),
    113–17; and Piskarevskoe
    Memorial Cemetery, 31–32,
    118–19, 126–29; and reconstruc-
    tion, 102–5; society, 95–100; and
    Stalin's death, 105–6; the thaw,
    109–13. *See also* Great Patriotic
    War cult
POWs. *See* Prisoners of war
"Prague Spring," 132
Pravda, 39, 61, 71, 74, 93, 104
Precocious Autobiography
    (Yevtushenko), 106
Price of Victory, The (Sokolov), 206

Prisoners of war (POWs), 50, 71–72, 110

Propaganda: and *glasnost*, 185–86, 192–94; military, 55, 57, 59, 63, 150–55; and Victory Day, 28–29, 31, 37

Ravdina, Tamara, 146–47
Reagan, Ronald, 30, 37, 38
"Red Pathfinders," 14, 152. *See also Dozor*
Red Star (Krasnaia Zvezda), 71, 73–74, 81, 91
Religion, 63–64, 170–71; and Orthodox Church, 43, 125–26, 167–68; and war memorials, 217–19
Remnick, David, 166
Requiem memorial, 146–50, 163–64, 193
Rest After Battle (1951), 100
Riesman, David, 131
Roosevelt, Franklin D., 87–88, 95
Rostov, 70–71, 230*n*22
Rzhev: battles of, 20–21; and *Dozor*, 11–12, 18, 203–4

"Sacred War," 62
Samsonov, Marat, 139
Savicheva, Tania, 70
Savitskii, Mikhail, 140
Search organizations. *See Dozor*
Second Shock Army, 212
Shamshykova, Liza, 79–80
Shelepin, Aleksandr, 177–78
Shpilianskii, Serega, 11–12, 17–18, 23
Shtrafniki (Danilov), 203
Shukshin, Vasilii, 65
Shvechkov, Aleksandr, 136–37
Simferopol grave robbings, 158–63
Simonov, Konstantin, 58, 73, 74–75, 81, 111
Skorobogatova, Tania, 139

Smaragdova, Marina, 150–51
Smertnyi medalion, 18
Sokolov, Boris, 206
Sokolov, S. L., 39
"Soldier-Liberator" memorial, 17
Soldier's Field Memorial, 46–48
Solomin, Nikolai, 139, 191–92
Soloukhin, Vladimir, 172–73
Song of Igor's Campaign, The (Nabokov), 52–53
"Soviet People's Immortal Valiant Deed, The" (Gorbachev), 34–35
"Special Report to the Twentieth Congress of the Communist Party of the Soviet Union" (Khrushchev), 107–9, 131–32
Stalin, Joseph: cult of, 35, 53–55; death of, 105–6; and *Dozor*, 13–14, 15; military diplomacy of, 55–60, 197–98, 211–12; "Not a step back" order, 71, 102–3, 203; speeches of, 58, 63, 91; vs. Hitler, 189–90, 202–3, 207–8. *See also* De-Stalinization; Stalinism
Stalingrad: battle of, 81–82, 114; renaming of, 109. *See also* Volgograd
Stalinism, 56, 90–92, 99–100; development of, 52–55; and Khrushchev, 106–10. *See also* De-Stalinization; Stalin, Joseph
Surkov, Aleksei, 73–74, 230*n*26
Suvorov, A. V., 13
Suvorov, Victor, 211–12

Tarkovskii, Andrei, 112
Teheran Conference, 87
Thirst memorial, 146
Toidze, Iraklii, 75–76
Tolstoy, Leo, 19, 85–86, 214–15
Tomb of the Unknown Soldier memorial, 41–42, 127–29, 143–44
Truman, Harry, 95
Tvardovskii, Aleksandr, 80–81, 111

22 June 1941 (Nekrich), 135

Voznesensky, Andrei, 158–63

"Valley of Death" (Yerkhov), 22
"Valley of Glory" memorial, 24–25,
    161–63
Vasilevskii, Aleksandr, 104
Victory (1948), 100
Victory Banner, 137–38, 216
Victory Day (*Den Pobedy*), 28–29,
    38–41; and *glasnost*, 199–201; and
    Leningrad, 29–32; and "Minute of
    Silence," 41–43; and Moscow,
    33–38; parade, 92–94; postwar,
    104–5, 110; and Volgograd,
    46–49; and war cult, 43–46
Vlasov, Andrei, 86–87, 212
Volgograd, 34; memorial, 47–48, 51,
    143; and Victory Day, 46–49
Volkogonov, Dmitrii, 210–11

War and Peace (Tolstoy), 85–86,
    214–15

Yazov, Dmitrii, 213–14
Yegorichev, N. G., 128–29
Yerkhov, Vladimir, 22, 163
Yevtushenko, Yevgenii, 106,
    119–21
Youth. See Iunost

Zaraev, Mikhail, 165
Zastoi. See Stagnation era
Zhdanov, Andrei, 102
Zhukov, Georgii, 92–93
Zone of Oblivion (Yerkhov), 163